Rilke's Russia

Rilke's Russia

A CULTURAL ENCOUNTER

Anna A. Tavis

NORTHWESTERN UNIVERSITY PRESS / EVANSTON, ILLINOIS

Northwestern University Press
Evanston, Illinois 60208-4210

ISBN: 0-8101-1152-7

Library of Congress Cataloging-in-Publication Data

Tavis, Anna A.
　　　Rilke's Russia : a cultural encounter / Anna A. Tavis.
　　　　　p.　　cm. — (Studies in Russian literature and theory)
　　　Includes bibliographical references.
　　　ISBN 0-8101-1152-7 (alk. paper)
　　　1. Rilke, Rainer, Maria, 1875–1926—Journeys—Russia. 2. Rilke,
Rainer Maria, 1875–1926—Knowledge—Russia. 3. Authors,
German—20th century—Biography. 4. Russia—Description and travel.
5. Russia—Intellectual life—1801–1917. 6. Russian literature—
Appreciation—Europe, German-speaking. 7. Russian literature—20th
century—History and criticism. I. Title. II. Series.
PT2635.I65Z898　　　1994
831'.912—dc20　　　　　　　　　　　　　　　　94-12817
　　　　　　　　　　　　　　　　　　　　　　　　CIP

The paper used in this publication meets the minimum requirements of the American National Standard for Information Sciences—Permanence of Paper for Printed Library Materials, ANSI Z39.48-1984.

Contents

Acknowledgments

This book would not have been possible without the faith and daily support of my family: my husband, Michael; my daughter, Anyuta C.; and my mother, Tai-cia Fiodorovna. I would also like to thank my friends and colleagues who helped me at various stages of this book's painful gestation. Foremost among them are: Ralph Freedman, my dissertation adviser, who launched me into the profession; Caryl Emerson, the tireless seeker of new talent; Saul Morson, a perceptive judge; and Clarence Brown, who taught me the art of translation. My special gratitude goes to Sue Bottigheimer, who read and reread these imperfect pages and encouraged my effort. In the end, the Northwestern University Press staff—particularly Susan Harris, the managing editor—made the final stages of this work specially exciting.

Rainer Maria Rilke:
A Russian Chronology 1875–1926

1875 December	René Maria Rilke born in Prague, the capital of Bohemia, a Czech province in the Austro-Hungarian empire. Prague's German-speaking population lives in a "double ghetto" of language and class. Rilke's mother, Phia Rilke, brings her son up as a girl until the age of seven, forbids him to speak Czech, and teaches him French instead. Rilke's father, Josef Rilke, a railway official and a retired military officer, wants his son to go into military service. The parents separate in 1884.
1886–1890	Rilke studies at a military school at St. Pölten and excels in academic subjects (including Czech), reads avidly, and begins writing.
1891–1892	Transfers to Lintz Trade Academy, reads Russian classics, decides to become a poet.
1893–1896	Through Valerie von David-Rhonfeld (Vally), his first serious love relationship, meets her uncle Julius Zeyer, the leading Czech neoromantic poet. Writes prolifically in all genres, edits the journal *Jung-Deutschland und Jung-Elsaß*, publishes his first collections of poetry: *Life and Songs, Offerings to the Lares,* and *Wild Chicory.*
1896–1897	Moves to Munich, meets the writer Jackob Wassermann, who introduces him to Lou Andreas-Salomé. Reads Turgenev, Dostoyevsky, and Peter Jens Jacobsen. Writes autobiographical novella *Ewald Tragy.*
1898	Travels to Italy, which he later remembers as a foreshadowing of Moscow. Keeps The Florentine Diary, dedicated to Andreas-Salomé. In Viareggio meets the Russian Helene Voronina. Prepares for his first Russian journey.

25 April 1899–18 June 1899
First Journey to Russia

25 April	Arrives in Moscow on Easter eve. Attends Easter services in the Kremlin. Meets the artist Leonid Pasternak and the sculptor Pavel Trubetskoi.
28 April	Visits Tolstoy for afternoon tea. Tolstoy warns his visitors against the idealization of Russian religiosity.
3 May–18 June	Arrives in St. Petersburg at the time of Pushkin's centenary celebrations. Visits museums, private collections, and theaters; immerses himself in the study of Russian religious art. Returns to Germany.
Summer	Devotes eight weeks to the study of Russian language, literature, history, and art at Frieda von Bülow's summer house in Meinigen. Publishes *Two Prague Stories,* the poem "The Tsars," and completes the play *The White Princess*.
September 1899–May 1900	Enrolls in Russian courses at Berlin University. Completes first draft of "The Book of Monkish Life" and the essay "Russian Art." Writes the original version of *The Lay of Love and Death of the Cornet Christoph Rilke*. Translates Chekhov's *Sea Gull* and Dostoyevsky's *Poor Folk*. Makes acquaintance of Sophie Schill, becomes her regular correspondent. Schill sends him Russian books, periodicals, and general information on Russia.

7 May–24 August 1900
Second Journey to Russia
Moscow, Kiev, Dnieper, Volga, Moscow, Petersburg

31 May	On his way to Kiev, Rilke meets Leonid Pasternak and his family.
1 June	Visits Tolstoy at Yasnaya Polyana.
2 June	Visits Pechersky monastery near Tula.
3–17 June	Stays in Kiev, visits churches, cathedrals, and the monastic caves.
19–21 June	Travels across the Poltava region.

21–24 June	Takes the train through Kharkov and Voronezh to Saratov, visits the Pushkin Museum. Volga journey on the steamer *Alexander Nevsky*.
24 June–2 July	Visits Volga cities: Saratov, Simbirsk, Samara, Nizhni Novgorod, and Yaroslavl. Travels to villages.
6–18 July	Stays in Moscow. Visits private collections, researches materials for a biography of a preimpressionist landscape painter, Fjodor Vasilijev. Owing to money shortage, abandons plans to travel to the Urals and into the Asian part of Russia.
18 July–24 July	Stays with Spiridon Drozhzhin and visits Novinki, the property of a minor poet, Nikolai Tolstoy. Writes a short autobiography in Russian for Drozhzhin.
28 July–22 August	Left by Andreas-Salomé in Petersburg. Reads about Russian art and painting. Visits Alexander Benois and plans a translation of his history of nineteenth-century Russian painting. Does research on biographies of two Russian artists, Alexander Ivanov and Ivan Kramskoy.
1900–1901	Lives in Worpswede, Berlin, and Westerwede. Marries the sculptor Clara Westhoff. Daughter Ruth is born.
1902–1903	Lives in Paris. Works with August Rodin.
1903	Writes *August Rodin* and *Worpswede*.
1903–1910	Travels in Italy and Sweden, lectures in Germany and Austria, lives in France.

Major Works of This Period

1904	*The Lay of Love and Death of the Cornet Christoph Rilke*.
1905	*The Book of Hours*.
1907	*New Poems*.
1908	*New Poems, the Other Part*.
1910	*The Notebooks of Malte Laurids Brigge*.
1910–1922	Works on *Duino Elegies*.

1913	Writes *The Life of Virgin Mary*.
1914–1919	Spends war years in Munich and Vienna.
1921–1926	Werner Rinhart rents Castle Muzot and gives it to Rilke.
1923	Finishes *Duino Elegies* and *Sonnets to Orpheus*.
January–mid-August 1925	Last stay in Paris. Meets former Russian acquaintances and Russian celebrities in emigration.
1 November 1925	Tsvetaeva moves from Prague to Paris.
December 1925	Celebrations of Rilke's fiftieth birthday. Greetings from Leonid Pasternak.
14 March 1926	Rilke replies to Leonid Pasternak, praises Boris Pasternak's poetry.
12 April 1926	Boris Pasternak's letter to Rilke.
3 May–22 August 1926	Rilke's correspondence with Tsvetaeva.
29 December 1926	Rilke dies at Muzot.
January 1927	Tsvetaeva learns of Rilke's death. Dedicates to him the poems "A New Year's" and "The Poem of the Air"; writes an essay, "Your Death," and "Some Letters of Rainer Maria Rilke"; translates Rilke letters.

The Neighbor's Soul

Umom Rossiu ne poniat'
Arshinom obshim ne izmerit'
U nei osobennaia stat'
V Rossiu nuzhno prosto verit'
Fjodor Tyutchev

One cannot rationally fathom Russia
One cannot measure it with a measuring stick
It has a special nature
One can only believe in it

RAINER MARIA RILKE made two eventful trips to Russia, the first in the spring of 1899 and the second in the summer of 1900. He was a fledgling poet then, uncertain of his aesthetic affiliations. In searching for the "Russian soul," Rilke was guided by the Nietzschean conviction that although God had died in the West, he continued to live a harmonious life in Christian Russia: "If I had come on this earth as a prophet, I would preach all my life that Russia was the chosen land over which lies God's massive sculptor's hand as though in a provident delaying action: everything it needs is to come to this land, but the fulfillment of its destiny is to be slower and clearer."[1] Rilke, like Dostoyevsky, professed the world's salvation through spiritualized beauty—"beauty will save the world"—and God served him as an overarching metaphor for all art. People in Russia, just like gods, could find for themselves different destinies and nurture their unrealized talents: they could eventually all become poets and artists, as they had been born to be: "I can hardly express what Russia was and is for me. Unknowingly, I brought with me a certain predisposition which right from the first moment there and absolutely completely made it seem like home to me."[2]

This study's starting point is the existing biographical and textual evidence of Russia's importance in shaping Rainer Maria Rilke's aesthetic perception. As such, it is an essay in cultural interpretation that aims at reclaiming Rilke's image of Russia as a valid cultural document. It situates Rilke's writings within the context that informed their creation and meaning and

xiii

that established the requirements for authority and legitimacy in their interpretation. Probing into the fundamentals of Russia's historical and cultural experience, Rilke was engaged in a fin-de-siècle search for origins: of art, of Russia, and of himself. A perceptive observer of human nature, he witnessed and chronicled the Russian Revival, a brief but pivotal period in Russian cultural history. To examine Rilke's Russia is to recapture the past that he shared with his Russian contemporaries, but memory of that past was lost in the historical turmoil of the Russian Revolution and the following years of the Communist state. Only in the last two decades has contemporary Russia gradually begun to reclaim its past, and it is now timely to retrace Rilke's steps.

It would be easy to consider Rilke's idea of Russia as an ideological construct arbitrarily imposed by an impressionable outsider on an exotic culture, and then to dismiss that image as false, while perhaps granting it some limited legitimacy. Yet by doing so we would ignore the obvious fact that cultures, like individuals, have multiple developmental lines and the choices which we have made for ourselves may limit our vision.[3] Without doubt, Rilke did not look at Russia with pristine eyes. His cultural attitudes had been defined by a set of customs and institutions of Western thinking about the Slavic lands. His belief in Russia's special mission had been anticipated by the entire development of European ideas about Russia since the days of Peter the Great, and his particular version of the Russian cultural myth had been prefigured by Herder and Hegel, de Vogüé, and Nietzsche. It had also been institutionally endorsed by the success of such European journals as the French *Revue des deux mondes* and *Nouvelle revue* and the German *Die freie Bühne* and *Neue deutsche rundschau*. But there was much more to the poet's involvement with Russian culture than the then fashionable passion for the exotic and fascination with the Orient. While contemporary Europe was searching in vain for a compelling positive self-definition, a new post-Emancipation Russia was unfolding to its East.[4] It was a time when there were very few givens, when almost every aspect of the culture rested on unstable ground and it was not clear what shape it would take or what roles the various elements of the new social order would play in its design. Russia's historical quandary, the state of being torn between two developmental lines—nostalgic reenactment of the national past and nihilist futurist experimentation—was again making itself felt.[5]

Rilke sought and found mentors on the Russian side, Russians who helped him steer his way through the country's cultural unknowns. Moreover, he had read literature on so broad a range of subjects that most of his evocations of Russia could, in fact, be seen as a form of cultural quotation. Rilke, a poet, allowed himself to represent as much as to invent, to imitate as much as to appropriate the culture he had claimed to be his own: "Russia became for me reality, and at the same time the profound, daily insight: that reality is something distant, which comes with inexpressible slowness to him who has patience."[6] Rilke defended himself against future accusations of an inaccurate vision of Russia in a letter to a Petersburg friend, in which he explained:

> So much has been written here [in the West] about . . . things (good and bad) that they no longer have any meaning except as imaginary crossing points between different theories. Whoever wants to say anything . . . speaks only about the views of his predecessors in the field and loses himself in the half-polemical spirit which, as a matter of fact, contradicts the naively productive approach with the help of which alone one can understand these [Russian] things.[7]

Subjectivity became Rilke's main virtue. Poetry served him as the best guarantee of continuity and integrity in the general atmosphere of uncertainty and disturbance. In his *Seventh Duino Elegy*, Rilke eloquently captured his characteristic "transcendence downward":[8]

Nirgends, Geliebte, wird Welt sein, als innen. Unser
Leben geht hin mit Verwandlung. Und immer geringer
schwindet das Außen. Wo einmal ein dauerndes Haus war,
schlägt sich erdachtes Gebild vor, quer, zu Erdenklichem
völlig gehörig, als ständ es noch ganz im Gehirne.
Weiter Speicher der Kraft schafft sich der Zeitgeist, gestaltlos
wie der spannende Drang, den er aus allem gewinnt.
Tempel kennt er nicht mehr. Diese, des Herzens, Verschwendung
sparen wir heimlicher ein. Ja, wo noch eins übersteht,
ein einst gebetetes Ding, ein gedientes, geknietes—,
hält es sich, so wie es ist, schon ins Unsichtbare hin.
Viele gewahrens nicht mehr, doch ohne den Vorteil
daß sie's nun *innerlich* baun, mit Pfeilern und Statuen, größer! (SW 1:711)

Nowhere, beloved, can world exist but within.
Our life is spent in changing. And ever lessening,
the outer world disappears. Where once was a durable house
pops up a fantastic image, crosswise, belonging completely
to the conceivable, as though it stood whole in the brain.
The spirit of the times makes vast storehouses of power,
formless as the stretched tension it gathers from
everything.
Temples it knows no longer. We hoard these heart-squanderings
more secretly. Yes, where one still lasts, a thing once
for prayer and devotion and kneeling, it holds its own,
as it is, already in the invisible world.

Many can see it no longer and pass up the profit
of building it now within, with pillars and statues, greater![9]

By maintaining an aesthetic distance, Rilke was able to refer to Russia by allusion rather than by category and to represent the country without denying or sacrificing its indigenous cultural qualities. It may be argued that lyric poetry as a genre of representation is too vulnerable to fluctuations of mood, too given to infinite variety of emotion, and too liable to swift changes of tone to claim any factual validity. Yet on another level, the poetic field is a restricted one: the scope for arbitrary tampering with the material is constrained by its reference to the unchanging elements of human nature. The poet's primary obligation to language makes his interpretive task even more exacting than that of the fact-bound ethnographer. In the end, Rilke expressed his insights in an unfamiliar artistic idiom and thus "defamiliarized" or challenged the accepted patterns of thinking about Russian religious and aesthetic experience. Considerations of what Rilke *really* should have known, read, or understood are therefore marginal in a study of the poet as a cultural critic.

Rilke himself was partly responsible for the initial lack of interest in his Russian past on the part of his Western biographers and critics. Russia entered his major works primarily in the form of distant allusions, metaphors, and aesthetic attitudes. Even though the Baltic German scholar Sophie Brutzer collected and presented overwhelming documentary evidence of his extensive Russian involvement as early as 1934, the majority of Western scholars contented themselves with passing remarks about his early Russian experience.[10] Most frequently mentioned among the poet's Russian references were his two essays on Russian art: "Russian Art" ("Russische Kunst") and "Modern Russian Art Movements" ("Moderne russische Kunstbestrebungen"); "The Book of Monkish Life" ("Das Buch vom mönchischen Leben"), the first book in *The Book of Hours* (*Das Stunden-buch*); three tales in the early collection *Stories of God* (*Geschichten vom lieben Gott*); two episodes in the novel *The Notebooks of Malte Laurids Brigge* (*Die Aufzeichnungen des Malte Laurids Brigge*), and three original poems, "Night Ride" ("Nächtliche Fahrt"), Sonnet 20 of the first part of the *Sonnets to Orpheus* (*Die Sonette an Orpheus*), and the elegy to Marina Tsvetaeva-Efron.

E. M. Butler, Rilke's skeptical British biographer, was primarily responsible for the dismissive attitudes that dominated biographical treatments of Rilke's Russian experience until the mid-1970s. In her 1940 biography, Butler contended that Rilke's interest in Russia was comparable in its striking geographical and racial affinity with Lawrence of Arabia's and Lady Hester Stanhope's obsession with the Middle East. For Butler and her followers, Rilke's travels in Russia were no more than paradigmatic journeys into the paradigmatic exotic elsewhere (Orientalism, in current critical jargon): "We do not know the laws of Rilke's Russia, we have never met its mythical inhabitants, the dreaming, inarticulate peasant-poets, fit temples for the Russian soul, humble incarnations of God. . . . To read about it . . . is to be steeped once more in the unconvincing glamour of some Never-Never land."[11] Rilke's predisposition for imitation and occasional kitsch in the early writings had become a biographical cliché,[12] and Russia served as a fitting illustration of one of the poet's youthful indulgences. Furthermore, the methodological reductionism of dominant critical methods—formalism and deconstruction—highlighted formal and thematic aspects of Rilke's later poetry, thus banishing all considerations of the author from the text. Politically motivated anti-Slavism might have acted as yet another reason for eradicating Russia from Rilke's past.

New documentary evidence, which surfaced from German and Russian archives at the time of Rilke's centenary celebrations in 1975, rekindled interest in the topic of Rilke in Russia.[13] Dr. Joachim W. Storck, one of Germany's leading Rilke scholars, launched a series of publications aimed at vindicating Rilke's ostensible cosmopolitanism. Storck explained Rilke's exaggerated Slavophilism and, by extension, his professed love for France and Scandinavian countries as the poet's defensive stance against Austro-Hungarian imperialism and as an antidote against the German ideology of ethnic superiority, which eventually lead directly to Hitler's *Mein Kampf*.[14]

Konstantin M. Azadovsky, a Russian scholar working in cooperation with German colleagues, produced a sequence of three important volumes in which he assembled, edited, and annotated a broad range of documents pertaining to Rilke and Russia: Rilke's extensive correspondence, diaries, and drafts of major works, as well as memoirs of him left by his Russian contemporaries, were all conveniently gathered in three complementary anthologies: the comprehensive *Rilke und Rußland: Briefe, Erinnerungen, Gedichte* (1986), the painstakingly detailed *Rainer Maria Rilke, Marina Zwetajewa, Boris Pasternak: Briefwechsel* (1983), and *Rainer Maria Rilke und Marina Zwetajewa: Ein Gespräch in Briefen* (1992).[15] In a series of well-documented articles, Azadovsky uncovered and made public Rilke's lesser known Russian contacts. Besides, he offered a new interpretation of Rilke's meetings with Leo Tolstoy, the artist and art historian Alexander Benois, the translator Pavel Ettinger, and the artist and illustrator Sergei Malyutin.[16]

Broad interest in Rilke's poetry among North American readers in the 1970s motivated two Slavists, Patricia Pollock Brodsky and Daria Reshetylo-Rothe, to explore Russia's place in Rilke's creative career.[17] The resulting monographs complement each other in a variety of ways. Reshetylo-Rothe's chronological account documents Rilke's journeys through Russia and the Ukraine in great detail. Poetry serves to support factual evidence. Brodsky's task is different; her orientation is primarily comparative, aimed at tracing possible textual references and allusions to Russian literature, folklore, art, and history.

The publication of Rilke's brief but emotionally charged exchange of letters with Marina Tsvetaeva and Boris Pasternak has provided scholars with a new entry into Rilke's Russian world. By engaging in correspondence with younger Russian poets, Rilke relived the nostalgia of his youth.

Attention to Rilke and the Russian theme has thus far come from different quarters, and it has become all the more urgent to acknowledge his contribution as a cultural interpreter.

THE STRUCTURE OF THIS TEXT

Constructed thematically, this study draws on earlier biographical and critical material and contributes a portrait of the writer as a worthwhile interpreter of Russian culture. It reclaims the poet's approach as a valid though idiosyncratic representation of Russian life at the turn of the last century.

Chapter 1 opens with a description of Rilke's cultural marginality vis-à-vis his own German-speaking community in multilingual Prague. His fascination for Russia was Pan-Slavic in origin, and his contacts with Czech modernists, particularly Julius Zeyer, provided a creative outlet for his anti-German feelings. Chapter 2 engages in the current debate concerning the authority of a cultural interpreter. It argues against the privileging of the "native point of view" and introduces the turn-of-the-nineteenth-century corrective to the contemporary polemic about Orientalism and feminism. Chapter 3 follows Rilke on his visits to two Russian capitals and demonstates how he was able to reconcile the polarities of Russian life by putting them to creative use. Moscow's authenticity and St. Petersburg's cosmopolitanism inspired Rilke to write in two very different styles—the deeply religious *Book of Hours* and the new thing-poems (*Ding-Gedichte*)—and these styles are analyzed here as culturally determined. Rilke's memorable journey into the Russian heartlands is the subject matter of chapter 4. The analysis focuses on Rilke's deeply religious though anticlerical position in the debate on the peasant soul, and on his ideological disagreement with the Russian intelligentsia as well as with avatars of Russian public opinion such as Tolstoy. Rilke's admiration for the peasant poet Spiridon Drozhzhin is treated as the major inspiration for his Russian poems, distantly related to the later *Ding-Gedichte*.

Chapter 5 examines Rilke's aesthetic position on religious, pictorial/iconic, and storytelling arts in Russia, which overlapped in part with that of the writer Nikolai Leskov. His observations on the tug-of-war between tradition and innovation in Russian society led to the paradoxical conclusion that the unique in art must evolve slowly from within the canonical tradition. Nikolai Leskov served as a guide in Rilke's search for authenticity in Russian culture and provided a welcome preparation for the complex world of Leo Tolstoy. The discussion in chapters 6 and 7 examines Rilke's and Andreas-Salomé's confrontation with Tolstoy and concentrates on their essays written in response to Tolstoy's "What Is Art?" as well as on their willing participation in Tolstoy's mythmaking. The creative product of his visit to Tolstoy's estate, Yasnaya Polyana, was Rilke's creative dramatization of the scene in the drafts of his novel *The Notebooks of Malte Laurids Brigge*. Rilke's image of Tolstoy (to be followed by Rodin and Cézanne) evolved from "the raging elder" into a revered antimodel.

The two concluding chapters focus on the last year in Rilke's life, when the dying poet was hoping to recapture the epiphany of his youth in Russia. The opening section throws new light on his attitude toward the Russian Revolution and its spokesman proto-Bolshevik Maxim Gorky. Correspondence between Rilke, Boris Pasternak, and Marina Tsvetaeva is presented in closing as the poets' concerted effort to preserve in poetry the culture that had been lost to politics. When it came to Russia, Rilke's resistance to history resulted in unusual cultural perspicacity of quite another, poetic kind, which merits recognition in its own terms.

Chapter One

Russia before Russia

PLACES OF ORIGIN: PRAGUE AND RUSSIA

Rilke called two places his home: Bohemia and Russia. Two Slavic lands, two ethnic neighbors, formed opposite poles in the psychological landscape of his imagined biography. When speaking and writing about his artistic origins, Rilke traveled between two counternarratives: the story of the young poet's estrangement from home and the tale of his self-discovery in a chosen land. Bohemia did not offer Rilke a useful concept of home: "kein brauchbares Heimatbewußtsein," as he put it in German. It is the thesis of this study that to complete his difficult journey from the margins of culture to the forefront, Rilke needed his two homelands: Prague, which made him aware of his needs, and Russia, which nurtured his talent. The more resentful Rilke was of his misbegotten Bohemian origins, the more determined he became to engage in creative self-ethnicity. Rilke belonged to a generation of artists who, in Walter Benjamin's description, "stood under the open sky in a countryside in which nothing remained unchanged but the clouds, and beneath the clouds . . . was the tiny, fragile human body."[1] He needed a new expression that could compress his subjective experience into the universal language of art.

In Prague, Rilke had already witnessed the rise of Pan-Slavism as a nationalist alternative to the dominant eurocentric model of social hierarchy and historical progression. For a young writer looking to define himself, the observation of a nation in the making had to be a liberating experience. If national lives could be opened up, reshuffled, and put together again in a new and meaningful way, so too, perhaps, could individual destinies be reconstructed creatively.

To make use of these new possibilities, Rilke decided to reclaim his past: "Nothing strange happens to us but only that which has belonged to us for a long time."[2] He believed in continuity and did not want to lose sight of or forget anything he had previously experienced.[3] But Rilke soon realized the

1

immense difficulty of raising himself "from the bottom of his narrow talent, meager language, ambitious youth, against the impediments imposed by place and time."[4] The sensation of Russia was one of light, promise, and hope which had been long in waiting. Rilke did not "discover" Russia but, as it were, revisited it. He later remembered experiencing a strange sensation like déjà vu upon his arrival in Moscow:

> The uneasy and confused youth had been lost for me; it reemerged again as a sunk city. And when I stood in the Kremlin on Easter night with my small candle, the clock on the Ivan Velikij Cathedral struck so powerfully and large that I believed to have heard the beating of the heart of the land which awaits its future day after day.[5]

Rilke blamed his native city for his feeling of nonbelonging, which became all-consuming to him. By leaving Prague for Munich in 1896, he followed in the steps of the majority of his fellow Prague German writers, who fled the provinces for the German-speaking cultural centers.[6] But despite his hopes, Munich made him even more acutely aware of his cultural marginality, and he relentlessly interrogated the emotional and cultural significance of Prague for his life and career.

THE PAN-SLAVIC PREDICAMENT

In the last years of the Hapsburg empire, a vigorous Pan-Slavic ideology gained momentum at the frontiers of Slavic lands. As a form of consolidated response to expansionist German policies, Pan-Slavism combined in itself German romantic thought and indigenous Slavic nationalism.[7] Prague and Belgrade more than Petersburg and Moscow insisted on close association between the Slavic lands and Russia, the only independent Slavic state. The focus of nationhood shifted from the institutions of statehood to the latent collective genius of the ethnic group. The ideal of a collective Slavic "soul" thus replaced the eurocentric Hegelian *Geist*.[8] This enabled the Slavophiles, in Dostoyevsky's spirit, to define national essence as the organic growth of the people's moral consciousness uncorrupted by the greed of Western capitalism. Pan-Slavs described themselves as different from, hostile to, and superior to the rationalist West.[9] The rising Slavic self-confidence and national pride coincided with a period of self-conscious soul-searching in the Nietzschean West; at stake were old cultural stereotypes of the Slavs as genially inert peoples existing on the margins of European civilization.[10]

Throughout the nineteenth century, the Czechs vacillated between Austro-Slavism and Pan-Slavism and by the century's end found themselves firmly placed on the side of Russia.[11] The newspaper *Pokrok* (Progress) editorialized, "We will be only coldly polite to Austria, but for the Slavs we will remain friends and brothers." Earlier, the nationalist organ of the Young Czechs, *Národní listy* (*National News*), had urged its readers: "The Czech people may rely on Russia; the Russians are aware of our distrust of Austria, and so will not deceive our hopes. . . . Russia is aware that the eyes of all Slavs are turned towards her, and that she must lead them to liberty and independence."[12]

By 1870 the Czech nationalist movement had entered a new stage of political radicalism: a broadly based "Revival of the Czech Nation" (*Obrození naroda*) followed in the steps of the "National Revival" (*Na'rodní obrození*), a cultural movement among the intellectuals.[13] With "the discovery of the people," the period of gestation of anti-Western nationalist consciousness was over. The dual meaning of the Russian word *narod* (cf. the German *das Volk* and the Czech *národ*) embraced two different concepts, the "nation" and the "folk," and thus little distinction was made between folk and national traditions. Cultural interests of young Czech patriots were chaneled in the direction of folklore: folk literature was seen as a treasure-house of shared national myths and legends open for political appropriation.[14] A Czech insistence on a common Slavic identity "in folk spirit" led to the heretofore unprecedented popularity of the Russian heroic epos, which in fact became more important to the Czechs than to Russians.[15] Russian folklore was used to demonstrate that the Slavic peoples had a great and glorious past of their own; many valued this folklore higher than Russian romantic poetry and realistic prose.[16] Almost every writer and poet of the time was engaged in planning or writing an epic on the subject of national history or a folkloric tale or legends.[17] Moreover, the transfer of written literature into folklore and, conversely, of folk into a literary mode was accepted as a matter of course. This nationalist impatience for historical legitimation eventually resulted in an episode of cultural embarrassment, of which Rilke was an interested witness.

The scandal had to do with the "discovery" in 1817 and 1819 of two collections of lyric and epic poetry, the *Queen's Court* and *Green Mountain* manuscripts (*Rukopisy kràlovedvorsk'y a zelenohorsky*). The two manuscripts were presumed to date from the ninth and thirteenth centuries and were felt to demonstrate the high level of Czech culture independent of German hegemony. But in the decade between 1875 and 1886, the two manuscripts were proved to be forgeries.[18] The disclosure met with nationalist resistance and resulted in soul-searching and questioning among leading Czech intellectuals. "Generally, it is infinitely better to have no history than to keep up in the people the inclination to falsehood," wrote a French commentator, Ernst Denis, expressing liberal European sentiment.[19]

The scandal surrounding the *Queen's Court* and *Green Mountain* manuscripts confirmed Rilke's negative reaction toward the radicalization of Czech nationalist politics. Rilke was convinced that true Czech identity, to

3

the extent that it existed, manifested itself in the primordial "childishness" of the people, while the intellectuals who forged the two manuscripts wanted them to "become old without getting older . . . Queen's Court Manuscript, indeed!"(*SW* 4:183). The protagonist of Rilke's *Two Prague Stories* speaks for the author when he pronounces his verdict on the hypocritical union between the intellectuals and the people. The abstract adoration of the "people" finds its counterpart in intellectual elitism and contempt for the dumb masses. "Hundreds of years divide them," argues Rilke's disappointed nationalist, Rezek. "We have only elders and children when it comes to culture. We have our beginning and our end, all at once. We cannot last. *That* is our tragedy, not the Germans" (*SW* 4:183).

To argue his case against the radicalization of nationalist politics, Rilke took up, in the first phase of his writerly career, the tragic events associated with the activities of the underground terrorist group Omladina. The group came to public attention in 1893, after a series of arrests of its leaders and the subsequent execution by group members of the police informer who had penetrated the movement.[20] Rilke's first novella in *Two Prague Stories*, "King Bohusch" ("König Bohusch"), portrays events from the viewpoint of the group's victim, the informer, who turns out to be a defenseless little hunchback known as König Bohusch. The events of the second novella, "Brother and Sister" ("Die Geschwister"), take place in the wake of the Omladina affair and dramatize the effects of radical politics on the general morale of the people. The heroes are a poor Czech family that moves from the provinces to Prague to enable Wanka, the son, to attend medical school. The character of Rezek, the informer's executioner in "König Bohusch," appears in the second novella as well to act as the mouthpiece for Rilke's ideas on nationalism. From the beginning, Rezek's character combines the idealism and the austerity of a blind revolutionary who gradually comes to realize the destructiveness of his actions. Rilke makes Rezek understand that his nation's tragedy lies not in its oppression by the Germans but in the tragic split between the nation's mind, its intellectuals, and its soul, the folk. Toward the end of "Brother and Sister," Rezek makes the following statement to the disenchanted Wanka:

> Our hatred of the Germans is by no means political but . . . — how shall I say it?— something human. It's not the fact that we have to share our home with the Germans that we complain about, but we are saddened that we have to grow up under such a mature people. It is the story of a child who has to grow up with adults. He learns to smile before he learns to laugh. (*SW* 4:182–83)

Rilke responded to the historical contradictions of Czech nationalism with the ambivalence characteristic of a liberal German. Being young and ambitious, he sought inspiration by plunging into the stream of a foreign nation-

4

ality.[21] But even though he rejected the German stereotype of the Czechs as a "strange, fanatical, narrow-minded, and romantically realistic nation," and supported the nationalist desire for independent nationhood, he could never think of assimilating into the Czech culture completely.[22] The difference between the Czechs and the Germans always remained for Rilke one of essence rather than of power and politics. "They are certainly not of today," Rilke wrote about the Czechs after he had left Prague. "They are a childish people, full of unfulfilled wishes having ripened overnight" (SW 4:182–83). Czech "childishness" revealed itself, in Rilke's view, in an irresponsible appropriation of Western models to forge their past; or, as the current German verdict had it, "appropriating it inwardly, reshaping it in their own way until all foreign traces have been replaced."[23] Characteristic in this connection is the mixture of admiration and fear expressed in Rilke's poetic homage to Jan Hus, the founder of Czech nationalist ideology:

> Bis zu uns her ungeheuer
> ragt der Reformator Hus,
> fürchten wir der Lehre Feuer,
> neigen wir uns doch in scheuer
> Ehrfurcht vor dem Genius. ("Superavit," SW 1:34)

> Before us towers
> Hus the reformer,
> and even though we fear his fiery teaching
> we bow down in timid
> reverence for his genius.

In Prague, Rilke already clearly separated radical nationalist politics from the national folk tradition. He rejected politics to promote aesthetics.[24]

RILKE'S PRAGUE

The outward impression of Prague was of a quiet and self-contented sleepy provincial capital neglected by Vienna.[25] The city's labyrinthine passageways—the distinguishing feature of its mixture of architectural styles—added a touch of claustrophobia to the general atmosphere of social decay: "You can walk through entire areas of Prague without having to use the open street for more than an occasional crossing," remembered Egon Erwin Kisch, Rilke's younger contemporary.[26] For someone with Rilke's energy and ambition, the German community of Prague offered little room for self-expression. The city's pale inhabitants resembled, in his description, the "heavy, enigmatic furniture" that cluttered the city's apartments. "It is the past that is kept alive in the chairs and wardrobes and pictures," Rilke wrote. "[T]he tiny rooms, three flights up, are innocent of this strange past, like people whose faces have inherited the name of a feeling from some ancestor and which they cannot wear because of their own weak hearts."[27] Rilke's compatriots were people of the past, always on the defensive against encroachments by the future. The Prague people, wrote Rilke, "Live their own past all their lives. . . . They are like corpses who cannot find peace and therefore live their death again and again in the secrecy of the night. The only progress they know is when their coffins rot to pieces or their garments fall apart . . . and they tell about it in voices long dead, such are people in Prague."[28]

Rilke's early stories capture the ghost of Prague's "vanished age," the aged, lethargic citizenry paralyzed by a general feeling of hopelessness and inertia. Depictions of "ghostliness which shuts itself off from reality" became the characteristic signature of Prague German writers. Ernst Wodak, one of Rilke's compatriots, confirmed his image of a city sunk in its past: "Particularly in beautiful weather one could see the old, white-haired men taking their dogs for a walk in the public gardens, passing the time in peaceful solitude or lively discussion with their peers about events that had taken place decades ago."[29]

Prague's outward cultural stagnation concealed the deepening social rifts among the three ethnic groups: the Germans, desperately clinging to their privileges; the Czechs, clamoring for cultural recognition and political representation; and the Jewish minority, struggling to survive in the political crossfire between the Germans and the Czechs. "In Prague the Germans live in quicksand," wrote the Prague novelist Paul Leppin. "The political tension of the last few decades has made coexistence between the Germans and the Czechs an extremely uncomfortable matter, creating a climate of repressed violence which limits above all the spontaneity of bourgeois life." Rilke himself mentioned "the street unrest" in a letter to his Prague fiancée, Valerie von David-Rhonfeld.[30]

Prague's social paralysis was translated into the linguistic sphere, and by the end of the nineteenth century the stream of German language in Bohemia threatened to dry up. "In Prague, we have no German people from whom the language can be reproduced, we are nothing but cultural Germans," complained Heinrich Teweles, editor of the monthly *Böhmen* (*Bohemia*), on the theme of social homogeneity in the predominantly middle-class German community. Franz Kafka commented on the puritanical sterility of Prague German writing to a Czech correspondent: "This is something a German does not dare to expect from his language, he does not dare to write so personally."[31]

Linguists generally agreed that the linguistic particularity of Prague German consisted in its abstract nature and relative poverty of expression.

Loss of spontaneity and melody, frozen in distorted syntax, resulted in rigid "literalization" of meaning.[32] While High German was still perceived to be the vehicle of universal intellectual expression and distinguished literature, Prague German, like so many local dialects, fell victim to linguistic hybridization. The only remaining stronghold of German influence in Bohemia, Prague German was richly shaded by Slavic, Czech, and Yiddish influences.[33] Outside the capital, the dry "paper German" (*papiernes Deutsch*), originally intended for official use only, mutated when spoken with Slavic intonation, idioms, word choice, and grammatical flow. Rilke deplored Prague's linguistic pollution, particularly in the marginal areas of contingent languages; he saw an "uneasy confusion of words" in the contact of the two linguistic bodies. In a letter to Alfred Sauer, a Prague literature professor, he identified language as the main culprit in Prague's cultural deficiency: "As a result, anyone who was raised in Prague, who was nourished therefore with the rotten refuse of language, later developed an aversion, even a sort of shame, for everything that had been taught to him during his tender childhood."[34] The "refuse of language" criticized by Rilke refers not to High German or native Czech but to *Kuchelböhmisch*, a German-Czech dialect used for communication between the two nationalities.

During these years, the language question became political for the majority of young Prague Germans. Regardless of talent, they turned to literature to seek escape from the confines of their cultural ghetto. "It was normal to ask every young Prague German abroad if he had written many books," remembered the Prague linguist Fritz Mauthner, "for one automatically assumed that he had."[35]

Nor was Rilke immune to this insecurity, which, in a not uncommon move, he managed to transform into a strength. Throughout his life, he tried to overcome what he believed was the barrenness of his native German dialect. Linguistic homelessness made him seek self-expression in the languages of his choice. His phenomenal gift as a translator and as a writer in foreign languages was an expression of a "jubilant and positive confession of belonging to the universal."[36] While direct Prague idiom surfaced only occasionally in Rilke's mature work,[37] his aversion to its baroque gaudiness (feigning wealth to hide poverty) resulted in his concentration on a single word and a single object in his search for a personal style. Rilke quickly abandoned the overwrought pathos of his earlier prose and cultivated increasingly lucid and sober expression in his "thing-poems."

At a time when Rilke found it difficult to attach himself to any coherent language or culture, Czech offered the most obvious and easily accessible linguistic and cultural alternative to German. Critical opinion has been divided between those who dismiss Rilke's occasional use of Czech phrases as ungrammatical and pretentious and those who insist on his genuine interest in participating in the Czech cultural revival.[38] Some even see his use of

Czech as a personal defiance of his mother's arrogant order not to use the language of servants.[39] But for Rilke, knowledge of the Czech language and its use in his work was a political rather than an aesthetic statement. Prague politics always stood in the way of any free artistic borrowing and cross-fertilization. In a letter to Pavel Ettinger, a Petersburg translator and scholar, Rilke explained his attitude toward the Czech language in the following way: "I do not know Czech because our family was the leading German family in Prague and it would have been seen as betrayal were one to let oneself as a child learn and understand the language of his neighbors, the people of Bohemia, whom I value so much. Now I often regret this omission."[40]

Rilke left Prague with the feeling of "anxious, heavy childhood" weighing him down: he was painfully self-conscious about the imperfections of his native language. But he was driven not just by a need to overcome his German ethnicity. For him, it was fascinating to explore the creative possibilities of an alternative cultural identity, and he committed himself to taking his future in his own hands.[41] In Prague, however, the standoff between the three ethnic groups, and the social taboos of the ruling German minority, prevented him from attempting such creative experimentation.

FIRST SLAVIC MELODIES

In contrast to his prose portrayals of sickly and haunted Prague, in Rilke's poetry folk Bohemia emerges as gay and optimistic. The poems of the *Offerings to the Lares* (*Larenopfer*) (1896), his first collection of poetry, are dedicated entirely to native Bohemian themes. While stylistically tentative, the poems are remarkably focused in theme: portrayals of landscapes, scenes of folk life, and objects of everyday use. The underlying concern of most of the poems, despite their exterior simplicity, is the resolution of the Czech national dilemma. Rilke described his intentions in *Offerings to the Lares* in a letter to an appreciative Czech correspondent. His poetry, Rilke wrote, expressed the sympathy he felt for the Czech people in their national effort; he offered to serve as a witness to the "supreme empire above the caste division of the nations: the empire on which the sun of art never sets." The universal nature of art, he believed, made him accept the common people and respect their naïveté more readily than the arrogant Germanophilism of literary and society circles in Prague. Rather than imitate foreign models, Rilke insisted, the Czech people should seek self-expression in traditional art forms: in singing, dancing, and music flowing in peaceful harmony with the smiling Bohemian landscape. Rilke considered his poems to be a "sounding of a gentle chord of peace amidst the clash of battle."[42]

The poem "Land and Folk" ("Land und Volk") is thematically central in *Offerings to the Lares*. It advances Rilke's argument that the Czech nation should look for authenticity and original self-expression in its indigenous traditions:

> . . . Gott war guter Laune. Geizen
> ist doch wohl nicht seine Art;
> und er lächelte: da ward
> Böhmen, reich an tausend Reizen.
>
> Wie erstarrtes Licht liegt Weizen
> zwischen Bergen, waldbehaart,
> und der Baum, den dichtgeschart
> Früchte drücken, fordert Spreizen.
> Gott gab hütten; voll von Schafen
> Ställe; und der Dirne klafft
> vor Gesundheit fast das Mieder.
>
> Gab den Burschen all, den braven,
> in die rauhe Faust die Kraft,
> in das Herz—die Heimatlieder. (SW 1:22–23)

> . . . God was in a good mood. Greediness
> was not his way;
> and he smiled; so became
> Bohemia rich with a thousand riches.
>
> Wheat like petrified light lies
> between the mountains, hairy with forest,
> and the tree, bending
> under hearvy fruits, demands props.
>
> God gave huts; stalls
> full of sheep; and lasses whose bodices
> were almost bursting from health.
>
> Gave all the lads, the good fellows,
> strength in their feasts,
> and native songs—in their hearts.

In Rilke's Bohemian poems, his mythical Czech folk live by nature, not by nurture; they are God's happy creatures who go through life singing folk songs to the accompaniment of simple folk fiddles. The self-conscious presence of an outsider, a voyeur, disturbs the naive simplicity of their existence.

The outsider spies on their merriment through the windows of a country inn and withdraws to record their "songs." Rilke's "The Folk Way" ("Volksweise") is inspired by such a chance observation:

Mich rührt so sehr
böhmischen Volkes Weise,
schleicht sie ins Herz sich leise,
macht sie es schwer. (*SW* 1:39)

I am so touched
by the ways of the Bohemian folk;
it silently creeps into my heart,
it makes it heavy.

In "The Folk Song" ("Das Folkslied"), he introduces the image of an accidental observer, a poet who forgets his worldly sophistication and immerses himself in the unreflecting idyll of folk life. Czech national poets, Rilke concluded, would succeed only by returning to their people and looking inward, into themselves:

Und große Dichter, ruhmberauschte,
dem schliechte Liede lauschen sie,
so gläubig wie das Volk einst lauschte
dem Gotteswort des Sinai. (*SW* 1:40)

And a great poet, intoxicated with fame,
listened to simple songs
as piously as the people once listened
to the word of God on Sinai.

Rilke believed that the future of the Czech nation depended on the people's ability to guard against the cosmopolitan dissipation of their newly discovered national pride and self-awareness. "Sounds of Freedom" ("Freiheisklänge") emphasizes his concern with the seductive attractivenesss of uncritical cosmopolitanism: adopting a rhetorical position with time-honored credentials in European romanticism, Rilke insisted that the legendary folk tradition alone, not poor imitations of the West, could provide nourishment for the national Slavic spirit.

Böhmens Volk! In deinen Kreisen
weckt ein neuer Genius
alte, heiße Freiheitsweisen,
und die mahnen nicht mit leisen

Worten, daß ein Fesseleisen
ganz zerschmettert werden muß.

Diese Streitpoeten blasen
lockend; und in Stücke haun
kannst du, Volk, in deinem Rasen
des Gesetzes Marmorvasen,
doch du kannst aus ihren Phrasen
keine Zukunft dir erbaun.

Tief in Herz und Sinn in treuer
Hoffnung senkt die Liedersaat,
sind dir deine Dichter teuer,
daß daraus ein Lenz, ein neuer,
keime.—Was dann blieb vom Feuer,
das entflamme dich zur Tat. (SW 1:45–46)

People of Bohemia! Among you
A new genius is awaking
old, heated ways of freedom,
and with no longer quiet words they are warning
that the iron fetters
have to be completely destroyed.

These fighting poets sing
enticingly; and you can, O people, in your rage
break to pieces the law's marble vases,
but you cannot build a
future for yourself from their phrases.

Deep into heart and mind
sink the songs in true hope,
and your poets are dear to you
then the spring will come, a new one,
young.—What will then remain from the fire
which inflamed you to action.

While in Prague, Rilke learned about the mythological hero Dalibor, who seemed to him to be the Czech national prototype of the artist. As the old Czech legend had it, the captive soldier Dalibor succeeded in freeing himself from his prison cell by turning into a musician. He enchanted his jailers with the sounds of the fiddle, which he had mastered in prison.[43] As

11

far as Rilke was concerned, there could have been no better and no less violent resolution to the Czech standoff with the Germans than Dalibor's. In his
Prague novella "Brother and Sister," Rilke has the disenchanted radical
Rezek talk nostalgically about Dalibor's miraculous escape from his captors.
Rezek guides the Wankas, brother and sister, who are confused about the
nationalist movement, through Daliborka, the tower in which the knight was
kept prisoner. In Rilke's presentation, Daliborka is transformed from the site
of Dalibor's captivity into the monument of his liberation. Dalibor's fiddle
becomes the instrument of his escape. He is the essence of the contrast
between the Slavic temperament and Western rationality.[44] The Dionysian
Slavs transcend confinement, mental and physical, owing to their unlimited
capacity for aesthetic feeling and profound emotion. In the poem "Neverthe-
less" ("Trotzdem") Rilke describes how once, while reading Schopenhauer,
he suddenly felt imprisoned in a "cell full of mourning," but the memory of
the legendary Dalibor liberated him from his intellectual captivity.

> Manchmal vom Regal der Wand
> hol ich meinen Schopenhauer,
> einen "Kerker voller Trauer"
> hat er dieses Sein genannt.

> So er recht hat, ich verlor
> nichts: in Kerkereinsamkeiten
> weck ich meiner Seele Saiten
> glücklich wie einst Dalibor. (*SW* 1:35)

> Often, I pick up
> my Schopenhauer from the bookshelf on the wall,
> he called this Being
> "Prison cell full of mourning."

> So, he was right, I have not lost
> anything: in the loneliness of jail
> I wake up my soul's different sides,
> happy as once was Dalibor.

In future years, the rich tradition of Russian narrative poems, *byliny*,
offered Rilke a broader folkloristic base on which to experiment with epic
Slavic themes. The three knights or *bogatyrs*, Ilya Muromets, Nikita
Dobrynin, and Alyosha Popovich, along with their antagonist, the mischie-
vous Solovei Razboinik, the Robber Nightingale, succeeded Dalibor in
Rilke's gallery of folk heroes. For Rilke, the transition from his earlier admi-

ration for Czech folk music to a love of Russian peasant poetry, choral singing, and *khorovod* dancing was a natural one to make. There was an important shift in Rilke's mythopoetic attitudes, however: the Russian tradition was similar and yet in some fundamental ways different from its sister Czech tradition. In Russian lore, tradition did not obscure but illuminated the peculiar existence of its individual members, particularly poets. As enunciators of collective creativity, folk bards affirmed the tradition without losing their distinct personal style. The broad strokes used earlier by Rilke to extol folk creativity gave way to particularizing portrayals of individual performers. In *Offerings to the Lares*, he tampered with the individual characters of real poets in order to produce a gallery of ideal national types measured against the model of the legendary Dalibor.

Four Czech poets were of personal importance to Rilke: Svatopluk Čech (1846–1908), to whom Rilke wrote a letter;[45] Kajetan Týl (1808–56), whose museum he visited; and two cosmopolitan contemporaries, the modernists Julius Zeyer (1841–1901) and Jaroslav Vrchlicky (1853–1912), to whom Rilke was particularly close in temperament and aesthetic vision.

Rilke's individual portraits of these different national poets clearly fit his overall Czech agenda. Most didactic in this respect is the poem "Kajetan Týl," in which the image of the poet is primarily of a national hero, an icon for his people to worship and imitate. Written in response to an ethnographic exhibition of 1895 honoring Týl's dedication to his people, the poem attempts to create a museum in its own right. Rilke was among the few Germans who visited the exhibition, in defiance of a general German boycott. Particularly important for Rilke was Týl's loyalty to his people and his decision to return to Bohemia after many years of traveling in the West. The poem concludes with a reference to Týl's popular tune "Kde domov můj" ("Where My Home Is"), which had become the Czech national hymn of liberation.[46]

> Doch wär er nicht für tausend Louis
> von Böhmen fort. Mit jeder Fiber
> hing er daran.—"Ich bleibe lieber,"
> hätt er gesagt, "kde domov můj." (*SW* 1:39)

> But not for a thousand louis
> would he have gone from Bohemia. With every fibre
> he was devoted to it.—"I'd better stay,"
> he said, "kde domov můj."

Svatopluk Čech, somewhat behind Týl in importance, was among those Czech national bards whose work celebrated Pan-Slavic unity with Russia. "It lives, it lives, the Slav spirit, defiantly it grows and flowers!" Čech wrote in his most popular poem, "Hej Slovane." "The Russian is with us, the

Frenchman will sweep away whoever is against us."[47]

Even though Rilke honored Čech's and Týl's unwavering commitment to the nationalist cause, he was cautious not to endorse their politicization of aesthetics. At this early stage, Rilke was still willing to strike a compromise between aesthetics and politics in the name of a higher ideal of individual and national independence. His aesthetic affinities, nonetheless, were with the Czech writers of cosmopolitan orientation. The modernists Zeyer and Vrchlicky were no less dedicated to their people than were Týl and Čech, but they accepted the national ideal only as long as it did not prevent their access to the broader world of modern culture. Russia was their compromise between the national ideal and the foreign exotic. Russia was seen as a source of tremendous potential strength and the home of a highly literary culture. Above everything else, Julius Zeyer's personal commitment to Russia served as a foundation for Rilke's future image of the country.

JULIUS ZEYER AND THE RUSSIAN SOLUTION

Rilke's acquaintance with Julius Zeyer profoundly influenced his future aesthetic orientation in general, not just his views of Russia.[48] Those idiosyncracies which strike Rilke's biographers as untraditional for a German were largely due to the "Czech" origins of his view of Russian culture. Zeyer's interest in Russia was of a purely aesthetic nature: nationalist and Pan-Slavic sentiments served him only as an occasional backdrop.[49] More important for Zeyer was to discover Russia's simple, unquestioning faith in God, which purified and mystified aesthetic experience. It was precisely because of Zeyer's ability to convince Rilke of Russia's aesthetic importance beyond the ideological constraints of Pan-Slavism that he was able to make Russia attractive to the young poet.

Zeyer stood out among his Prague contemporaries as a truly cosmopolitan figure. The son of a rich Prague industrialist of Alsatian descent and a German-Jewish mother, Zeyer spoke German and French better than Czech, but early in life he chose to write primarily in Czech in a gesture of opposition to repressive Viennese policies in Bohemia.[50] A great part of his life was spent traveling; Bohemia always seemed too narrow to accommodate his restless imagination.

Zeyer first went to Russia as a student in 1873, driven by an almost religious anticipation of a holy land: "The gates of the Slavic Mecca will open to me; for me it is like Odysseus sitting on the banks of the sea," he wrote to a friend.[51] After arriving in Petersburg, Zeyer lived in the house of an Old Believer, Shubin, who told him many fine things about his life in the North. Zeyer's friend Professor Kašpar reported that Shubin "also explained the Old Believers' faith and rites, all of which interested Zeyer greatly, so that he thought little of home."[52] In Petersburg, Zeyer found work as a reader and clipper of economic articles from foreign papers for Prince Golytsin, but he soon changed employment to become a tutor and companion to the son of Count Valuev, a Russian minister. The Valuevs were a highly educated, intellectual family who knew Russian culture well; they introduced Zeyer to Russian folklore and religion and encouraged him to study the Russian epic tradition and to begin writing on his own. On his second visit to Russia, in 1880, Zeyer was employed as a tutor in the household of a veteran of the Russo-Turkish War, General Popov. His work for the Russian war hero did not make Zeyer any more pro-Slavic. Although he longed for Slavic unity, he was becoming less rapturous and naive about the Russian Empire and more pessimistic about European realpolitik. His political views expressed a growing sense of futility, and he was particularly critical of tsarist absolutism.

> The Germans do whatever they wish, the world now actually belongs to them. What tricks they play against Russia everywhere and Russia does nothing. What trouble they [the Russians] could make for them if they set up something on the very border of Bohemia. And if they left off the persecution of the Poles, then they could have a fine dance in Germany itself, in Poznan, for example. But they are not even interested in the Russians in Hungary.[53]

In order to understand the enigma of the Russian people and their deeply religious character, Zeyer sought material that revealed primitive passions and desires; he turned to folklore and religion. He was only marginally interested in the great Russian psychological novel. For him, the attractiveness of a foreign Slavic lore lay both in its linguistic similarity with the Czech and in its remoteness, which allowed it to be answered creatively. Typical of Zeyer's desire to create his own mystical world was his passion for collecting objects of religious art. No doubt, when Rilke was first brought to Zeyer's house by Valerie von David-Rhonfeld, the writer's niece, he was introduced to Zeyer's stories and impressions of Russia as well as to his treasury of Russian Orthodox objects: old lamps, icons, and even an icon screen.[54]

At the time of his first meeting with Rilke in 1893, Zeyer had just returned from a five-month journey to Russia, his third, in the course of which he had traveled to Kiev, down the Dnieper, through Crimea, and to the Caucasus (Rilke would follow a similar route on his own second Russian journey). It was on this trip that Zeyer had heard the blind singer recite the song of Aleksei, the man of God, about whom he wrote a story, "Aleksei, Man of God" ("Alexej, člověk Boži'").[55] Zeyer's last visit to Russia, in the summer of 1899, almost coincided with Rilke's first trip.

Much of Zeyer's work involved Russian subjects. He started by writing historical works (*Ondrej Cernysev*, a novel; *Darija*; and a song about Igor based on an ancient Russian chronicle account, *Revenge for the Death of*

Igor [*Zpev o pomstê za Igora*][56] and finished his career by responding to the Russian epos. Zeyer was among the first to draw Rilke's attention to Russian literature, and his peculiar taste must have affected Rilke's own highly selective readings. Rilke's 1905 translation of the twelfth-century Russian epic song *The Lay of Igor's Campaign* (*Slovo o polku Igoreve*) bears the subtitle "From the Translations of the Igor-Tale" ("Aus den Übersetzungen des Igor-Lieds"), which undoubtedly refers not only to the available modern Russian versions of the original epic but also to its Czech imitations and interpretations, known to him long before he had read the original.[57] Zeyer approached the Russian epic material with the desire to refocus it, and his method remained consistent throughout his career: he retained the outlines of the original to develop them organically, filling in details and characteristics. (Of course, both Zeyer and Rilke understood "translation" in the very broad eighteenth-century sense of cultural transmission.) He freely added themes from other songs to heighten the interest and emotional effect of his story. Zeyer's touch is visible in Rilke's future work with the Russian folklore material: his translation of *The Lay of Igor's Campaign* and the three Russian stories in his collection *Stories of God*. Rilke echoed the motifs of Zeyer's "Aleksei, Man of God" in his own version, "The Song of Justice," included in *Stories of God*. In addition, Zeyer's personal gift of "Three Legends of Crucifix" ("Tri legendy o krucufixu") (1895) inspired Rilke's religious cycle "Christus Visionen," started in 1896.

By this time, Zeyer had been discovered by the younger generation of writers in Prague as a leader in the emerging Czech decadent movement, and he became a local celebrity of sorts. Rilke remembered in a letter to Otilie Malybrok-Stieler, a German translator, how Zeyer's encouragement at their first meeting was flattering to him: "I felt richly rewarded, on the one hand, by his open and warm acceptance which he accorded me with his tone and look and, on the other hand, with anecdotes and stories which had been given to him by his extensive travels and which he knew how to relate in most polished ways."[58]

Rilke has since been reproached by critics for having altered Zeyer's character in his later poetic tribute to "the Master."[59] Even though Rilke was well aware of Zeyer's personal aloofness, his elitist tastes, and his idiosyncratic attitudes, he had historical and literary reasons for picturing the leader of Czech modernism as a folk bard. If in the West decadence and nationalism represented two radically opposed trends, the decadent movement in Bohemia took root in the historical situation of Czechs as a subject nation. Czech modernism had its psychological basis in the melancholy and depression of an elite isolated within a radically nationalist society. Unprecedented emphasis on individualism was a reaction to German oppression, on the one hand, and a rejection of the homogenizing ideology of the radical nationalist movement, on the other.[60] As far as Rilke was concerned, the aesthete Zeyer transcended the nearsightedness of a narrow nationalism and bequeathed to his people a vision of the future as seen from within the legends and myths of their past, thus tying them in with the international cultural tradition. Zeyer and the circle of modernist writers that gathered around the journals *Moderní revue* and *Lumír* attracted a following of young people who adopted the modernist agenda as an opening for self-expression and a new sensibility. Rilke hoped that Zeyer's message would eventually be heard.

Du bist ein Meister;—früher oder später
spannt sich dein Volk in deinen Siegeswagen;
du preisest seine Art und seine Sagen,—
aus deinen Liedern weht der Heimat Äther.
. . . .
Es hat dein Volk sich seine Ideale
noch nicht versetzen lassen zu den Sternen,
die unerreichbar sind und Sehnsucht glasten;

du aber mahnst, ein echter Orientale,
es möge in dem Ringen nicht verlernen
auch im Alhambrahof die Kunst zu rasten. (*SW* 1:35-36)

You are the master;—sooner or later
your people will harness themselves into your triumphant carriage;
you glorify their art and their legends,—
the ether of homeland wafts in your songs.
. . . .
Your people have not yet let their ideals
rise high to the stars,
which are unreachable and radiate longing;

and you warn them, as a true Oriental,
one should not unlearn in his struggle
to find time for art even at the court of Alhambra.

   The young Rilke was too ambitious and restless to commit himself to any political cause or to seek any definitive literary affiliation. He participated in practically all intellectual and cultural activities available to him in Prague: he joined the leading artistic associations, embarked on a variety of publishing ventures, promoted his own writings, did journalistic work for *Jung-Deutschland und Jung-Elsaß*, and edited his own journal, *Jung-Deutschland und Jung-Österreich*. He used Slavic motifs and words in his writings only to add local color and an exotic quality to his first, aesthetically quite unremarkable, literary productions. In 1896, in the draft of an entry for a lexicon of nineteenth-century German poets and prose writers, Rilke described himself in the following manner:

> René Maria Rilke . . . currently editor of "Young Germany and Young Austria." My motto: patior ut potiar. For the present I nourish a striving towards light; for the future, one hope and one fear. The hope: inner peace and joy of creation. The fear (burdened as I am with an hereditary nervous condition): madness! I am active in the fields of drama (*Free and Equal, Hoar-Frost*), the novella and sketch (many scattered in over 20 journals, soon to be collected), lyric poetry, psychodrama, criticism, etc.[61]

EWALD TRAGY: THE PRODIGAL SON'S DEPARTURE

Rilke completed his story *Ewald Tragy* (1898) two years after he left Prague for Munich. Writing this profoundly autobiographical novella must have played a cathartic role in his life. In writing it, Rilke sought to liberate himself from his dark childhood fears binding him to his Slavic homeland.[62] *Ewald Tragy* stands out among the rest of Rilke's Prague tales—"Pierre Dumont" (1894), "The Seamstress" ("Die Näherin") (1894), "The Gym Hour" ("Die Turnstunde") (1899), and *Two Prague Stories* (*Zwei Prager Geschichten*) (1899)—as the closest anticipation of his later autobiographical novel, *The Notebooks of Malte Laurids Brigge*. Rilke appropriates in his early novella the biblical legend of the prodigal son. Beginning with Ewald, all Rilke's heroes become perpetual leave-takers: the itinerant bards of the *Stories of God*, the rebellious Russian monks, the icon painter of "The Book of Monkish Life," the Parisian artist Malte Laurids Brigge, and the lyrical subject of his Elegy to Marina-Tsvetaeva Efron. This image completes its full circle in the *Eighth Duino Elegy*:

> . . . daß wir,
> was wir auch tun, in jener Haltung sind
> von einem, welcher fortgeht? Wie er auf
> dem letzten Hügel, der ihm ganz sein Tal
> noch einmal zeigt, sich wendet, anhält, weilt—,
> so leben wir und nehmen immer Abschied. (*SW* 1:716)

> . . . we have the bearing
> of a man going away? As on the last hill
> that shows him all his valley, for the last time,

he turns, stands still, and lingers, so we live,
forever saying farewell.[63]

Chronologically, Ewald's story unfolds on three different levels: his Prague past, his Munich present, and his expectations for the future. The story's opening scene depicts the family's last gathering in Prague, convened on the occasion of Ewald's departure. Even though Ewald's decision has already been announced, it still remains to be explained and justified to the disapproving relatives. Ewald's father grudgingly yields to his son's argument that leaving home is central to his education and personal growth: "Good, have your experiences. I have nothing against that." The elder Tragy admits that in these matters he is no longer up to date and cannot identify completely with Ewald's reasoning. When Ewald senses his father's defensive position and willingness to compromise, he ventures a new attack: "That is exactly it, from sometime ago, from *anno olim,* you are dusty and dried up" (*SW* 4:517).

Herr Tragy's wavering and the aging aunts' resentment are the easiest obstacles to overcome in Ewald's battle for independence; self-doubt is his more enduring enemy. At the family's last dinner, the most feared question is put to Ewald by the outsider to the family, the French governess Fräulein Jeanne: "Are you a poet then?" To his horror, Ewald has to admit that he is not sure of the answer: "That's just it, I do not know. And one should really know one way or the other. *Here* I can't get it clear: one can't get outside oneself, I need quiet, and room, and perspective. . . . and I have so many doubts myself. Really—I lie awake sometimes the whole night . . . and torment myself with the question, 'Am I worthy?'" (*SW* 4:530–35)

Jeanne is an accidental visitor from the world to which Ewald wants to belong. Her words "And—are you leaving?" sound interrogatory to his ear and he replies with a hasty "yes." To Ewald's prudish family, this exchange resembles a scene of seduction by the French girl, a fitting explanation for his departure.

Ewald's first few weeks in Munich make him realize that his departure from Prague was the easiest part of his life journey; he sinks into deep despair: "All to no end. He remains forgotten. He can call and make signs [*Zeichen geben*]; his voice reaches nowhere and he reaches no one." In despair, Ewald composes a letter to his mother in which he asks for her sympathy and compassion. It immediately becomes clear to him, however, that "this thin and nervous woman" understands him least of all. At this painful moment of realization, Ewald slowly burns his letter, "in small shivering flames." He continues to live with the feeling of a heightened expectation of a great future for himself: "But it is precisely in those days that his desire for participation is so strong; it continues to grow in him and becomes an unquenched dry thirst, which does not discourage him but makes him bitter and defiant" (*SW* 4:566–67).

In Rilke's personal life, to the extent that he repeated Ewald's trajectory, the solution came unexpectedly. In May 1897 he met Lou Andreas-Salomé. Fourteen years Rilke's senior, Andreas-Salomé was an established author and journalist who had just embarked on a new intellectual venture: the study of Russia. Rilke embraced Andreas-Salomé's Russian idea with enthusiasm. "It was so essential for me, with my different interests, to concentrate at last on something—and I have chosen Russia," he explained to his mother in a letter. "I must stick with it, don't you think?"[64] In Russia, in Andreas-Salomé's analysis, the man in Rilke finally caught up with the emerging artist. The two lived in harmony with each other for a brief while, until ultimately the artist overtook the man completely.[65] Rilke could not predict the long-lasting effect that Russia was to have on him, but he captured the first moments of his arrival in Moscow with poetic accuracy:

> In the dusk, the giant outlines of the church projected straight into the sky and to its sides, in the fog; there were two silver chapels. On their steps, pilgrims awaited the opening of the doors. This sight so unusual for me shook me to the depth of my soul: for the first time in my life I had an inexpressible feeling, something like a feeling of home—I felt strongly that I belonged to something, my God, to something in this world.[66]

Chapter Two

Mapping the "Russian Soul":
Lou Andreas-Salomé

"OCCIDENTALISM" AND ITS DISCONTENTS

Rilke's image of Russia as a site for an imaginary escape from Prague took tangible form under the guidance of Lou Andreas-Salomé (1861–1937). Born and raised in a German-speaking family in the center of St. Petersburg, Andreas-Salomé was no more Russian than Rilke was Czech. But even though as a child she took little interest in events outside her German home, school, and church, she always insisted that the Salomés felt themselves as a family to be not only in the Russian military "service" but Russians.[1] Being the only girl, she was the only one of the six children to pursue higher education in Europe. At the age of eighteen, she followed the common route of young Russian women of her age and class. While in the West, Andreas-Salomé kept her Russian passport until the Bolshevik Revolution, and committed herself to no single culture, state, or—for that matter—man. In everything she did, she tacked between the "inside" and "outside" of events and relationships, between experience, interpretation, and identification.

At the time of her meeting with Rilke, Andreas-Salomé's interest in Russia was of a fairly recent vintage, encouraged by her acquaintance with the group of Berlin naturalists associated with Die freie Bühne (the free stage). After returning to Russia in 1895, she embarked on a schedule of fairly regular "expeditions" covering the Russian cultural scene for the German and Austrian press. Andreas-Salomé's Russian surveys earned her the reputation of being a well-informed expert. Her attitude toward language was purely pragmatic: she did not seek to attain native "virtuosity" in Russian but to develop an efficient comprehension of it that would allow her to read it and to observe the culture.

Andreas-Salomé's position of cultural relativism conferred on her an advantage over the "insider's" partialities and the "outsider's" biases. She represented a new type of cultural interpreter who resented totality in any of its forms. One is tempted to apply to her style of cultural commentary the interpretative model of "outsidedness" currently associated in the Slavic tradition with Mikhail Bakhtin: "In the realm of culture, outsidedness is a most powerful factor in understanding."[2] She approached cultures first and foremost with an anthropocentric concern for the subject; more specifically, she focused her readings of Russian culture on the Russian character type in its multiple manifestations. The imposition of coherence on unruly cultural material became for Andreas-Salomé a matter of the interpreter's choice, a choice that she acknowledged had to be responsibly made. As for herself, she offered to act as a mediator between Russia and the West, unmasking both Western "Orientalism" and its counterpart, Slavic "Occidentalism."

Andreas-Salomé's competence as an interpreter of Russian culture has been challenged on many occasions in connection with the ongoing critical investigation of Western biases in representing non-Western civilizations.[3] Her critics saw her principle of a psychological approach to cultures replace the more traditional ethnographic approach and, in the end, felt that it collapsed into self-indulgence: "What better way was there to keep at a safe distance than . . . to extol their virtues without really having anything to do with them?" To assert that Andreas-Salomé (and later Rilke) did not know much about Russia ("she had no authority to prophesy about Russia") is to suggest that there was only one "real" Russia to represent—the essential Russia— and to assume that all Western "visions" and "textualizations" suppressed the authentic native humanity.[4] It is also to read Andreas-Salomé out of her own time. Andreas-Salomé began writing when Russia had already established itself as a mighty colonial empire and had begun talking back to Europe in a strong nationalist voice. The myth of the Russian soul had penetrated the West through popular Russian novels and had successfully competed with Western ideologies of cultural superiority. Andreas-Salomé did not intend to submit the undifferentiated "Russian essence" to a systematic Western interrogation; instead, she wanted to initiate a creative dialogue between the two cultures. Although she studied her new subject assiduously, she never planned to complete an inventory or a comprehensive description of Russian culture. No single definition was conclusive to her, and she decided to focus on specific cultural features that could function as types for a cultural synthesis.

Rilke's role as a poet and a sympathetic observer fitted well with Andreas-Salomé's scenario of the "Russian drama." She saw clear parallels between an artist's psychological state of anticipation and Russia's fin de siècle belief in the country's great future. She often described Rilke and Russia in similar terms: both were "humanly alive, driven, young and confident."[5] Besides, Andreas-Salomé's human investment in Rilke was not entirely without self-interest. Without him, her encounter with Russia would have remained purely cerebral and platonic, and she could not have written after their adventure together, "Only now am I young, only now can I be what others become at 18, entirely myself."[6] A perceptive psychologist, Andreas-Salomé welcomed an opportunity to launch a young poet on a career by giving him a spiritual home, and Rilke cooperated fully with her plan. Russia bonded them in a spiritual marriage: the mature, independent, and established Andreas-Salomé became more important to the young Rilke than any other woman would be in his life.

Rilke and Andreas-Salomé turned to Russian culture neither to "merge" with it nor to impose traditional Western values on the "underdeveloped" Russian cultural landscape. They sought a new and enriching experience for themselves. Most important, they brought to Russia those questions for which there were no answers in the West. They complemented each other in this joint cultural venture: Andreas-Salomé controlled the word while Rilke excelled at capturing the image.

ORIENTALIST AND FEMINIST PERSPECTIVES

When Rilke reported to his mother that he had met two "splendid women: the famous writer Lou Andreas-Salomé and the African explorer Frieda von Bülow,"[7] he could not help identifying the two women by their remarkable careers. Andreas-Salomé and von Bülow were unique, but at the same time representative of a generation of women who sought self-actualization in cultures other than their own. Although postcolonial critics have argued persuasively—if self-evidently—that Western colonial expansion produced corporate mechanisms for dominating and restructuring other cultures and peoples, rarely have they discussed the concomitant emergence of powerful alternative, nonreductive ideologies and movements that undermined attitudes of cultural superiority.[8] Most prominent among the latter was Western feminism, which nourished itself in cross-cultural contexts. The generation of women to which Andreas-Salomé and von Bülow belonged emphasized a feminist ideology based more on the difference between genders than on their sameness. Writing, journalism, and the advocacy of underprivileged groups and nondominant ideologies became the most effective means to forward a woman's right to be involved in socially meaningful activity. The foreignness and pristine exoticism of Africa or Russia presented Western women with the freedom to live their lives the way they wanted.

Frieda von Bülow was a veritable German Isak Dinesen who ushered in a new type of Western sensibility about the African continent. The integration of individualism with social responsibility was important to von Bülow, and she earned the reputation of a dedicated "Africanist," a writer of notable talent and "colonist" in the positive sense of explorer.[9] At the age of thirty, she went to East Africa on behalf of the National Women's League (Deutsch-Nationaler Frauen Bund) to help Carl Peters, the league's founder, organize medical assistance for the natives in Zanzibar and Dar es Salaam. Andreas-Salomé left a psychological portrait of her friend in the novel *Das Haus* (*The House*) (1919) and in her memoir, *Lebensrückblick* (*Looking back*) (1931). She described von Bülow as a gifted and eccentric but repressed woman who had desired to escape from her strict upbringing in an aristocratic Prussian home. As soon as the opportunity availed itself, she escaped to Africa to look for deliverance from her periodic depressions and melancholy. For Andreas-Salomé, von Bülow's self-sacrificing work in African hospitals was motivated by a "crazy fascination for subordination" and ultimately reached the point of sadomasochistic self-indulgence. Andreas-Salomé's seemingly ungenerous and ungracious image of von Bülow in her later writing was no more than an exercise in psychoanalysis, of the kind to which she subjected most of her friends. Von Bülow rarely took offense and accompanied her friend on one of her Russian ventures. She also hosted Lou and Rilke in her summer home near Berlin while they were preparing for their second Russian journey.

If Andreas-Salomé knew about Africa from von Bülow, she was introduced to the Orient by her husband, a professor of oriental languages and cultures, Friedrich Carl Andreas.[10] Born to a half-European, half-Malaysian mother and a noble Persian father, Andreas was raised on the island of Java until the age of six, when his family moved to Germany. In his and Lou's German home, Andreas maintained a lifestyle of Eastern asceticism, marked by simple food and clothing. As a scholar, he was ahead of his time in insisting on the priority of ethnographic fieldwork and relying primarily on firsthand knowledge of other cultures. Andreas traveled widely in the Orient and lived in rural communities in Persia for extended periods of time in complete isolation from any European influence. His nonacademic approach to cultural studies, his unique talent for languages, and his insistence on accuracy and tact in the representation of other peoples' mores and traditions earned him more enemies than friends in German scholarly circles. He was able to secure a tenured teaching position in Persian and West Asiatic languages in Göttingen only after a major change in Bismarck's foreign policy had made it necessary to create several teaching centers, modeled on the Berlin Institute for Oriental Languages, to train competent diplomats and military and business personnel.

Partly because of Andreas's isolation within German academe, his circle of friends consisted primarily of literary and artistic personalities. Germany's new generation of cosmopolitan writers, actors, and artists appreciated the access to exotic cultures that Andreas's polyglot skills offered them. In the first years of their marriage, Andreas-Salomé took advantage of Andreas's connections in Berlin's cultural milieu; she met with the Danish literary critic and historian Georg Brandes;[11] the Berlin theater critic Otto Brahm; the editor of the magazine *Die Zukunft*, Maximilian Harden; the brothers Heinrich and Julius Hart; and the group associated with Die freie Bühne. Andreas knew Scandinavian languages and read untranslated works by Ibsen to his wife. Andreas-Salomé put her advantage to good use and produced pathbreaking studies of Ibsen's plays.[12] From the beginning, Andreas helped Andreas-Salomé to place her essays and reviews in the leading literary journals and worked closely with her on her style as an unbiased judge and critic.

Andreas-Salomé later remembered how she adapted herself to her husband's way of life "with great naturalness." She was even willing to leave Europe with Andreas and to immerse herself in oriental cultures. The 1899 visit to Russia was originally conceived as an oriental journey with Andreas: they wanted to visit the monastery region of Echmiadzin near Yrevan, continuing on to Armenian Persia via Moscow and Petersburg. Eventually, Rilke's participation prompted her to refocus the original version of the plan exclusively on Russia.[13] As it turned out, the oriental joint family venture demanded too much subordination from a free spirit like herself, and she decided to stage an unconventional homecoming visit to Russia in the company of her husband and her young lover.

Andreas-Salomé's return to Russia was both sentimental and theatrical. She presented herself as a prodigal daughter who had come home after a decade of wandering through Europe. Her journalistic writings on Russia ranged in genre between psychological studies and sociocultural analyses; the sentimental homecoming motif she reserved for her autobiographical prose. Rilke's role in this scenario was to provide the vessel for her emotional outpourings. In the long run, the combination of her Russian homecoming and her love affair with a sensitive young poet prepared her for her subsequent interest in Freudianism.

CONTESTING THE "RUSSIAN SOUL"

Even though Andreas-Salomé had never lost contact with her family in St. Petersburg, Russia did not become important to her intellectually and culturally until she discovered Russian literature: "The Russians interest[ed] me in other than a literary sense. I had not taken much interest in literature before. . . . I was uneducated in it."[14] Her earlier perception of Russia as a backward and hopelessly faltering Eastern empire was replaced by an image of a land of messianic promise.[15] Like the majority of Western intellectuals assaulted by the genius of the Russian novel, as if out of nowhere, Andreas-Salomé was overwhelmed by the psychological depth of Russian literary expression; a realization that made her feel a "joyful incentive, the movement of youth and self-confidence." The most amazing feature of the newly valorized Russian character was its combination of hope and hopelessness, a "promise of a new spirit [that] was not clouded by the fact that their treatment of these themes was sad and gloomy."[16]

Andreas-Salomé's involvement with Russia was relatively short-lived: starting in 1895, it ebbed in the early 1900s, and all of her subsequent publications merely repeated ideas she had developed in earlier work. The corpus of her Russian writings falls into three chronological periods: the early sociological survey of 1896, five major cultural and literary essays of the middle period (1897–98),[17] and her occasional late reviews and publications (1909–13 and 1919–21). Her two autobiographical novels, *The House* (1919) and *Rodinka* (1923), complete the Russian cycle. In her Russian publications, Andreas-Salomé dealt with a broad variety of issues ranging from informed cultural and political commentary, to analyses of Russian philosophy and literature and personal reflections on Russian life and the national character. A sensitive observer, though never a powerful or creative thinker, Andreas-Salomé possessed a remarkable synthesizing mind. She acted as a barometer of her generation's attitudes toward Russia, the tone and focus of her publications changing frequently.

Any European writing on Russia at the end of the nineteenth century was responding to the major breakthrough in Western perceptions pioneered by Melchior de Vogüé's study *Le roman russe* (1886). Andreas-Salomé was also well acquainted with the more skeptical tradition articulated by, among others, Georg Brandes in his *Impressions of Russia* (1889). Andreas-Salomé was able to develop her distinct style of commentary largely thanks to her ability to gauge the contemporary Russian intellectual scene and her knowledge of Western views on Russian society.

For much of her critical Russian material, Andreas-Salomé depended on the views and opinions of the heretical Petersburg critic Akim Lvovitch Volynsky (a pseudonym for Akim Flexer, or Flekser, 1863–1926), the writer and leading reviewer for the cosmopolitan journal *Severny Vestnik*.[18] Volynsky was one of the most hated personalities in the St. Petersburg literary establishment: his acrimonious renunciations of civic-mindedness in literature, his cosmopolitan attitude, and his uncompromising defense of marginalized dissident authors such as Nikolai Leskov earned him more enemies than friends. Volynsky's caustic expositions revealed to the fascinated Andreas-Salomé the intricate inner tensions of the Russian literary establishment. As a good student of Volynsky's "alternative" school of Russian culture, Andreas-Salomé learned not to be sentimental about Russia's past, and her occasional enthusiasms for Russia's historical role were deliberate and self-consciously theatrical. Like Volynsky, Andreas-Salomé advocated a happy synthesis between Western rationality and Russia's Eastern spirituality and believed in fundamental affinities between the Jewish and Russian religious aspirations.[19] To rely on Volynsky for information might not have guaranteed accuracy, but it gave Andreas-Salomé a provocative and unconventional angle on Russian literary politics. Volynsky translated and published Andreas-Salomé's and Rilke's work in *Severny vestnik*, and she generously reciprocated by promoting his critical writings in Germany.[20] We will return to Volynsky when we consider Rilke and Leskov.

A brief comparison of Andreas-Salomé's two Russian essays—the 1896 review of "thick journals"[21] (*tolstye zhurnaly*, a uniquely Russian institution which alone provided a venue for literary, social, and political debate) and the two-part essay "Russian Letters and Culture" ("Russische Dichtung und Kultur") (1897)—will help us locate her more precisely as a cultural critic. Andreas-Salomé's principal skill—or, as some would have it, vice—as a cultural commentator was her ability to guide Western readers through the thick maze of Russian topical publications. Her principal strategy in reviewing Russian journals was to condense their long-winded articles and simplify their convoluted messages for foreign readers. The review for 1896 is characteristic in this respect. Of the major genres in Russian "thick journals"—theoretical treatises, fiction, translations, light prose, and news reports from the provinces—Andreas-Salomé held theorizing of any kind in the lowest esteem. She believed that the Western tradition of structured logical argument was alien to the Russian associative mind and found Russian theoretical compositions lacking in organization and structure and, even at their best, imitative of the West. Russia's contemporary infatuation with Marxist economic theory was, she felt, highly inappropriate for a country with its social and national traditions and could not promise its people any viable solution. Although Andreas-Salomé mentions the emerging workers' groups and clubs, she viewed them exclusively as a symptom of social dislocations within the "folk organism." They represented to her the enormity of the social and economic transformation facing Russian industrial centers and the countryside.[22] If Russia were ever to develop an indigenous philosophy, it would do so not by rejecting God and embracing Marxist dogma but, like the Jews, by recasting God from a spiritual reality into an abstraction.[23]

In her 1896 review, Andreas-Salomé describes the local reports sent to journals by professionals working in the Russian provinces as authentic and accurate. Historically, publicist discourse had served as the principal means of political expression in Russia, and it saw its heyday at the end of the nineteenth century. Andreas-Salomé was thus calling her readers' attention to the genre of the *ocherk*, the "sketch," an effective genre for circulating opinions in a society where public concerns largely displaced private interests.[24]

Although in her review Andreas-Salomé pays little attention to the literary sections in the journals, dismissing them as largely imitative light entertainment, a radical change in her attitude can be seen only two years later, in her overview "Russian Letters and Culture," written under Volynsky's instruction. Russian literature, she now claimed, was unrivaled, for the same reason that other genres of Russian intellectual expression were wanting. Russian novels assimilated into their formless narratives the most difficult philosophical, theological, and social concerns right alongside the most ordinary daily doings. Andreas-Salomé used the metaphor of a tree to illustrate the distinct quality of the Russian literary tradition. In the West, literature constituted only one branch of a complex cultural tradition; in Russia, it formed powerful national roots. She remarked on the Russian authors' artless fascination with experience and authenticity as opposed to the Western weariness of life.

Andreas-Salomé's broad though sketchy two-part account of nineteenth-century Russian cultural life followed the chronological development of Russian letters from Pushkin and Belinsky to contemporary writers, journalists, and poets. A psychological sketch of Leo Tolstoy as an archetypal Russian writer formed the centerpiece of her survey. According to Andreas-Salomé, Tolstoy was the most deliberate of Russia's "untechnical and formless" writers; his seeming artlessness resulted from his sustained cultivation of the Russian nation's best talent. Although Tolstoy's self-questioning and inner struggle were reminiscent of Western introspection, the naive and sublime way in which he wrestled with his personal issues lifted him above Western rationalizations. Tolstoy's personal charisma supported the power of the cultural myth surrounding him, and he perfected this role over many years. He was wise to realize that preaching alone could not sustain the international following he had inspired, and that the irresistible magnetism of his personality could help convert those who doubted his teachings. Essentially Russian, he belonged to the world community at large and knew how to appeal to an untutored peasant, an innocent child, and a gray-haired sage. Tolstoy's powerful cultural presence both fascinated and puzzled the West, and Andreas-Salomé later continued to explore her ideas about the Tolstoy phenomenon in a study provocatively titled "Leo Tolstoy, Our Contemporary."

Andreas-Salomé concluded her series of articles on Russia with an overview of Russian literary criticism. In her presentation, she followed Volynsky's anti-Belinsky campaign and declared that the narrow dogmatism of Russian literary critics reflected negatively on the greatness of Russian writers. Russian critics' stubborn insistence on the primacy of social and ideological concerns over individualistic and aesthetic ones prevented them from recognizing the free and inspired quality of Russian writing.

The distinguishing feature of Andreas-Salomé's exploration of Russia's role in European history was her personal search for the mythical "Russian soul." She used this cultural cliché to frame her overriding philosophical concern: to understand Russia vis-à-vis the West. Although she never developed a clear definition of the Russian soul, its meaning took shape in a gradual accumulation of definitions in various works of journalism and fiction. Writing of Russia, she emphasized first and foremost the moral and mental makeup of the Russian people, the system of their beliefs reflected in their psyche and behavior. Andreas-Salomé embraced the idea of Russia's special role with nostalgia, lamenting the corrosive effects of the capitalist urge for profit at the expense of traditional paternalism and collectivism.

CONTESTING THE "NATIVE" POINT OF VIEW

Andreas-Salomé's evocations of peasant culture (*narod*) as the essential and inherent backbone of Russian society sounded anachronistic in the context of the new pragmatic mood emerging in post-Emancipation Russia. In the 1890s educated Russian society had been wrestling with the old question, Who is the Russian peasant?[25] Psychology and morality were no longer adequate explanations for the institution of the village commune. The peasant came under national scrutiny by specialized professional analysts of the countryside; the fields of statistics, economics, demography, and ethnography were called upon to investigate *narod* as an economic agent in the nascent market economy. The positive Slavophile aura surrounding *narod* had come under attack in the wake of the failure of the "going to the people" movement. As Dostoyevsky had predicted in 1876, educated Russian society found itself disappointed at what it actually discovered in the countryside and "immediately renounced them [the peasants] without regret."[26] Consequently, Andreas-Salomé's and Rilke's nostalgic recourse to a romantic image of Russia went against the grain of the "native" change of guard: the homogeneous and often idealized collective identity of the "folk" had disintegrated into a picture of ignorant and underdeveloped individuals, not yet capable of "human qualities and thoughts." Even though Andreas-Salomé and Rilke drew inspiration from the same conceptual trinity as their Western counterparts—the peasant's morality, psyche, and system of beliefs—they diverged from Russian intellectuals on the issue of the psychological and cultural independence of the individual within the commune. For the Russian elite, the *narod* was doubly oppressed—bound by an economic yoke and kept in the dark by pagan prejudice and ignorance. Those who went to the villages were guided by the vision of the dark masses patiently awaiting their liberation through enlightenment. The need to supervise and protect the peasants ultimately surfaced in the urge to control and act on them. The most striking confrontation between the intelligentsia's ideal and the *narod*'s actual existence was well captured by Gleb Uspensky in an 1888 sketch: "Looking at these healthy, free people who were neither hungry nor cold, who were dressed well, warmly and attractively in clothes they wove and made themselves, listening to their expansive, intelligent speech, I completely forgot the word *muzhik*. Yes, these were authentic free people, precisely people . . . these were not *muzhiks*."[27]

Andreas-Salomé and Rilke were fascinated by the peasantry, but they had different expectations of the Russian village than their Russian counterparts did: they came to visit, to observe, to record, and to learn without any desire to colonize, educate, or simply intrude on the course of village life. It was the peasants' individual creativity and artistic intuition they came to witness. In Western and Central Europe, the relationship between the city and the country was far less strained than in socially polarized nineteenth-century Russia. German, Czech, and Slovak social and political structures allowed for a freer flow between town and country; almost every European village could boast of its own doctors, lawyers, and teachers. There was never such a tremendous feeling of guilt and alienation from their own people as was experienced in Russia.[28] The ambivalence in Russia's writers toward these shifting images of the *narod* during the last decade of the century is exemplified by Tolstoy.

When Tolstoy met Andreas-Salomé and Rilke in 1899, he shared in the general discomfort with a tidy definition of *narod,* but he took the opposite position from that in Uspensky's sketch quoted above. Having started his literary career with the portrayal of Platon Karataev as an ideal carrier of national consciousness, he then offered the ambiguous character of Levin's serf, Fjodor, and finished with a photographic dramatization of the cruelty of rural life in *Power of Darkness*. Tolstoy's naturalistic play was welcomed by European naturalists as a stark revelation, and it became a staple in the repertoire of major European stages. Tolstoy's answer in the debate over the powers that ruled the Russian village was unequivocal: he scorned assertions that the peasant worldview was shaped by the powers of the land and argued that they had no such sentimental attachments in the village. Peasants lived and acted in moral darkness, "stealing firewood, horses, drinking to excess and beating their wives."[29] During their meeting in Yasnaya Polyana, Tolstoy warned Andreas-Salomé against her unrealistic association of the peasants with the force that would carry Russia into the future.

The reflections of Sophie Nikolaevna Schill (pen name Sergei Orlov) on her acquaintance with Andreas-Salomé and Rilke reveal the same disparity between her "German visitor's" vision of Russia and her own position as a veteran member of the Russian intelligentsia. Having met Andreas-Salomé and Rilke in Berlin in 1899, Schill quickly became an intimate and volunteered to be their local guide and adviser during their Russian travels. Most striking among Schill's records is the description of Andreas-Salomé's and Rilke's visit to the Pretchistensky Night Courses for workers, where Schill taught. Many years later, she remembered the scene and commented on the rapport between her students and the foreign visitors:

> It was exciting to witness this rare encounter between our workers of peasant stock and these representatives of Europe's most refined cultural circles. They were not

interested in the first attempts of the Russian workers to actively participate in politics, but in their true nature, their daily village life, their healthy roots—in the "peasant soul which had not yet been completely silenced by the city and the workers' barracks."[30]

A populist, people's educator, writer, and coworker at Tolstoy's publishing house Intermediary (*Posrednik*), Schill agreed with the familiar populist persuasion that the *narod* provided moldable human material waiting to receive society's projected ideals. Education was her solution. The German visitors' disregard for the "initial attempts of the Russian workers to actively participate in politics" struck Schill as inexcusably nearsighted. She was writing her notes in 1927, the time of the first collectivizations, deportations, and purges in the countryside. She perceived any indulgence with the peasants as a threat to the proletarian leadership of Russian historical "progress."

Schill also misjudged Andreas-Salomé's and Rilke's place on the German cultural scene. Neither belonged to "Europe's most refined cultural circles," but they were themselves the exotic representatives of Germany's Slavic diaspora. Cultural marginality guaranteed their intellectual mobility: they skirted the margins of a variety of Europe's modern artistic movements but remained nonaffiliated. Russia's temporary vogue in Europe legitimized Andreas-Salomé's and Rilke's Slavic affinities and helped them to overcome them and move beyond, to the next stage in their careers.

Schill concluded her observations by saying that Andreas-Salomé's and Rilke's "warm and lively" attitude toward Russia was "unusual and rare" in Germany.[31] In fact, their interest in Russia was by no means as unusual as it might have appeared to the Russians. Unusual, rather, were their sincerity, intensity, and degree of personal commitment, which surpassed the mere fashion for Orientalism.

Rilke and Andreas-Salomé looked for "Russia's true face," and the more it was removed from the Western sophistication of the capitals, the more authentic and representative it appeared to them. They did not take the "native" interpretation as the ultimate truth, while challenging Western stereotypes as well. Perhaps the greatest compliment one could pay these "intimate outsiders" was that they were not trying to save or convert others; they were honestly on a cultural quest for their own solely aesthetic purposes. Schill wrote about Rilke: "He observed the busy Russian life of 1900 with sympathy; he wanted to understand it in full, and to enrich himself through it and take it in as a whole in his creative superconsciousness."[32]

Andreas-Salomé denounced the "progressive'" separation between peasants and workers. Bolshevik ideology was all the more terrifying to her for its appropriation of Russian religious utopianism. She felt that "those most radical fanatics" thrust a wedge between two blood brothers: the peasants, whose life of devotion and resignation came to an abrupt end, and the proletariat, who were pushed by the Marxists into an "orgy of willed action."[33] At the end of her life, Andreas-Salomé refashioned in fiction an image of a *narodnik* into a Marxist ideologue; she had observed this character evolution in Sophie Schill: "This fine, good little soul that recently spoke words as bloody as if she were herself capable of throwing a bomb."[34] Andreas-Salomé was intuitively aware of the latent extremist tendencies among the radical Russian intelligentsia and imparted her mistrust to Rilke.

THE POET'S POINT OF VIEW

Rilke did not come to Russia for Russia's sake alone but for his own as well. From the start, there were two different Russias in Rilke's life: the one he readily shared with others and the one he kept private. To claim Russia exclusively as his own, Rilke had to go through a painful separation from Andreas-Salomé—and a reunion three years later, but in friendly correspondence only. He described his mental state before going to Russia as one of primordial nakedness in spirit: "I do not know whether I will ever reach that condition when I can walk in my own clothes. In any case, I will become all naked first, then I will find out the rest."[35] In Andreas-Salomé's sound judgment, Rilke needed his own point of departure, and Russia offered him that wholeness in which the mind is still inseparable from the soul; the man "totally and unself-consciously absorbed in the artist, and the artist in the man."[36]

Andreas-Salomé prepared the ground for Rilke's transformation into a great poet with remarkable clear-sightedness. The process of life creation that she designed for him closely followed the great scenario of her own life: "I submit to the great plan of my life without knowing it. It holds a surprise for me over and above all reasoning and expectation." She concluded her experiment with Rilke and Russia by reclaiming her independence from them both: "I submit to it with deep humility and see clearly now that the time has come to call you: go your own way to meet your dark God."[37]

In Andreas-Salomé's orchestration, Rilke's preparation for Russia started with a name change. "It was not too much longer before René Maria Rilke became Rainer," she wrote shortly after meeting Rilke in Munich.[38] Her next move was to require that Rilke cultivate a distinctive, controlled handwriting, and as an exercise, he had to diligently copy Andreas-Salomé's Russian essays, thus acting as her first reader and silent judge. Rilke's manuscripts would eventually become artworks of calligraphy. Finally and most importantly, she sent him on an Italian journey (spring 1898) with instructions to keep a diary of his impressions, later published as *Florentine Diary* (*Das florentzer Tagebuch*).[39]

For at least three reasons, the former mecca of Western artists fell short of Rilke's expectations. First, the overcrowded tourist sites on the Baedeker-packaged tours were distressing to him. "An Italian textbook whose goal was to guide to enjoyment should contain only one word and only one single piece of advice: Look!" Rilke decided.[40] Second, the connection between objects of art and real things had been hopelessly lost: "Instead of finding a connection to things, visitors stare into the gap between the rush of sight-seeing and the solemn preaching of pedantic art professors."[41] And most disheartening of all for Rilke was the discovery that contemporary Italian artists had surrendered their privileged position as teachers and secular spiritual leaders of their people to become servants of the philistine class. An Italian artist had become "some sort of a household uncle who provides Sunday entertainment for his nephews and nieces (his favorably inclined audience)."[42] In his critique of Italy, Rilke expressed his general discontent with the post-Renaissance state of Western civilization. His search for authenticity led him to the pre-Renaissance cultures of the European Middle Ages, Russia, and Asia. He mistrusted Apollonian rational order, preferring, like Nietzsche, Dionysian spontaneity.[43]

In Italy, Rilke developed a characteristic pattern of recording several parallel accounts of his experiences. Besides his diary, he kept two personal notebooks, wrote daily letters addressed to a variety of correspondents, and tried out ideas and drafts for future works in different forms and genres. His first collections of poetry, *In Celebration of Myself (Mir zur Feier)* and *In Celebration of You (Dir zur Feier),* and several of his prose pieces and essays began as such shadow compositions. In the course of his relationship with Andreas-Salomé, Rilke became particularly aware of the dangers of intimacy, and he defended the privacy of his artistic experiments. "Know then, that art is a road to the fulfillment of an individual," he appealed to Andreas-Salomé. "The material of the solitary artist is the world and he must set his works in this world. But they are not for you. Touch them not, and stand in awe."[44]

Rilke failed to find in the overcrowded Italy a personal space, which made his anticipation of the journey into pre-Renaissance Russia even more urgent. He perceived his visit to Moscow as a rare complement to his Florence spring.[45] "See you soon in the East," he wrote to Helene Voronina, his acquaintance from St. Petersburg whom he had met in Viareggio. "I want it to be so. And I tell myself in reassurance: wishes are the memories of our future."[46]

Even though Russia became for them both an intensely personal experience, Rilke was emotionally and intellectually more open to absorb new ideas and images than his worldly guide, Andreas-Salomé. For Rilke, Russia offered images and symbols that had been waiting to be articulated and released in a new form of artistic expression. For Andreas-Salomé, the experience was freighted with the sentimentality of return, the intoxication of emotional rebirth, and the almost bodily experience of immersion in the endless future. Or, as she wrote:

> It was an extraordinary experience for each of us. His was contingent on the breakthrough of the creative self, and Russia offered fitting images while he was still mastering his own language; for me it was simply intoxication from the encounter with Russian reality in its immediate fullness. All around me spread the land of these people in its breadth; this human misery, resignation, and expectation. This reality so overwhelmingly absorbed me that I have never again experienced such powerful emotions, except in personal relationships.[47]

In all of her recollections of Russia, Andreas-Salomé recognized the independence of Rilke's experience from hers. She was a necessary catalyst, but he had to absorb the experience and transform it into art on his own.

Chapter Three

Two Russian Capitals

RUSSIA: EXPERIENCE AND MEMORY

Russia's two capitals, like bookends, bracketed Rilke's experience of Russian life. Throughout its history, the Russian national identity had been split between two opposing poles—pagan Kiev and Christian Byzantium, Ortho-dox Moscow and Muslim Kazan, indigenous Moscow and cosmopolitan Petersburg—forcing into the open the question of divided Russian nation-hood. Even though Rilke became emotionally attached to Moscow in the beginning, several years later Petersburg grew more important to him as a writer. Moscow was Rilke's only "Easter city," the home of Tolstoy; Peters-burg, by contrast, was Dostoyevsky's "most premeditated city in the world." Even after Andreas-Salomé abandoned him in unfriendly, cold St. Peters-burg, he insisted with optimism that Russia was the happiest time in his life: "Are you happy? I am, despite all my troubles, I am happy so deeply, with such trust, so triumphantly happy. And I thank you for this."[1]

Rilke at first felt content with the high and hymnic experience of Moscow. "Learning to see" was his principal way of engaging with Russian reality. "I feel," he wrote to Helene Voronina, "that Russian things can offer the best images and names for my personal feelings and confessions. And if I can grasp them thoroughly, with their help I can express in my art every-thing that clamors for voice and clarity." Yet it became increasingly clear that as long as he held Russia sacred, as "a kind of lived myth," he could not draw on it as a source of artistic imagery.[2]

At this point a brief philosophical excursion might be helpful. Two sets of concepts—experience and memory—underlie Rilke's reflections on the interdependencies between the life and the art of a poet, and here German terms are more precisely calibrated than English ones. Human experience and memory interact at two levels: the here and now of an event (*Erlebnis*) and reflection at a temporal distance (*Erfahrung*).[3] Experience can be an involuntary remembrance (*Gedächtnis*) or a willed recollection of the past

(*Erinnerung*). The lived event (*Erlebnis*) represents the here and now of being; it is always contextual, always located in a particular space and time, and always accompanied by fleeting impressions and feelings. An idea of an event (*Erfahrung*) first recedes into the past, acquires certain distance, and undergoes transformation. As Malte wrote, "Verses are not, as people imagine, simply feelings [read *Erlebnis*] . . . they are experiences [*Erfahrungen*]. For the sake of a single verse, one must see many cities, men and things, one must know the animals, one must feel how birds fly and know the gesture with which the little flowers open in the morning."[4] In order to reproduce past experience (*Erlebnis*), one needs to dramatize whole scenes in characters and images. Nonetheless, remembrances (*Erinnerungen*) of things as they were are not enough; they have to be forgotten and come again, "till they have turned to blood within us, to glance and gesture, nameless and no longer to be distinguished from ourselves—not till then can it happen that in a most rare hour the first word of a verse arises in their midst and goes forth from them."[5] Otto Reik's explanation of the workings of memory is appropriate in Rilke's case: "The function of remembrance [*Gedächtnis*] is the protection of impressions; memory [*Erinnerung*] aims at their disintegration. Remembrance is essentially conservative, memory is destructive."[6] Only after Russia, in Paris, did Rilke's memory begin its destructive work of creation, and the result is the Russia-inspired *The Book of Hours, New Poems, The Notebooks of Malte Laurids Brigge*, followed by *Sonnets to Orpheus* and the *Duino Elegies*.

PORT OF ENTRY: HOLY MOSCOW

Rilke, Andreas-Salomé, and her husband, Dr. Andreas, arrived in Moscow at the most opportune time for a spiritual pilgrimage. As soon as their Warsaw-Moscow train pulled up at the Brestsky train station on Maundy Thursday, 27 April 1899, the three newcomers were swept away by the festive crowds filing out of the city's countless churches.[7] One of Rilke's first impressions of Russia was the sight of an Orthodox cathedral flanked by two silver-domed chapels with pilgrims on the steps. He remembered the image as both unusual and strangely familiar: "For the first time in my life I had an inexpressible feeling, something like a feeling of home—I felt strongly that I belonged to something, my God, to something in this world."[8] His expectations made it possible to see renewal where his intellectual Russian friends registered only hypocrisy and loss. In contrast with the theatricality of Western religious rituals—Rome, for example, was no longer "an Easter city . . . which knows how to lie under great bells. It is all extravagance without piety, a festive performance without festivity"—Moscow's celebration of Easter appeared to Rilke as a paragon of sincere spontaneity. Rilke wanted to believe in Russia's pre-Renaissance authenticity:

For me there was only one Easter; it was then, in that long and uncommonly, unusually exciting night when all the people crowded in and as Ivan Velikij struck me in the dark, stroke after stroke. That was my Easter, and I believe that it sufficed for an entire lifetime. The message given to me on that Moscow night was unusually powerful, and it went deep into my blood and my heart. I know it now: Christ is risen! [9]

For many years thereafter, Rilke and Andreas-Salomé ritualistically exchanged greetings on Orthodox Easter. "Christ is risen! He is risen, indeed!" (*Khristos Voskres, Vo istinu Voskres!*) was their pledge of loyalty to the Russia they had shared.[10]

"I have been out. I saw: . . . " Rilke could have written these opening lines of his *Notebooks of Malte Laurids Brigge* on his first day in Moscow. And yet the distance between his diverse urban experiences and Malte's was not in time or geography but in the eye of the beholder: an engaged participant in Moscow city life could not be further detached from the lonely Parisian *flâneur,* a voyeur of the human condition. Sophie Schill described Rilke's and Andreas-Salomé's memorable excursions into the city, their visits to churches, marketplaces, and beer and tea halls in the "gloomy" parts of town. Everywhere they went, they encountered good-natured openness and a readiness to talk.[11] Motherly Andreas-Salomé and the youthful-looking Rilke made for an unusual sight.

Souvenir shopping was an important part of Rilke's cultural expedition: to create around himself his own Russian world, he had to collect and display Russian artifacts. He started his collection by striking an unexpected bargain at Moscow's Sukharevka Market, picking out for himself a remarkably crafted seventeenth-century silver cross, once owned by a noble *boyar.* The name of the cross's original owner was engraved on the reverse side, and the face of the cross was inlaid with miniature plates, the ancestral seals. Every seal portrayed a scene from Christ's passion in the style of an old Russian icon. Rilke's acquisition was of the highest artistic value, and he triumphantly displayed his treasure, wearing the cross over his clothing like a Russian priest.[12] Russian clothes and, later, a study decorated with Russian icons and artifacts became his way of creating a secure personal world inside external disorder.[13] He became convinced that only in Russia could one gain direct access to things and engage them in an aesthetic exchange; the Westerner could only fetishize and consume things. He explained his position in a letter to a Russian friend: "Here one gains for the first time a direct access to things and remains with them in a continuing exchange which seems to be almost reciprocal; even though one remains the guest of all these things in every sense of the word."[14]

While in Moscow, Rilke and Andreas-Salomé deliberately distanced themselves from everything European and intellectual: "One can understand what lies ahead only from the point of view of old Russia," they concluded.[15] Except for the visit with Tolstoy and a few artists who helped arrange that visit (Leonid Pasternak and Pavel Trubetskoi), Moscow excursions served as the source of purely Russian imagery and ideas, the "unforgettable *skazka* [fairy tale]" contacts with Russia's Westernized intellectual and cultural elite had to be postponed until St. Petersburg. The striking paradox of Rilke's and Andreas-Salomé's "willful" aesthetics lies in the fact that their remarkably farsighted psychological vision went hand in hand with deliberate ideological shortsightedness. Their Russia was a "long-term nomad" who had covered great distances preparing itself for the final synthesis between East and West.

"VENERABLE FATHER AND METROPOLITAN"

The poetic segment "Venerable Father and Metropolitan" ("Ehrwürdiger Vater und Metropolit") resonates with a cry for an urgent solution to Russia's central cultural dilemma: the need to reconcile the emerging individualism with the national, communal tradition. Written shortly after Rilke's return from his first Russian trip, this lyrical piece was ultimately omitted from the final version of *The Book of Hours*. Rilke's editing demonstrates that, for all his trying, he remained in every sense a Western guest,[16] unable to endorse wholeheartedly the nationalist Slavophile agenda. The segment's conservative message contradicted the liberating spirit of the entire cycle of poems. It is interesting to us here primarily as the beginning of Rilke's Russian aesthetics.

The action of "Venerable Father and Metropolitan" takes place at one of the monasteries of St. Anargyren, common in the Suzdal-Yaroslavl region. The poem's colorful protagonist, Apostle, leads his monkish life painting holy images in the canonical Orthodox style:

> Mein Leben is im Ganzen wie mein Kleid,
> und meine Seele is wie mein Gesicht,
> und meines Tages Werke sind geweiht
> von einem Willen, der nich von sich spricht. (*SW* 3:361)

> My life is like my dress, and my soul is like my face, and my day's work is preordained by a single Will which does not speak for itself.

The poem is written in the form of a letter addressed by Apostle to Father Metropolitan. Confused by the messages reaching him from the outside world, the monk is facing a spiritual turning point. He has to make a decision whether to faithfully observe the Orthodox prescription or to opt for the individualist Western way:

Sie haben Gott vergeudet, und wir sparen
mit unserm Gotte und wir legen jede
getane Tat und Alles, was uns freute,
in kühle Kästen, glüten jedes Heute
so wie ein Kleid . . . (SW 3:363)

They have squandered God, and we are sparing with ours and we lay our every
deed and everything that gave us happiness in cool caskets, smoothed out each day
like a garment.

The problem has reached crisis proportions, since Russia, the last bastion of
Christian dogma, is tempted to forfeit its purity to Western enticement:

Ich fühle man fingt
auch bei uns schon an,
Ihn zu bekennen in falscher Art. (SW 3:366)

I feel that here, too, we have begun to acknowledge him in false images.

Apostle decides to uphold the canon and to fulfill the Slavophile hope
that the Russian people will carry on their sacred mission of saving the world
from squandering its gods:

Ein jedes Volk hat seine Pflicht und Rolle.
Und wenn wir uns um *eine* Fahne scharen
dann ward uns wahrlich eine wundervolle:
Wir müssen dämmernd unsern Gott bewahren.

Every people has its own duty and role. And if we gather around a *single* banner
then our fate is truly exceptional: we must guard our God in twilight.

Apostle's reference to the single character of the people is not so much a
"nationalistic or chauvinistic" statement, as some interpreters suggest,[17] but
a reference to the evolutionist worldview, which attributes one dominant
character to an entire people and looks for unity in diversity. Andreas-
Salomé also noted in this connection the striking consistency she had
observed in the Russian character: "Throughout the vast stretches of the
land . . . along its rivers, between the White and Black Seas, between the
trans-Urals and the European borders, it seems as if we were constantly
meeting one and the same man, as if he came from the nearest village—
regardless of whether he had a standard Russian nose or that of a tartar."[18]
The truth of the matter was that Rilke's overrefined European individuality could not sustain the sacrifices required by Apostle's complicity with

the canon. Apostle's decision to take the conservative route guaranteed stability without inspiration, God without art, and an East ignorant of the West. Besides its doctrinaire ideology, the poem is stylistically weighed down with excessive details and allegorical allusions that contrast with the inspired lightness of Rilke's lyrical work. By editing Apostle's letter out of the final version of *The Book of Hours,* Rilke decided against the easy solution to Russia's difficult quest for identity.

THE BOOK OF HOURS

The Book of Hours (*Das Stunden-Buch*) chronicles Rilke's gradual aesthetic appropriation of Russian culture: "Everything seen truly, he trusted, must become poetry."[19] Even though "The Book of Monkish Life"("Das Buch vom mönchischen Leben") is the most identifiably "Russian" among the three books, its decorative monastic setting makes universal rather than exotic the cycle's central theme: the protagonist's quest for authentic subjectivity within a universal harmony. The solution would come to Rilke in his *Duino Elegies*: "Nowhere, beloved, can the world exist but within" (*SW,* 711).

In Rilke's "Russian" cycle, the individual's gradual "disengagement" from the external world is dramatized in a dialogue between man and God, who are now neighbors:

> Du, Nachbar Gott, wenn ich dich manchesmal
> in langer Nacht mit hartem Klopfen störe,—
> so ists, weil ich dich selten atmen höre
> und weiß: Du bist allein im Saal. (*SW* 1:255)

> You, neighbor God, if sometimes in the night
> I rouse you with loud knocking, I do so
> only because I seldom hear you breathe;
> I know: you are alone.[20]

The book's protagonist is a nameless Russian icon painter who, unlike the earlier Apostle, refuses to comply with the tradition and subjects the external order of things to radical questioning:

> Was wirst Du tun, Gott, wenn ich sterbe?
> Ich bin dein Krug (wenn ich zerschrebe?)
> Ich bin dein Trank (wenn ich verderbe?)
> Bin dein Gewand und dein Gewerbe,
> mit mir verlierst du deinen Sinn. (*SW* 1:275)

Two Russian Capitals

What will you do, God, when I die?
When I, your pitcher, shattered, lie?
When I, your drink, go stale or dry?
I am your garb, the trade you ply,
you lose your meaning, losing me. (Deutsch trans., 15)

In this new state of self-awareness, the icon painter takes charge by constructing his own representations of God's world:

Da neigt sich die Stunde und rührt mich an
mit klarem, metallenem Schlag:
mir zittern die Sinne. Ich fühle: ich kann—
und ich fasse den plastischen Tag.

Nichts war noch vollendet, eh ich es erschaut,
ein jedes Werden stand still.
Meine Blicke sind reif, und wie eine Braut
kommt jedem das Ding, das er will. (SW 1:253)

Now the hour bows down, it touches me, throbs
metallic, lucid and bold:
my senses are trembling. I feel my own power—
on the plastic day I lay hold.

Until I perceived it, no thing was complete,
but waited hushed, unfulfilled.
My vision is ripe, to each glance like a bride
comes softly the thing that was willed. (My trans.)

After living through the prodigal days of search and indecision described in the second and third books ("Ich war zerstreut; an Widersacher / in Stücken war verteilt mein Ich" [I was dispersed; into rivaling / parts was I divided]), Rilke's wayward monk arrives at a resolution. The pantheistic image of St. Francis of Assisi brings the confused world together into one flowing continuum:

Er kam aus Licht zu immer tieferm Lichte,
. . . .
Und ihn empfing das Große und Geringe.
. . . .
Und als er starb, so leicht wie ohne Namen,
da war es ausgeteilt: sein Samen rann
in Bächen, in den Bäumen sang sein Samen

41

und sah ihn ruhig aus den Blumen an.
Er lag und sang. Und als die Schwestern kamen,
da weinten sie um ihren lieben Mann. (*SW* 1:365–66)

He came from light to even deeper light . . .
And was received by the small things and big. . . . .
And when he died, so easy as if nameless,
then was he divided: his semen ran
in the streams, in the trees sang his semen
and quietly stared at him from the flowers.
He lay and sang. And when the sisters came,
they wept over their dear man. (My trans.)

    Thus, with the theme of St. Francis of Assisi, which concludes *The Book of Hours,* Rilke has come full circle in joining together his Russian experience and his Western religious and philosophical background. St. Francis was highly respected among Russian thinkers, including Tolstoy, for his striking affinity with the Russian institution of the religious elder, the *staretz,* who conjoined the world of man and the world of nature. Franciscan pre-Renaissance mysticism advocated communion with all God's creatures, and its asceticism did not reject, condemn, or despise the body. For anyone so intensely searching for spiritual bridges between Western and Russian Christianity as Rilke, St. Francis and his teaching became the most obvious choice. St. Francis's teachings, his personality and spiritual leadership, were dramatized with new urgency in Tolstoy's controversial persona.[21]

GATE OF DEPARTURE: PETERSBURG "THING-POEMS"

Only in Petersburg could Rilke fully appreciate Russia's cultural divisions. After the chaotic hustle and bustle of Moscow street life, solitary Petersburg threw him back on his intellectual resources; he sought out the company of cosmopolitan Russian intellectuals and the silence of the city's libraries and museums. In Moscow, Rilke was a guest "showered with presents"; in Petersburg, he felt the urge to learn. He rigorously studied Russian history, literature, and art and wrote letters and poetry: "For the first time I felt the call to research and find out. A truly scholarly inclination."[22] Moscow always remained a dream, an "unforgettable *skazka*"; Petersburg as an "alien city" dominated his later memories. His remedy against loneliness and anxiety in St. Petersburg was the same as Malte's in Paris: Rilke wrote.[23]

    The Petersburg cluster of poems began with the three short pieces addressed to Rilke's Petersburg aquaintance Helene Voronina. The daughter of a member of the Russian Imperial Academy of Sciences, Voronina had traveled widely, was well read, and spoke several languages. Rilke chose Voronina, whom he had met in Viarregio, to play the role of Andreas-Salomé's counterpart; she was a part of the organic Russian world that Andreas-Salomé could at best rationalize and explain. At a time when his entire audience consisted of a small circle of sympathetic friends, Voronina became his "dear listener" ("Meine liebe Lauscherin"). Rilke became particularly protective of Voronina's "Russianness," advising her against dangerous infatuations with Western ideas: "Read little German . . . leave Nietzsche alone. . . . Nothing good comes to Russia from the outside."[24] Rilke's mentoring of Voronina is often misinterpreted as condescension toward her intellectual capabilities; all it reveals, however, is his legitimate concern that Russia would be pushed violently toward foreign Western ideas just as those ideas had come to seem inadequate in the West. Moreover, enriching as it was, Rilke's exchange with Andreas-Salomé made him feel poor from mere taking: "Nothing can I give you, absolutely nothing: my gold turns into cinders when it reaches you and I feel impoverished."[25] His relationship with Voronina offered him a welcome opportunity to master some confidence and to try out the role of a giver instead: "I have more power in myself than I can express in words and will use it to free people from the fear from which I myself have come . . . as my Russian neighbor has given me when we went out at 9 in the evening to the sea . . . her silent trust so that I felt like her father in my desire to protect and defend her."[26]

Rilke's three poems to Voronina emerge as rhymed conversational pieces in the linear "here and now" of their relationship. The first two, "Let Every Joy Happen" ("Laß Dir jede Freude geschehen") and "A Song for Helene" ("Lied für Helene"), are written in the tone of an older well-wisher instructing his attentive young listener:

Laß Dir jede Freude geschehen
wie der Garten
an allen Alleen
wie ein Fest
sich den Frühling gefallen läßt.
Denn der Freuden sind viele—
Sie warten
bis Du sie rufst zum Spiele.
Lass Dir jede Freude geschehen
welche immer auch Dir gescheh—
aber aus den sieben Wehen
Wähe Dir Dein Weh! (SW 6:1225)

Let every happiness happen to you
as a garden

43

in all its alleys
as a holiday
which lets spring happen.
For there are many joys—
they wait
till you call them to play.
Let every happiness happen to you
whatever might happen to you—
but from seven woes
choose one for yourself!

The second poem matches the first in its utter artlessness:

Wir alle brauchen solchen warmen Regen
wie er in diesen Nächten flutend fiel,—
so muß der Himmel seine Hände legen
in unsrer Seelen sanftes Saitenspiel
damit ein Frühling drin beginnt.
Dann laß den Wind
allein mit Deinem Liede,
und sei nicht bang, daß er es Dir entreißt:
Aus Deiner ersten Furcht kommt lauter Friede
wenn Du Dein Lied auf Flügeln weißt. (*SW* 6:1224)

We all need such warm rain
which fell in torrents last night—
in such a way the sky must have put its hands
on the tender lyre of our souls
so that spring can start there.
Then the wind starts alone with your song,
and do not be afraid that it will take it away from you:
total freedom comes from your first fear
when you let your song fly on those wings.

These first two "feeling" poems were written in the overflowing Bohemian style and contrast with the third poetic sketch dedicated to Helene, which in its style anticipates Rilke's aesthetics of "things":

Für Helene
Ich höre von weit—von weit
die Uhr aus Ihrem Gemache.
Sie singt in sinniger Sprache

und spricht
als ob sie noch anderes bedeute
als Zeit.
Wie wenn Perlen zerreißen
aus einem reichen Geschmied;
Silben der Zärtlichkeit—
so müssen die Elfen heißen . . .
Wie ich ihrer mich freute
wenn sie begann
und in klaren runden
Schlägen ihr Geläute
Über die Stirne der Stunden
wie ein Lächeln rann . . . (SW 6:1223-34)

I hear from afar—from afar
the clock in your chamber.
It sings in a singing language
and speaks
as if it could tell more
than time.
As pearls ripped out
of a rich garment;
the syllables of tenderness—
so must the elves be called . . .
How much I have enjoyed their chimes
when they began
and in clear rounded
strokes their sounds
over the forehead of the hours
ran as a smile . . .

Helene's world is defined by her cosy Biedermeier living room; her silver clock is its centerpiece. When the clock comes alive it acquires a human face, a voice, and a smile; it fills up the entire living space, and without Helene's noticing it, the clock begins to dominate her life.[27] Helene is still unaware of the dangers involved in breaking up hierarchies between the human and material worlds. This world becomes a much more dangerous place when objects start making claims on human lives and their course.

This first *Ding-Gedicht* of Rilke's will have impressive progeny. Nine years separate Rilke's unpretentious verses to Helene's clock and his poetic dedication to Rodin's statue of Apollo exhibited at the Louvre exhibition. "Apollo's Archaic Torso" ("Archaïsche Torso Apollos") (1908) has been recognized as one of the highest achievements in the genre of thing-poems.

Wir kannten nicht sein unerhörtes Haupt,
darin die Augenäpfel reiften. Aber
sein Torso glüht noch wie ein Kandelaber,
in dem sein Schauen, nur zurückgeschraubt,

sich hält und glänzt. Sonst könnte nicht der Bug
der Brust dich blenden, und im leisen Drehen
der Lenden könnte nicht ein Lächeln gehen
zu jener Mitte, die die Zeugung trug.

Sonst stünde dieser Stein entstellt und kurz
unter der Schultern durchsichtigem Sturz
und flimmerte nicht so wie Raubtierfelle;

und bräche nicht aus allen seinen Rändern
aus wie ein Stern: denn da ist keine Stelle,
die dicht nicht sieht. Du mußt dein Leben ändern. (*SW* 1:557)

We did not know his unheard-of head, in which the eyeballs ripened. But his torso still glows like a chandelier in which his gaze, screwed in just then, lingers on and glows. Or else, the curve of his chest could not blind you, and in the slight turning of his loins a smile could not go toward that center which bore procreation. Otherwise this stone would stand disfigured and short beneath the transparent fall of the shoulders and would not break out of its contours thus like a star: for there is no place that does not see you. You must change your life.

    Both poems reflect on the connection between people and objects, but they belong in two altogether different worlds. The family clock is the keeper of domestic routine; it participates in the life cycle of births, marriages, and deaths. In the poem, the clock mediates between the "Ich" of the lyrical hero and the "Du" of his girlfriend. No words are exchanged between them, but the chimes of the clock are friendly and inviting. Apollo's headless torso is a lone artifact from times long gone; it comes alive for each of us in our own way. There is no eye contact; the statue's face and head are made redundant. There is no need for words; its frank male sexuality asserts power and control over the viewer. The torso simply radiates the command that all great art issues to us: "You must change your life!"
    Although Rilke explores the aesthetics of "thingness" in both poems, he applies it differently and comes to opposite aesthetic decisions. In the poems to Voronina, he still needs "things" to channel his nostalgic attachment to the domestic security of sentimental living rooms. In "Apollo," the

mature Rilke exploits verbal economy and stylistic discipline to convey the depth of imagery and ideas; his aim is to dislocate the viewer from his secure world. Rilke once clarified the psychological mechanisms underlying his late thing-poems. If we imagined that individuals could be rooms of different shapes and sizes, large and small, most people would know their own corner and their one spot near the window; one narrow strip on which they keep walking back and forth. In this way, they secure a sense of stability and learn how to build their lives around familiar objects.[28] Besides, portrayals of feelings were no longer legitimate vehicles of representation for him. The poet's task was to suggest feelings via "things" and not to indulge in experiences themselves: "We do not know the contours of feeling / we only know what shapes it from without" (SW, 1:697).

PETERSBURG INSOMNIA: "NIGHT RIDE" AND MALTE'S PETERSBURG NEIGHBORS

The St. Petersburg that had once alienated the impressionable young poet now challenged Rilke intellectually; it provided the environment that led him to the idea of the *Ding-Gedicht* and the authorship of *The Notebooks of Malte Laurids Brigge*. The poem "Night Ride" ("Nächtliche Fahrt") (1907) belongs with Rilke's cityscapes in his collection *Neue Gedichte* (*New Poems*): Paris, Chartres, Bruges, Furnes, Ghent, Naples, Rome, and Venice. St. Petersburg is by far the most remote of them all in the author's memory, and the poem complements nicely the three Russian episodes in the novel *Malte Laurids Brigge*.

Since its beginnings, Russia's most Western city has engendered endless literary explorations of the Petersburg theme. Despite the diversity of opinions, the majority of interpreters have conceded that the city has a tendency to drive its inhabitants, if not crazy, then into melancholy and delusion. The product of Peter the Great's rational mind, that enormous art object had broken loose from its creator's control and proceeded to warp its inhabitants' lives. Petersburg's sinister play with the human psyche had made the city's reputation notorious.[29]

Just as an impressionist painter is concerned with capturing the most revealing lighting for his model, Rilke was fascinated with times of transition and uncertainty: mornings and evenings were his favorite times of day to portray. Venice, for example, was portrayed as a city in the early morning in late fall, abandoned by tourists and still recovering from the nightly visitation of its ghosts ("Late Autumn in Venice" ["Spätherbst in Venedig"]). Like Dostoyevsky before him, Rilke chose to describe Petersburg during the time of its delirious white nights: the sun goes down only for a few hours, and the city slumbers in the uncertainty of twilight. In "Night Ride," the observer's glance

moves from one weightless object to another, and the peculiar lighting skews
the city's arrow-straight streets and avenues flanked by heavy stone palaces:

Damals als wir mit den glatten Trabern
(schwarzen, aus dem Orloff'schen Gestüt)—,
während hinter hohen Kandelabern
Stadtnachtfronten lagen, angefrüht,
stumm und keiner Stunde mehr gemäß—,
fuhren, nein: vergingen oder flogen
und um lastende Paläste bogen
in das Wehn der Newa-Quais,

hingerissen durch das wache Nachten
das nicht Himmel und nicht Erde hat,—
als das Drängende von unbewachten
Gärten gärend aus dem Ljetnij-Ssad
aufstieg, wärend seine Steinfiguren
schwindend mit ohnmächtigen Konturen
hinter uns vergingen, wie wir fuhren—:

damals hörte diese Stadt
auf zu sein. Auf einmal gab sie zu,
daß sie niemals war, um nichts als Ruh
flehend; wie ein Irrer, dem das Wirrn
plözlich sich entwirrt, das ihn verriet,
und der einen jahrelangen kranken
gar nicht zu verwandelnden Gedanken,
den er nie mehr danken muß: Granit—
aus dem leeren schwankenden Gehirn
fallen fühlt, bis man ihn nicht mehr sieht. (*SW* 1:601–2)

Then as we on the smooth trotters
(black ones from the Orlov stables)
while behind high chandeliers
nocturnal city facades lay, in the early morning
mute and no longer aware of hours of the day—
rode, no: slid or flew
and curved around weighty palaces
into the flow of the Neva Embankment,

enraptured by the sleepless nights,
which know neither heaven nor earth—

as the longing of unguarded
gardens seething from the Letnii Sad
arose as its stone figures
giddily were disappearing
behind us into fainting contours, as we rode—:

at that moment the city
stopped existing. All at once it confessed
that it had never existed for anything but peace
begging; like a madman whose insanity
is suddenly lifted which betrayed him,
and who no longer has to think
his sick and unavoidable thoughts of many years standing:
it felt like—granite—fallen from an empty and wandering brain,
until it was no longer seen.

The opening stanza introduces the poem's main theme: the susceptibility of the human psyche to the uncertainty of light and time. Disconnected objects crowd the first five lines, until the verb is finally introduced in the sixth: "Then, as we on the smooth trotters / (black ones from the Orlov stables) . . . rode." The uncanny image of pitch-black riding horses sweeping through the city adds a touch of Russia to the otherwise un-Russian portrayal. Those black horses dispel the evil charm of the white night and take their passengers away into the realm of art and fantasy. The rhythm accelerates as the ride progresses through the city. The city's victory over time is only a fleeting moment of lucidity between sanity and madness.[30] There was something particularly menacing in the way Petersburg provoked moments of awakening in the middle of a nightmare which made the timelessness of the night even more unbearable.

The image of St. Petersburg as a city of timeless phantoms is ironically replayed in *The Noteboooks of Malte Laurids Brigge* (1911). The novel's protagonist, Malte, tells the story of his Petersburg neighbors, who suffer from their city's common affliction: insomnia. "My two Petersburg neighbors for example attached little importance to sleep. One of them stood and played the fiddle, and I am sure that as he did so he looked across into the over-wakeful houses which never ceased to be brightly lit during those improbable August nights. Of my other neighbor on the right I know at least that he lay in bed; during my time, indeed, he no longer got up at all."[31] In "Night Ride," Rilke diagnosed lucid delirium as a Petersburg state of mind; in Malte's story about his neighbors, he examines insomnia's effects.

Nikolai Kusmitch, Malte's neighbor on the right, is a typical lowly clerk with a Petersburg curse on his character. He "discovered" one day that time was money, and since he expected to live a long life, he decided that he would become uncommonly rich by earning interest on his time. To his horror, time was slipping away from his room with the draft. Shaken by the unfairness of this waste, he confined himself to bed to save the little time he had left. His time was spent in reciting poetry from memory. Pushkin's and Nekrasov's rhythms provided structure for his otherwise shapeless reality: "When one recited a poem slowly like this, with even stressing of the rhymes, one had, to some degree, something stable on which to keep a steady gaze, inwardly, of course. Lucky, that he knew all these poems."[32] Music and poetry have, as it were, become the only real constants in Petersburg's delirious existence.

Rilke's autobiographical novel *The Notebooks of Malte Laurids Brigge* was his first confrontation with himself and his Russian experience as subjects for fiction. It is not a mere accident that Malte's story begins in St. Petersburg. [33] Rilke called his Malte "one who hears a glorious language."

> [He] feverishly conceived plans to write, to create in it. He had still to experience the dismay of learning how difficult this language was; he was unwilling to believe at first that a long life could pass away in forming the first short fictitious phrases that have no sense. He flung himself into this study like a runner into a race; but the density of what had to be mastered slowed him up. Nothing more humiliating could be thought out than this apprenticeship.[34]

Malte's fate illustrates Rilke's best-learned Russian lesson: it is not success that counts but one's dedication to the goal. The time had now come for Rilke to be left alone with his "dark Russian God."[35] By the time of his departure, Rilke knew that he wanted to take with him the sacred Russia of bearded peasants, folk bards, village storytellers, Tolstoy and his "real things"— but he was leaving behind the troubled tsardom of profane poverty, ignorance, despair, and revolutionaries. In the next few chapters we will look at four separate intersections between Rilke and real-life Russians: the peasant poet Spiridon Drozhzhin; the master of Russian realistic prose, Nikolai Leskov; the Revivalist painter Victor Vasnetsov; and the powerful presence of Tolstoy.

Chapter Four

In the Heartlands: Spiridon Drozhzhin
and Rilke's Russian Poems

THE GERMAN WANDERER

On their second Russian trip (spring and summer 1900), Rilke and Andreas-Salomé followed the path of Russian pilgrims (*stranniki*), crisscrossing the Russian heartlands from Moscow to Kiev, stopping en route for a day's visit at Tolstoy's country estate, Yasnaya Polyana. After Kiev, they took a steamer down the Dnieper River to travel across the Ukraine, and then came back to Russia on the northbound train.[1] From the city of Saratov they sailed up the Volga to the old Russian cities of Simbirsk, Kazan, Nizhni Novgorod, and Yaroslavl. Rilke recorded his impressions of the endless Volga landscape: "One learns all dimensions here; one discovers: the land is huge, water is something tremendous and the biggest of them all is the sky. What I have seen so far was a single picture of the land, the river, and the world. Here, however, everything is by itself. It seems to me that I have witnessed creation here."[2] On this journey, Rilke and Andreas-Salomé wanted to relive the two periods in Russian history that fascinated them the most: the time of the Rurik dynasty (which ruled from 856 to 1598) and the Battle of Poltava (fought in 1709 between the armies of Peter the Great and the combined forces of the Swedes led by Charles XII and the Cossack chief Mazepa).

Sophie Schill, who helped Rilke and Andreas-Salomé arrange their travel itinerary, was in private critical of her country's sociopolitical conditions. She even warned her visitors about the dirt, poverty, and ignorance of daily life in the Russian villages. Nonetheless, she wasn't entirely free of the time-honored Russian habit of trying to camouflage the unappealing aspects of Russian life. To their future village hosts, she described the two travelers as idealistic German tourists who loved everything Russian so passionately that she felt obligated "to convey to them only the most pleasant impressions" and to try to spare them the disappointment of uncovering Russia's

51

"unwashed face."[3] Schill was not alone among Rilke's and Andreas-Salomé's Russian acquaintances in mistaking their interest in the peasants for youthful romanticism, an outsider's naïveté, and cultural shortsightedness.[4] But they wanted to be not common tourists but wanderers through the Russian land who could be trusted with the most awkward truths. The two travelers saw their ethnographic foray into the Russian countryside as the most effective way of escaping from cultural stereotypes while creating their own Russian mythology. In doing so they did have a few impressive models to follow: their circle of Russian friends included well-known writers-travelers such as Vasily Yanchevetsky, who had crossed Russia on several occasions. Yanchevetsky remembered how in a conversation Rilke mentioned that "truth" would be coming to the West from Russia and from the still living Russian Christ. He also recalled an anecdote current among his Russian friends about Rilke's meeting with Tolstoy. In response to Rilke's romanticized image of the fairy-tale Russian Christ, Tolstoy replied that if such an imposter were to appear in his village, the local peasant women would jeer at him (*"baby osmeiut"*). The Russians were, in fact, Rilke's harshest critics, but most of them, like Yanchevetsky, found in Rilke's deeply rooted mystical attachment to their country some strangely Russian quality.[5] In response, Rilke translated, published, and promoted obscure Russian writers like Yanchevetsky and Drozhzhin.[6]

SPIRIDON DROZHZHIN AND RILKE'S RUSSIAN POEMS

Rilke's enthusiasm for the peasant poet Spiridon Drozhzhin (1848–1930) was an eloquent manifestation of his consistently nonconventional predilection for untrodden paths in Russian culture. Rilke learned about Drozhzhin from Schill, who sent to Berlin Drozhzhin's collection of poems *The Songs of a Peasant* (*Pesni Krest'anina*) (1898). The unassuming simplicity of Drozhzhin's verse impressed Rilke, and he promptly wrote him an appreciative letter at Rilke's and Andreas-Salomé's request. Schill arranged a few days' stay at Drozhzhin's native village and a visit to the neighboring Novinki, an estate belonging to the regional landlord, Nikolai Tolstoy, a distant relation of Leo Tolstoy. Schill's remarks in this connection that Rilke's tastes were "simple and aesthetically weak" and that he overlooked some of the "greatest treasures of Russian literature" in favor of inferior ones reveal her own intelligentsia biases rather than Rilke's naïveté.[7] Rilke's intuition did not betray him in Drozhzhin's case. Although second best, Drozhzhin belonged to a new generation of peasant poets (*rzhenye poety*) who received considerable attention in post-Emancipation Russia.

Peasant poetry evolved as a socioliterary phenomenon from the merging of two folk traditions: storytelling and the village chronicle (*bytopisanie'*).

Drozhzhin occupied a middle position, both chronologically and in stature, in the movement, which besides him included Nikolai Kliuev (1884–1937), Sergei Esenin (1895–1925), Ivan Surikov (1864–1950), and Lev Trefolev (1839–1905), who all came from peasant stock and raised themselves above their social group by education, experience, and ambition. The desire of these poets to speak on behalf of Russian peasantry met with the support of liberal-minded intellectuals, who helped them with funds and promoted their publications in such prestigious "thick" journals as *Delo, Slovo, Svet, Semeinye vechera, Vestnik evropy,* and *Detskoje chtenie.* The more ambitious of these village bards moved permanently to the cities and made literature their career. Osip Mandelshtam described the peculiar originality of this Russian village genre as "daily routine [*byt*] and peasant speech lingering in Hellenic dignity and simplicity."[8] The movement reached its creative peak in the first decade of the twentieth century in the works of Kliuev and Esenin and ended tragically with Kliuev's death in the purges of the 1930s and Esenin's suicide in 1925.[9]

Although Spiridon Drozhzhin was among the first of the village poets to receive recognition in the capitals, his low political profile and generally optimistic outlook on life made him unpopular among the intelligentsia.[10] He did not care much for literary politics in the capitals and chose the life of his native village, working in the fields in the summer and writing his poetry in the winter. Writing was for him a part of the natural life cycle, and he believed in the nurturing power of the peasant community and in education as the only sensible way of improving the conditions of the Russian peasantry. As such, he was a natural focus for Rilke's profoundly apolitical aesthetic search. Drozhzhin preferred to be called a *pesnetvorets* (creator of songs) instead of the accepted foreign term *poet,* and he was always ready to burst into song and perform his poems (*pesni*) in a "strong, deep voice."[11] As a matter of course, Rilke and Andreas-Salomé were treated to Drozhzhin's spontaneous performances around the traditional Russian samovar. A photograph taken at the time of their visit shows them on the steps of Nikolai Tolstoy's house with Drozhzhin, who is holding an open book. "I lived happily among books and pictures in his small newly built hut," Rilke reported to his mother.

> He is the elder (*starosta*) of a small village community where everyone highly respects him. In the summer, he does the usual peasant's labor, and in the winter, when his hands are free from the fields, he becomes a poet again. As a poet he is known to all of Russia. . . . He is a gentle and kind person. He personally knows older Russian writers, keeps their portraits and letters, and owns an enviable library. The landscape spreads outside his window, wide meadows [with flowers] balance nicely with the volumes of his books.[12]

Rilke was not alone in choosing Drozhzhin over other Russian peasant poets. Drozhzhin's circle of fans included such unlikely bedfellows as Leo Tolstoy, Maxim Gorky, and the grand duke Konstantin Konstantinovich Romanov. Tolstoy received Drozhzhin in his Moscow home and questioned him at length about the changes taking place in village life after the Emancipation. At the end of their meeting, Tolstoy presented him with an autographed copy of his story "The Death of Ivan Ilyich." Maxim Gorky believed that had Drozhzhin been given proper schooling and encouragement earlier in life, he could have become one of Russia's major poets. Grand Duke Konstantin Konstantinovich, a reputed connoisseur and a sophisticated art critic, was asked to review Drozhzhin's work for an Academy nomination. He was particularly impressed with the spirit of optimism found in his poems. In the grand duke's opinion, Drozhzhin's personal integrity presented a sensible alternative to the dissatisfied upstarts "who imagined themselves to be poets but the best they could do was to complain without any reason."[13] What impressed Rilke most—and quite likely Tolstoy as well— was Drozhzhin's ability to move freely between poetry and hard peasant labor. Rilke tried to achieve the same pristine unity with his surroundings after he left Russia by joining the artists' community in Worpswede.[14]

According to Rilke's diary, the first Russian poems "unexpectedly occurred" to him in the Schmargendorf forest with a spontaneity of creation reminiscent of Drozhzhin's singing.[15] Between the end of November and the beginning of December 1900, he wrote six poems altogether, revising and adding two more in April 1901. In those Schmargendorf days, Rilke was still planning to return to Russia and settle there permanently. The imperfection of these poems is reminiscent of his Bohemian "feeling" verses, whereas their lucidity anticipates the language of his later Parisian thing-poems. Rilke's Russian poems demonstrate a translator's heightened sensitivity toward foreign idiom and style and a fine linguistic ear for thematically central motifs. Writing poetry in a foreign language was Rilke's way of staking new aesthetic ground for his own creations. A selective sampling of Drozhzhin's and Rilke's Russian poems reveals a surface thematic and stylistic affinity covering an underlying philosophical difference. We begin with Drozhzhin's declaration of his poetic credo:

Moia Muza

Moia muza rodilas' v krest'anskoi izbe
ni chitat', ni pisat' ne umela,
tol'ko serdtse prostoie imela
i, moi slavnyi narod, o tebe
mnogo iskrennykh pesen propela.
Moia muza rodilas' krest'ankoi prostoi

In the Heartlands

i prostym menia pesniam uchila
Iz derevni rodnoi chasto v gorod bol'shoi
za soboiu pevtsa uvodila
Kogda peli my s nei to bedniak zabyval
Vsio, chto v serdtse ego nabolelo
Kogda pashniu pakhal il' zhelezo koval,
s etoi pesnei rabota kipela
po selam.
derevniam, po bol'shim gorodam
ona tikhoiu grust'iu zvuchala
I uchast'e ko vsem goremychnym liudiam
u schastlivyjkh liudei vyzyvala.

My Muse

My Muse was born in a peasant's hut
it could not read or write
it only had a simple heart
and it sang many sincere songs
about you, my glorious people.

My Muse was born in a peasant's hut
and it taught me many simple songs
it often led its poet from his village to a big city
When she and I sang, a poor man forgot
everything that was aching in his heart
when he was sowing the seeds or casting iron
his work went smoothly with this song
In the hamlets, villages, and big cities
it sounded with quiet sorrow
and called forth happy men's sympathy for all suffering folk.

Moi pesni

Net, mne ne veselo nichut'
Kogda v izmuchennu'u grud'
Na kratkoie mgnovenie
Niskhodit vdokhnovenie . . .

My Songs

No, I am not a bit merry
when an inspiration descends

into my tortured soul
for a brief moment . . .

Untitled

Kuda itti, kakoi dorogoi,
Gde dum muchitel'nyi iskhod?
I kak svedu ia s zhizn'u strogoi moi neokonchennyi raschot?

Tak grud' szhimaets'a ot muki,
Tak tiazhelo i dushno zhit'
Chto ponevole khochesh v zvuki
Vse eti dumy voplotit'

Where should I go, which road should I take,
where is the outcome of my labored thoughts
how will I make my unfinished reckoning with this hard life?
My chest aches with yearning
it is so difficult and suffocating to live
that involuntarily
you want to put these thoughts into sounds.

Pesnia

Kak listok otorvan
S vetochki rodimoi
bez puti bez voli
bureiu gonimyi,—
Tak i ia po svetu belomy skitaius'
ne zhivu, a tol'ko goremychnui maius'.

A Song

As a leaf torn off
its native branch
without definite road or will
so do I wander around the world
not living but only, poor me, suffering.

In the Heartlands

Compare these to Rilke's Russian poems:

Starik

Vtse na poliakh: izbushka uzh privyk
k etomy odinochestvy, dukhaet
i laskaia, kak niania, potushaet
plachuschego rebionka tikhii krik.

Na pechke, kak by spal, lezhal starik,
dumal o tom chego teper' uzhe net,—
i govoril by, kak by kak poet.
No on molchit, dast mir emy gospod'.

I mezhdu serdtsa svoego i rot
prostranstvo, more . . . uzh temneet krov'
i milaia krasavitsa liubov'
idiot v grudi bolsh'tus'ach godov
i ne nashla sebe gudy,—i vnov'
ona uznala, chto spasen'a net,
i bednaia tolpa ustalykh slov,
chuzhaia, mimo prokhodila v svet. (SW 4:952)

The Old Man

The whole village is in the fields
but the peasant hut is already used to this loneliness
it sighs and affectionately like a wet nurse,
quiets the crying child's feeble scream

An old man lies as if sleeping, on the hearth
thinking about things that were already gone,—
and he could have spoken as if he were a poet.
But he is silent, God, give him peace.

There are distances and seas between his mouth and his heart
his blood is already darkening
and sweet love beauty swells in his chest larger than a thousand years
it did not find lips for herself,
—-and once again
she recognized that there was no salvation
that a poor crowd of tired words
passed by unknown, into the open world.
(Noon, 7 December 1900)

Unpretentious as they may seem, Drozhzhin's simple peasant tunes and Rilke's ungrammatical evocations of feelings produce vastly different effects: Drozhzhin is a direct participant in village life while Rilke remains a sympathetic outsider.[16] Drozhzhin's picture of the Russian countryside is far from idyllic: his main theme is the loss of the village tradition and the exploitative relationship between the city and the country. However, the forced loneliness of Drozhzhin's uprooted Russian peasants is tragic but not hopeless; they yearn for a return to a settled family life in their factory barracks in the city. Despite their melancholic mood, his poems ultimately celebrate the enduring national character and look toward the future with hope and optimism. He has trust in the natural cyclical course of events and believes in bringing the community together again through faith and enlightenment; thus the past meets the present in his characters.

Loneliness is sacred for Rilke. Whether it affects an old dying peasant or a child, they each become poets. Peasants are closer to truth than we are, and more authentic, since they are more in touch with their immediate surroundings. Rilke's Russian poems are his attempts to gauge the distance between himself and the unfathomable Russian soul: "Russia became to me what your landscape is to you: home and the sky," Rilke wrote to the painter Paula Becker.[17]

Vtoraia Pesnia

Ia idu, idu i vsë eshio krugom
rodina tvoia, vetrennaia dal'
ia idu, idu i ia zabyl o tom,
chto prezhde drugikh kraiov znal,
I kak teper' daleko ot menia
bol'shie dni u iuzhnogo moria,
sladkie nochi maiskogo zakat;
tam pusto vsio i veselo i vot:
temneet bog . . . stradaiuschii narod
prishol k nemy i bral ego kak brata.
(1 dekabria 1900) (SW 4:954)

Second Song

I walk and walk and all around me still
Your native land's windy expanse
I walk and walk and I forget
that I have known other lands before.

And those long days at the Southern sea
are already too far from me

58

sweet nights of a sundown in May;
everything there is empty and gay—but here
the God is dark . . . and this suffering folk
has come and took him as a brother.
(1 December 1900)

While visiting the village of Novinki, Rilke witnessed a conflagration that
provided the occasion for a poem, "The Fire." The fact that Rilke responds
aesthetically to a devastating scourge of Russian village life underscores his
fundamental aloofness from the concerns of the village bards. In the peasant
poetry tradition, coals and ashes are symbols of the peasant's difficult fate;
lamentation and mourning would be the order of the day, and never Rilke's
metaphysical pondering.[18]

Pozhar

Belaia usad'ba spala,
da telega uekhala
b noch', kuda-ta, znaet Bbog.
Domik, odinok, zakrylsia:
sad shumel i shevelilsia:
posle dozhdia spat' ne mog.

Paren' smotrel noch' i nivy,
to letel, ne toropias',
mezhdu nami molchalivyi
neokonchennyi rasskaz.

Vdrug on zamolk: dal' sgorela
ved' i nebosklon gorit . . .
Paren' dumal: trudno zhit'!
Pochemu spasen'a net?
Zemlia k nebesam gliadela
kak by zhazhdala otvet.
(5 dekabria 1900) (SW 4:955)

The Fire

The white estate house was asleep,
but the cart left
into the night, God only knows where.
The little abandoned house closed itself,
the garden rustled and stirred,
it could not sleep after the rain.

59

A young lad was looking into the night and fields,
as was carried on, slowly,
between us a silent
and unfinished conversation

Suddenly he stopped talking: the distance was afire
the sky was also burning . . .
the lad thought: it was hard to live!
Why is there no salvation?
The earth was looking at the sky
as if waiting for an answer.
(5 December 1900)

Although agricultural labor is being glorified in "The Face," by analogy the theme of creative writing is also presented: work as total abandonment in body and soul. The connection is made through the symbolic use of hands and faces. The artist's hands are always busy with creation, and only when his work is accomplished do his hands empty themselves of their hard-earned treasures. The face comes alive in the end like the cover of a book or the frame of a finished portrait. Rilke's poem is an attempt to argue for the necessity of the dialogue between the artist and the laborer. Artists turn to simple people for nourishment after a stringent regimen of creative work:

Litso

Rodilsia by ja prostym muzhikom,
to zhil by s bol'shim prostornym litsom:
v moikh chertakh ne donosil by ia.
chto dumat' trudno i chego nel'zia
skazat' . . .
I tol'ko ruki napolnilis' by
moeiu liubov'u i moim terpeniem,—
no dnem rabotoi-to zakrylis' by,
noch' zapirala by ikh moleniem.
Nikto krugom by ne uznal—kto ja.
Ja postarel, i moia golova
plavala na grudi vniz, da s techeniem.
Kak budto miagche kazhetsia ona.
Ja ponimal, chto blizko den' razluki,
i ia otkryl, kak knigu, moi ruki
i oba klal na schëki, rot i lob . . .

Pustyie snimy ikh, kladu ikh v grob,—
no na moëm litse uznaiut vnuki

vse, chto ia byl . . . no vsëtaki ne ia;
v etikh chertakh i radosti i muki
ogromnyie i sil'nee menia:
vot, eto vechnoe litso truda
(V noch na 6 dekabria 1900) (*SW* 4:951)

The Face
If I had been born a simple peasant,
I would have then lived with the big, broad face:
and in my features I would not have betrayed
what was difficult to think and what was impossible
to say . . .
And my hands alone would have been filled
with my love and my patience,—
if at daytime they would be busy with work,
the night would lock them up in prayer.
No one around would have known—who I was
I would get old and my head would flow down my chest with the current.
It seemed as if it got softer.
I realized that the hour of parting was coming close,
and opened my hands as a book
and put them both on my cheeks, mouth, and forehead . . .

I take them off when empty, place them in a coffin—
but my grandchildren will recognize in my face
everything that I used to be . . . but still not quite myself
in these features there is happiness and suffering
greater and stronger than myself
here is the eternal face of labor.
(In the night, 6 December 1900)

The harmonious interrelationship between experience and art which Rilke presents in his Russian poems and tales or in the *Sonnets to Orpheus* and the *Duino Elegies* would never be so undisturbed again in his work. There is no such continuity in the imagery of the novel *The Notebooks of Malte Laurids Brigge*. Only a few years later, Rilke writes that there were many faces in Paris, "for each person has several." A person's true face is the one freely chosen from a vast selection. There is no alternative to living but self-creation. In the worst scenario of life, one loses one's identity entirely as one loses one's face. In his Paris diary, Malte describes a street scene in which a woman "had completely collapsed into herself, forward into her hands. . . . Her face remained in her hands. I could see it lying in them, its hollow form. It cost me indescribable effort to stay with those hands and not to look at what had torn itself out of them. I shuddered to see a face from the inside, but still I was much more afraid of the naked flayed head without a face."[19]

In retrospect, Rilke's experiments with Russian poetry were none other than a coming to terms with his own language. Imitation and assimilation were central to his self-examination, and he was able to master the Russian language well enough to write letters and poetry in the original. Rilke remembered that he came "very close to making the Russian language, which was closest to [his] spirit, the means of [his] artistic expression." But he was well aware of the difficulties of writing in another language, and "it would have been, of course, impossible without huge losses."[20] If at this early stage Rilke's original work in Russian was of little aesthetic value, he excelled in the quality of his translations. In the course of the next two years, Rilke became Germany's foremost interpreter of the old Russian epic *The Lay of Igor's Campaign*, translated parts of Dostoyevsky's *Poor Folk*, and embarked on numerous other translation projects ranging from well-known writers such as Chekhov, Tolstoy, and Alexander Benois (a history of Russian art) to little-known "tertiary" authors such as Drozhzhin and Yanchevetsky.

As the years passed and Rilke grew more confident in his ability to put foreign idiom to use in his own writing, he returned to the long abandoned Russian imagery. One of his most striking Russian impressions was the memory of a "white horse with a peg on his feet which once toward the night sprang up in gallop in front of [him] on the Volga meadow"; it came back to him twenty-two years later, in 1922. Sonnet 20 of the first part of *Sonnets to Orpheus* includes the following lines: "He sprang to me across so many years, full of happiness, into wide open feeling."[21]

> Dir aber, Herr, o was weih ich dir, sag,
> der das Ohr den Geschöpfen gelehrt?—
> Mein Erinnern an einen Frühlingstag,
> seinen Abend, in Rußland—ein Pferd . . .
>
> Herüber vom Dorf kam der Schimmel allein,
> an der vorderen Fessel den Pflock,
> um die Nacht auf den Wiesen allein zu sein;
> wie schlug seiner Mäne Gelock
> an den Hals im Takte des Übermuts,
> bei dem grob gehemmten Galopp.
> Wie sprangen die Quellen des Rossebluts!

Der fühlte die Weiten, und ob!
Der Sang und der hörte—, dein Sagenkreis
war *in* ihm geschlossen.
            Sein Bild: ich weih's. (*SW* 1:173–74)

But to you, Lord, what shall I dedicate, say,
who taught the creatures to hear?—
My memory of a day in spring,
at evening, in Russia—, a horse . . .

The white horse came over from the village alone
a hobble on his fore fetlock,
to spend the night in the meadows alone;
how his curly mane struck his neck
in time with his high spirits,
with his high gallop clumsily hindered.
How the springs of stallions' blood sprang!

He felt the distances, and how!
He sang and he listened—, your saga's cycle
was enclosed within him.
    His image: I dedicate it.

Rilke's focus on peasant culture as a symbol of an untainted, unadulterated Russian nationhood was not unusual at the close of the nineteenth century; what *was* new and original was his continuing optimism and trust in the vitality of the peasant soul, which was by this time being regarded with increasing suspicion and hostility by the Russian urban intelligentsia. Suddenly thrust into the sphere of common citizenship by the Emancipation Act of 1861, the peasant became not only alien but threatening to society's influential political groups: populists, Slavophiles, and monarchists alike had to come to terms with a new self-assertive peasant identity.[22] With the evaporating myth of the ideal peasant, educated Russian society found it difficult to justify its paternalism and was slow to develop a new attitude. Rilke, free from such class biases, celebrated the unprecedented release of creativity in Russian peasants: they were patient and introspective enough to live in harmony with themselves and unself-conscious enough to still be nourished by their communities.

The most important aspect of Rilke's commitment to Drozhzin and his general attraction to peasant creativity was the role it played in providing him with access to the complex Russian personality of Leo Tolstoy. Drozhzhin proved real and convincing Tolstoy's advocacy of the peasant aesthetic, which made no sense in the West. But before discussing Tolstoy, we turn first to a potent force of Russian prose realism: Nikolai Leskov, who was to play a pivotal role in Rilke's aesthetic evolution.

Chapter Five

The Aesthetics of Icons and Tales:
Nikolai Leskov and Victor Vasnetsov

TOLSTOY BEFORE TOLSTOY

Those unfamiliar with Russian cultural politics in the second half of the nineteenth century may be surprised to encounter the name of Nikolai Leskov (1831–95) next to Leo Tolstoy's in Andreas-Salomé's surveys of Russian literary history. Leskov is featured as the "great portrayer of Russian spirituality" in her two-part esssay "Russian Letters and Culture" and becomes the protagonist in the discussion of the Russian religious aesthetic in "The Russian Holy Image and Its Poet" ("Das Russische Heiligenbild und sein Dichter").[1] In Rilke's writings, Leskov's presence is nowhere immediately visible: not in his lyrical cycle *The Book of Hours*, or in his *Stories of God*, or in the two essays on Russian art. Nonetheless, it is certain that Rilke knew his work and his thinking about Russian icons and tales, and his polemic with Tolstoy was largely shaped by an implicit dialogue with Leskov.

A gifted teller of tales from Russian provincial life, a passionate connoisseur and collector of old Russian icons, Leskov stood outside the Russian literary mainstream. He was resented by fellow writers on the right and left of the political spectrum for his uncompromising positions on major political issues. He was passed over by the leading literary critics for his acrimonious public manner and refusal to join any political party or literary clique. Ignored by mainstream criticism at home, Leskov was generally regarded in the West as an author of local color and minor importance.[2]

To defend a national writer of Leskov's popular appeal against his influential adversaries at home required from a Westerner an insider's grasp of the Russian cultural politics. Russian literary life struck Andreas-Salomé and Rilke as Western, predominantly urban, antireligious, and therefore dangerously superficial. They felt that if a change were ever to come to Russia, it had to originate in the organic religious and spiritual life of the Russian provinces. As described in chapter 2, Andreas-Salomé and Rilke were guided in their search for the authentic "Russian soul" by Akim Volynsky, the literary editor of a St. Petersburg monthly, *Severny vestnik*. As a Jewish intellectual of unorthodox convictions, Volynsky identified with Leskov's outcast status and acted as his staunch advocate and ally in the Russian capitals. In 1898, Volynsky published a series of five essays devoted to a discussion of the writer's origins, beliefs, and artistic goals. Leskov's main subject matter, according to Volynsky, was the "joyless daily routine which follows after celebratory contemplation of the deity, [it] envelops the soul as gray mist but deep down, there starts quiet ferment . . . which releases itself into liberating fantasies."[3]

As far as Andreas-Salomé and Rilke were concerned, Leskov came closer to expressing Russia's authentic folk spirit than did Dostoyevsky and Tolstoy. If Russia's two great novelists opened for the West the depth of the "Russian soul," Leskov's characters in their turn embodied those souls individually. They came directly from the vastness of the Russian heartlands and lived lives of routine, boredom, dreams, memories, fantasies, and worship. Leskov embraces the world of the common folk but resents the pretentious Westernized politics of the capitals. Even though Leskov's most powerful stories deal with Russian religious life, his emotional exuberance falls short of religious exaltation; churches, priests, icons, and chants are regular features of people's daily life. Leskov never achieved the scope of Dostoyevsky's and Tolstoy's psychological portrayals, to be sure, but his reputation as the supreme master of the mundane has yet to be challenged.

No other writer could speak better for the Russia that Rilke and Andreas-Salomé came to witness than Leskov did. They shared Leskov's obstinate faith in Russia's singular historical role, his deeply religious but radically anticlerical outlook, and his principled insistence on the observance of traditional Russian aesthetic norms in all artforms from icon painting to storytelling. Leskov's art was not one that naturalistically imitated life but one that approached the "art-for-art's sake" position through the back door of custom and tradition.

Having taken in Leskov's unpolished grassroots philosophy, Andreas-Salomé and Rilke prepared themselves for a confrontation with Tolstoy's more difficult and aggressive aesthetic. Leskov's stories exposed the rugged authenticity of human souls, which becomes veiled in Tolstoy's didactic and self-indulgent reflection. As Andreas-Salomé concluded, Leskov served them as a dress rehearsal, a "Tolstoy before Tolstoy."[4]

THE END OF THE STORYTELLER: WALTER BENJAMIN

Andreas-Salomé and Rilke admired Leskov for the same reasons that the radical Russian intelligentsia resented him: he was an inveterate outsider at everything he ever did or wrote. In post-Emancipation Russia, Leskov remained unswayed by foreign influences, and in the ideological crossfire between Westernizers and Slavophiles stubbornly upheld a self-sufficient Russianness. Having grown up as a Quaker, Leskov eventually embraced a rather rationalist, ethical version of Russian Orthodoxy. At one time, he professed a modified form of Tolstoyan moralism but rejected its ascetic and fanatic aspects.[5] The titles of Leskov's stories, "Cathedral Folk," "At the End of the World," "The Enchanted Wanderer," and "The Sealed Angel," reflect the centrality of religious themes in his writing. His protagonists are never ideologists of the elite or apologists for the dispossessed; they are instead "live and attractive characters" found in the most unremarkable walks of life.[6] Leskov was too busy creating healthy Russian heroes and deeply religious, whether honest or vicious, human types to take any interest in the characters of the "superfluous men" or the "new people" of Russian nineteenth-century realist novels.

In the age of the novel, Leskov obstinately continued to be a storyteller. He excelled in the minor genre of loosely assembled picaresque tales on a broad variety of topics. He did not play with time sequences or points of view, suppressed all commentary, and did not disturb the story's narrative flow with overt psychological analysis. Thus his stories served as channels of a sort for traditional Russian values. One of the nation's most serious problems, he believed, was its amazing forgetfulness.[7] In his art, Leskov advocated the importance of transmitting the national tradition from one generation to the next, but he was far from idealizing the past: "Now is no worse than then," he used to say.[8]

For Leskov, unlike the earlier romantics and contemporary social realists, there was nothing sublime or prophetic in being an artist or a writer. Beauty was of a primary, religious, and mystical nature and by no means the exclusive property of a select few. "Writing is to me no liberal art, but a craft," he never tired of repeating.[9] *Enchantment* (*ocharovanye*) was Leskov's word for the mystical state that was revealed in the peculiar sublime condition of "holy foolishness," known in Russia as *jurodsvo*. The Russian *jurodivyi* was never a recluse but a harmonious human being who lived among the people. Leskov's writings were marked by this distinctly Russian holy foolishness, which conspired with the common reader against the critics.[10] Were Leskov to slip into an analysis or explanation, he would have had to adopt the guise of a novelist, alien to him.[11]

Andreas-Salomé and Rilke joined a small but authoritative group of Leskov's advocates—Tolstoy, Gorky, and Volynsky—because he perfectly embodied their image of "other" Russia. In Andreas-Salomé's view, Leskov had a truly Russian talent—spontaneous, unphilosophical, impulsive, and unsystematic. A wanderer through the land, he had no formal university education, and captured in his narratives the slow, unpretentious flow of

Russian life.[12] Andreas-Salomé judged that as long as he confined himself to descriptions of daily Russian life, he remained an original and captivating author. Whenever he tried to draw philosophical conclusions from his portrayals, he slipped into self-contradiction and an irascible, defensive tone. It was her task as a critic to rescue the brilliant and spontaneous storyteller from the tendentious and unconvincing demagogue.

Andreas-Salomé's attempt to save Leskov from obscurity in 1898 may have been overoptimistic but not hopeless. But for Walter Benjamin, writing his essay "The Storyteller: Reflections on the Works of Nikolai Leskov," in 1938, the death of Leskov's storytelling art sealed humanity's apocalyptic fate. Whereas Leskov's art brought Rilke and Andreas-Salomé closer to their contemporaries, it made Benjamin aware of the unbridgeable distance between people.[13] It would have been hard for Andreas-Salomé to convince Benjamin's contemporaries that the Russians were a deeply religious and nonpolitical nation and that salvation of the world would come from their passive compliance with the course of history. The demise of storytelling was, for Benjamin, a dying out of the epic side of truth—wisdom. It was not a mere symptom of decay but "a concomitant symptom of the secular productive forces of history" whereby humankind had lost its ability to exchange experiences.[14] Both story (*Geschichte*) and history (*Geschichte*) were dead: narrative had been removed from the realm of living speech and oral forms would ultimately be subsumed into the written text.

The critical positions of Andreas-Salomé and Benjamin are almost half a century apart, and they capture different stages in the demise of the storytelling genre. Taken together, however, they demonstrate a remarkable complementarity of vision. Benjamin was prophetic in predicting the depreciation of storytelling in the twentieth century: he had lost Andreas-Salomé's faith in the survival of cultural fundamentals.

THE HOLY IMAGE IN THE AGE OF MECHANICAL REPRODUCTION

The industrial revolution came to Russia only in the final third of the nineteenth century and served to accelerate social dislocations and individual anxieties. Specific questions of traditional national identity, like the fate of Russian icon painting, received widespread attention. Put in most general terms, the discussion focused on the dangers of cultural loss occurring in the process of the mechanical reproduction and market circulation of icons. Moreover, individual artists also came under scrutiny for the difficult moral choices they had to make between merely reproducing and freely re-creating holy images. Leskov added his voice to the iconographic debate with characteristic abandon. His passion for collecting icons was second only to his love of telling stories, and his insistence on the interdependency between tradition and innovation was echoed by cultural observers who came after him—including the interested West Europeans, Andreas-Salomé, Rilke, and Benjamin.

Two specific events fueled the nationwide debate on icons. First, in 1873 a provincial Russian newspaper reported a case of heresy that scandalized the public. A peasant entered a parish church in the small provincial Russian town of Chugirin to ask the priest to consecrate his newly purchased icon. In the course of the ceremony, the top layer of the icon's paint peeled off, revealing underneath a devil's face peering over a blasphemous inscription. Subsequent investigation uncovered similar images of hell (*adopisnye ikony*) in neighboring villages and in the nearby convent. The discussion that unfolded in the metropolitan press revealed both the public's overwhelming ignorance about the basic principles of Russian iconography and the dearth of serious research and scholarship on Russian religious art.[15] Leskov responded to these revelations by publishing a series of articles in major national journals revealing a rare knowledge of the history, traditions, and techniques of Russian schools of icon painting. The Russian Orthodox canon, Leskov argued, was organically rooted in the national past, and any digression from the canon could potentially lead to the loss of the centuries-old tradition.[16] Moreover, iconic images had to be reproduced only by hand, and the dangers of blasphemous deviations from the rules had to be avoided.

The second public controversy concerning Russian icons flared up twenty years later, in 1893, in St. Petersburg. The discussion this time focused on the issue of Russia's cultural self-assertion vis-à-vis the West. The episode involved a group of French men visiting Stroganov's private collection of Russian art. They particularly admired the icon "Christ's Resurrection and Ascension from the Cross." Impressive to the foreigners was the Russian painter's imaginative rendering of the canonical biblical theme. The Frenchmen publicized their discovery in a Parisian paper and were stunned to learn that their hosts were deeply offended. During the ensuing international altercation it became clear that the French and the Russians viewed their religious art from opposing perspectives. For the Russians, any analogy between icon painters and contemporary secular artists was fundamentally sacrilegious. The unsuspecting French had unwittingly demonstrated the ignorance of Westerners about the deeply religious significance of Russian icons.

Leskov spoke up on the Russian side of the debate, arguing for the unique quality of the original Russian icons. In his telling of the emergence and development of Russian iconographic art, however, he neglected to take into account certain fundamental facts in the early history of the so-called old Russian originals (*podlennik*). Contrary to Leskov's insistence on their

original purity, ancient Russian tradition had consolidated itself by appropriating Byzantine models and indigenous pagan and folk pictorial forms.
The art historian Dmitrij Rovinsky (1824–95), Leskov's contemporary, had
convincingly argued that knowledge of Greek iconography reached Russia
indirectly, first in the form of verbal descriptions (*slovesnye opisaniia*) and
orally transmitted interpretations instead of original images (*litsevoi podlennik*). The message was clear: the first Russian icon painters had to trust their
own intuition and imagination as much as rely on the descriptions of Greek
messengers in order to reproduce those first "originals." Moreover, the icon
painters in Stroganov's workshops were, indeed, among the first to approach
icons as individual works of art rather than as prescribed models for copying.[17] It is clear that Leskov's insistence that the first Russian icons could not
have been individual artist's creations was historically inaccurate. How
deliberate his "ignorance" was still needs to be discussed.

The conservative position that Leskov took in his public statements
went against the free spirit of his art. In his rich and subtly humorous story
"The Sealed Angel," he displays an impressive knowledge of the difference
between the Novgorod and Stroganov schools of icon painting. The characters are an intriguing mix of no-nonsense Russian traditionalists and curious,
compassionate, but ultimately misapprehending foreigners. The plot
involves a construction company of Old Believers who carry their icons with
them on a bridge-building project under the general supervision of an English engineer. When their most cherished icon is stolen and defaced
("sealed"), they send their fellow worker, the narrator of the story, to a distant town to find the one painter who can produce an exact replica of the
original. Their trick works; the Orthodox bishop who had appropriated their
icon is deceived by the forgery. In his joyous celebration of simple people,
Leskov shows how they manage their lives by cunning, wit, and imagination,
even if in the end the whole community converts to the official church.
Commenting on Russian hagiographical writings, Leskov complained of
their standard conventionalism: "In the lives of Russian saints, in spite of
their great interest, there is one great shortcoming that has long been
noticed—in them the individualism of the person being glorified is scarcely
visible. There is much that is miraculous but very little that is of the everyday and specifically theirs."[18] In his stories, Leskov is willing, if not down-
right eager, to tamper with the original sources to communicate the desired
message; his essays, however, advocate a more disciplined approach to the
originals.

Walter Benjamin published his reflections on Leskov's craft as a storyteller and his essay on the work of art in the age of mechanical reproduction
in the same year, 1936. The essays turn Leskov's apocalyptic predictions
about the loss of national tradition into self-fulfilled prophecy: "The uniqueness of a work of art is inseparable from its being embedded in the fabric of

tradition."[19] The mechanical reproduction of art objects, as Leskov had warned in 1873, could only diminish the uniqueness of the originals to the point of their irrelevance. It became increasingly clear to Benjamin that when reproduced, works of art lose their organic cult value. In principle, of course, the work of art had always been reproducible, and reproduction in itself did not jeopardize the art object's sacred "aura." For Benjamin, moreover, handcrafted forgeries enhanced the cultic "aura" of the original, and for Leskov, the original itself represented a crafted rather than created object. The intensive intervention of mechanical means of reproduction in the second half of the nineteenth century in Russia led to different degrees of authenticity. All that Leskov and Benjamin could see was the loss, and they had little faith in technology's potential for creation.

Rilke and Andreas-Salomé were familiar with the nature of the Russian iconographic debate from Volynsky's accounts. The main issue was the battle between tradition and innovation in the process of shaping Russia's post-Emancipation identity. Influenced by their historical optimism, Rilke and Andreas-Salomé saw cultural gain where Leskov and Benjamin lamented cultural loss. Guided by their personal goals, they did not think in terms of global phenomena or national movements that "saved" or "mined" large cultural groups. They believed that the survival of the community had to be accomplished solely through the advancement of its individual members. Rilke's two critical essays "Russian Art" ("Russische Kunst") and "Modern Russian Art Movements" ("Moderne russische Kunstbestrebungen") reflect positively on the continuity in Russia's national tradition. Just because technology makes mechanical reproduction possible does not mean that such reproduction inevitably displaces cultural value. Rilke, for one, kept the storytelling genre alive in his collection *Stories of God* and in a miscellany of shorter narratives inspired by Russia: "The Dragonslayer" ("Der Drachentöter"), "Vladimir, the Painter of Clouds" ("Wladimir, der Wolkenmaler"), and "In Conversation" ("Im Gespräch").[20] Thus, subtle threads of continuity emerge between Leskov and Rilke, connecting both with Tolstoy.

THE STORYTELLER IN THE *STORIES OF GOD*

Rilke's collection *Stories of God* (1899–1904) follows the evolution of storytelling from craft to art in the modern age.[21] The stories are arranged in narrative layers that somewhat resemble iconographic design. Twelve tales of the cycle (thirteen, counting the introductory novella) are linked through the centerpiece storyteller, who performs his tales (old and modern, Russian and Spanish) in front of different audiences. The reader thus gets a sense of multidimensional narrative perspective; the landscape of a lifetime is laid out for him.

Different types of storytellers are represented in this collection. The principal narrator is a modern man, a traveler, who honors the tradition of telling each story as if he were telling his life: "The storyteller . . . is the man who could let the wick of his life be consumed completely by the gentle flame of his story." The technique of a story within a story allows the main narrator to surround himself with multiple doubles and to create an aura of authenticity for himself: "It is granted to him to reach back to a whole lifetime (a life, incidentally, that comprises not only his own experience but no little of the experience of others . . .)."[22]

The stories are connected through an invisible protagonist, a "dear God," who is a quintessential artist responsible for ongoing creation in the skeptical modern age. At the same time, an artist lives among people and bears responsibility for keeping community traditions alive. In each of the thirteen stories there is an embedded conflict, a moment of crisis when personal ambitions and creative desires go against communal mores and practices. The titles of Rilke's three Russian tales name their peripeteia but omit the resolution: "How Treachery Came to Russia" ("Wie der Verrat nach Rußland kam"), "How Old Timofei Died Singing" ("Wie der alte Timofei singend starb"), and "The Song of Justice" ("Das Lied von der Gerechtigkeit"). In Russian tales the conflict is miraculously resolved and an accommodation is reached between the individual and the community. In the act of naming the conflict, the storyteller gives counsel not for one situation, or for a few, but for many, as does a proverb.[23]

The first story, "How Treachery Came to Russia," introduces the mythic ancient Russia which "borders on God." God lives in Russia among people, and "one has the feeling that everything new is introduced by him, every garment, every dish, every virtue, and every sin must first be approved by him, before it comes into use" (*SW* 4:31). The story's protagonist, Tsar Ivan the Terrible, is traveling to pay his annual tribute to the Tartar khans and is desperately trying to figure out how to avoid the payment. While on his way, he comes upon a bearded little peasant (*muzhik*) who is building an onion-domed church. The peasant helps him with some sound advice on the condition that he later receive some of Ivan's gold. When the time for repayment arrives, the greedy Ivan is unwilling to part with his treasures and decides to cheat. He sends the peasant a barrel full of sand instead of gold. Thus the tsar fails God's test for moral integrity and allows treachery into his land (*SW* 4:315). In the original folk tale the roles were reversed: the peasant was portrayed as greedy and crafty while the tsar was frugal, guarding state coffers.[24]

Rilke's seemingly artless tale is making a contemporary argument. His tampering with the folk plot came at a time when educated investigators of peasant culture were scrutinizing economic relations in the post-Emancipation village. Disconcerting evidence of economic competition and social dif-

ferentiation had been turned up that belied the continuing vitality of mutual aid and a natural economy. The majority of urban intellectuals could recall
that even the great bard Leo Tolstoy had shifted his views: the familiar par-
adigm of the gentry exploiting the peasant was changed to one of peasant
exploitation of a fellow peasant: "Every peasant, if conditions are favorable,
will be the most excellent example of an exploiter of anyone else, be he lord
or peasant."[25] Egotism, individualism, and exploitation were perceived as the
peasant's new characteristics. The intention of Rilke's tale is to rehabilitate
the common peasant as a source of moral good without taking away from
him his individuality and his judicious intelligence.

Rilke's second tale, "How Old Timofei Died Singing," focuses on the
conflict between two generations of storytellers: the old singer Timofei and
his wayward son, Yegor. Timofei is a "resident" who never leaves his village,
while Yegor is a "wanderer" who yearns for distant places and new experiences.[26] In the beginning of the story, Yegor leaves his father's home with his
new bride to seek a better life in big, cosmopolitan Kiev. Yegor acts against
his father's wishes and the unwritten law of his village: he is the only son of
the local bard and has to take over his father's trade to continue the village
tradition. Old Timofei takes to his bed, and the villagers' life comes to a
standstill: there is no "soul anymore . . . without his songs. Nothing throbs,
nothing moves, no one weeps anymore, and there is no real reason to laugh
either" (SW 4:322). Meanwhile, Yegor hears the powerful call of his people
and decides that the time has come for him to leave his wife and return to
the village.

Upon his return, he locks himself up with his father for the winter to
learn the old songs. When Timofei finally dies, Yegor begins to sing for the
first time. Familiar songs are so powerful in Yegor's performance that no
one can listen to them without weeping: "He reportedly sang in such gentle
and sorrowful tones, the like of which no one had yet heard from any other
singer. This tone always occurred, quite unexpectedly, in the refrain, which
made the song's effects particularly touching" (SW 4:324). Yegor's art has
been enriched with "the lore of faraway places combined with the lore of the
past, as it best reveals itself to the residents of the place."[27] As before, Rilke's
story touches on one of Russia's most urgent post-Emancipation social problems: changes in attitude among the younger generation of Russian peasantry. At the turn of the century, the peasants became less observant, less
respectful of tradition, and generally discontent. In search of earnings, they
moved to the cities but kept their village ties. If they returned to their villages they usually spread general disaffection with life.[28] Rilke remains true
to his optimism about Russia's future: the peasant bard preserves the village
lore in a modern way: he is at once a wanderer and a resident who leaves
home and comes back, breaking old tradition to create a new one. For Rilke
personally, the story of Yegor's life was, in a sense, a Russian variation on the

theme of the return of the prodigal son. Yegor returns to a happy reconciliation with his past. Malte Laurids Brigge's return is much less hopeful. Only a few years after writing the story of Yegor, Rilke concluded his novel on a note of uncertainty: "We do not know whether he remained; we only know that he came back."

The story "The Song of Justice," the third tale in the collection, raises the same issue of continuity between generations, this time focusing on the theme of patriotism. The story's hero, Alyosha, the village shoemaker's son, refuses to follow any traditional paths: he does not learn his father's craft, nor is he happy with fieldwork or marriage. One dark Ukrainian night, the old and blind *kobzar* (bard) Ostap wanders into the village and begins singing songs about the glorious national past. Ostap's call for justice touches Alyosha; he raises his head for the first time and follows the *kobzar*'s call to join the noble cause of the liberation of his country from oppressors. Such is the power of song.[29] As in the other tales, Rilke's use of broad metaphoric strokes that brush aside psychological depth, hint at history, and allude to folklore—in short, that forgo art for the sake of didactic moralizing—is artistically not very convincing. Moreover, his romanticized version of peasant patriotism was historically inaccurate. Tolstoy, here citing peasant behavior with great approval, was a most emphatic opponent of the notion of peasant patriotism: "I have never heard any expression of patriotic sentiments from the people, but I have, on the contrary, frequently heard the most serious and respectable men from among the masses giving utterance to the most absolute indifference or even contempt for all kinds of manifestations of patriotism."[30]

Rilke carefully crafted his *Stories of God* to pay final tribute to the storytelling technique. His thoughts and feelings about the emerging new type of artist were channeled into these traditional images. His storytellers belong with the Russian cluster of artists' portraits: the icon painter and monk Apostle from "The Book of Monkish Life," the revivalist artist Vasnetsov from his essay "Russian Art," and the group portrait of modern Russian artists in the essay "Modern Russian Art Movements." Of course, as noted before, the eagerness with which Rilke was ready to embrace everything Russian resulted, at times, in an uncritical advocacy of what most took to be Russia's failings and a blindness to its shortcomings. Andreas-Salomé warned in her observations on Leskov and Tolstoy that an artist is always in danger of losing his ground when he feels committed to an idea over his own creative impulses. To be true, art had to become the artist's way to live, win, and celebrate life.[31] If Leskov showed Rilke how to be a modern storyteller, Russian artists introduced him to the world of Russia's modern icons. The Russian icon's dual identity—religious and aesthetic—answered his need to reconcile the contradictions of his own artistic temperament.

74

ICONS IN RILKE'S ESSAYS ON RUSSIAN ART

Rilke discovered Leskov in 1897, before his visits to Russia, while sitting silently at the literary discussions between Andreas-Salomé and Volynsky at her home in Wolfratshausen, and while copying Andreas-Salomé's essays on Russian literature. Most immediate to him was Leskov's central concern: namely, the question of how to reconcile the artist's uniqueness with his communal responsibilities. Rilke offered to answer this vexed question in his two essays on Russian art, "Russian Art" (1901) and "Modern Russian Art Movements" (1902).[32] He started his argument where Leskov had left off in his much debated icon essays: by asserting the individual artist's roots in his community and his obligation to keep his tradition alive. Rilke's artist possesses a free spirit, but although he knows the temptation of freedom, he remains true to his origins. Besides the two surveys of Russian art, Rilke planned to write full-lengh biographies of the Russian artists Ivan Kramskoy and Fjodor Vasilijev, as well as to translate Alexander Benois's two-volume history of Russian art.[33]

Rilke had two compelling reasons for writing his way into Russian culture by way of the visual arts. First, general Western knowledge of Russian artists lagged behind that of Russian writers: "Russian literature is known everywhere . . . but when the question about Russian painting comes up one is, perhaps, surprised to have to give the negative answer" (SW 5:613). In addition, Rilke was unhappy with contemporary Western discussions of Russian literature, for even the most sympathetic Westerners like Andreas-Salomé occasionally slipped into a condescending tone when speaking about Russian "formless" spirituality.[34] In order for the cultural dialogue between Russia and West to continue, Rilke felt, Russia had to be able to speak back to the West in her own voice.

Rilke revealed his more personal reason for writing about Russian art in a letter to Gerhart Hauptmann: his impressions of Russia were "still, intimate, and unliterary," and he was struggling with the proper form for expressing them.[35] Images helped him transcend words already overinhabited by other Western commentators. "Whether I could ever reach the point where I can walk around in my own clothes—I do not yet know. In any case, I will get naked first and then we will see what will happen," he noted in his Italian diary, anticipating his sense of renewal after his first trip to Russia.[36]

Rilke opens his essays on Russian art by pointing out the importance of locating Russian art in its national context: "It is impossible to discuss any particular event in Russian art without saying a few words about the country itself" (SW 5:493). He moves on to portray a series of lively biographical sketches of individual painters who marked important stages in the development of Russian art. For Rilke, genuine art had always been an extension of the artist's personality, and he wanted to re-create a composite character of the nation by studying its crafts and traditions.

As a Westerner, Rilke had two major criticisms of Russian artists: their preoccupation with subject matter at the expense of images, and their lack of stylistic independence. Russian visual art was weak for the same reason that its literature was so powerful: the nation's obsession with introspection. The Russians filled their days with worry about ever-present hardships and went through life with lowered brows, unable to enjoy the unencumbered beauty of the landscape. Russia's first modern artists came from the ranks of those who finally raised their eyes to enjoy their country's simple beauty. Second, even the most talented of Russian artists were either too willing to give up their personal ambition for communal interests or else too susceptible to Western influences. As a result, some truly original work had been submerged in a flood of imitations. Russia's best artists were those who successfully balanced traditional national strengths with characteristic weaknesses. To illustrate his observation, Rilke tells the exemplary story of an Italian architect, Aristoteles Fioraventi, who came to Moscow in the sixteenth century to rebuild the Moscow Kremlin. To accomplish this difficult task, Fioraventi lived in Russia in order to learn and absorb Russia's indigenous style. The resulting mix between national and borrowed traditions became Russia's stylistic signature.

The major part of Rilke's essay "Russian Art" is devoted to an analysis of the life and career of Victor Vasnetsov (1848–1926). Vasnetsov, one of the initiators of the Russian Revival movement, advocated in the visual arts what Leskov had been trying to accomplish in literature: the development of an authentic Russian language for national self-expression. Just as Leskov's stories were based on his thorough knowledge of old Russian literature, folklore, and the Old Believers' faith, Vasnetsov's paintings absorbed traditional Russian folk imagery. Vasnetsov was as narrative in his paintings as Leskov was visual in his narratives. P. N. Gay described Vasnetsov's style as a "synthesis of old Russian and Byzantine characteristics, the art of the pre-Raphaelites and even Michelangelo." Most importantly, he was a "realist at heart and if he were not, he would not have been a truly Russian person."[37]

Rilke chanced upon Vasnetsov's work on one of his visits to Tretyakov's Art Collection in Moscow. By that time, Vasnetsov had already received attention in the West and enjoyed a significant following at home.[38] His neoromantic canvases attracted attention for their forcefulness in reclaiming Russian national art forms both from cosmopolitan imitators of the West and from the nationalist realists of the Society of the Moving Exhibitions (Peredvizhniki). In true Revivalist spirit, Vasnetsov's art opened the floodgates for a new national pictorial self-consciousness; his folkloristic paintings were followed by similar stylistic developments in applied and decorative arts, theater design, book illustration, and architecture.

Rilke's most important personal revelation about Vasnetsov's art was the connection it helped him make between the image and the Russian soul (*SW* 5:617).[39] Vasnetsov claimed to have achieved immediate communication between the audience and his epic-size canvases with their mythological subjects. As an artist he did not dare to think of his *own* soul, Rilke explained, "but rather appealed to the vast, communal soul of the people, searching for it among peasants, in their traditions, beliefs and prejudices, in the old songs and *bylinas*" (*SW* 5:618). Events in Vasnetsov's life demonstrate that the artist in him was in no sense a naive amateur; he had hardened himself against both blind imitation of the West and conformity at home. While in Paris he cut short his apprenticeship and returned to Russia to reconnect with his people. At home, he was guided by his own intuition and refused to follow either the prescriptions of the academy or prevalent styles. Vasnetsov's rebellion resulted in his looking at the Russian landscape and rendering it in the idiom of Russian folk narratives (*SW* 5:499).

Vasnetsov's frescoes in the St. Vladimir cathedral in Kiev inspired Rilke to reflect on the changing role of religious painting in modern Russian culture.[40] Having acknowledged the icon's diminishing cult value, Rilke's essay offered a solution that would escape Benjamin's apocalyptic vision. Artists like Vasnetsov—and, we might add, Leskov—embodied a happy compromise between the modern age, the medieval icon painter, and the storyteller. Vasnetsov's paintings and Leskov's storytelling marked the difficult birth of a new tradition.

By the time Rilke wrote his second essay, "Modern Russian Art Movements," his focus had shifted from the iconographer Vasnetsov to modern psychological artists: Ivanov, Kramskoy, Isaak Levitan, Il'a Repin, and Nikolai Gay.[41] Rilke accomplished this transition after seeing Ivanov's canvas *Christ in the Wilderness,* which had a profound personal effect on him. The painting portrayed a lonely Jesus sitting on a stone in a desert, lost in melancholy meditation. "Russian art does not become more narrow with its growing nationalism," Rilke concluded. On the contrary, "it may be in a better position to express the higher human universals if it completely abandons everything foreign, accidental, and un-Russian."[42] Rilke's advocacy of Russian nationalism has often been misinterpreted by his critics. He was not proposing a return to the confines of a cult or mindless ritual, but he believed in art as a channel or a system of canals for focusing generally unformed national feelings and intuitions. To be authentic, Russian artistic images had to be intimately linked with millions of individual Russian souls (*SW* 5:618).

The artist's real challenge was to balance the personal and the communal in his work, Rilke insisted. And if looking at other artists' lives and careers helped Rilke articulate his personal artistic dilemmas, his poems and stories served as extensions of his inner dialogue. The three parts of *The*

Book of Hours and the three Russian novellas in the narrative cycle *Stories of God* all convey the same basic message: an artist is always a prodigal wanderer. All Rilke's artists start as rebels against external rules—religious, nationalist, political, and the profane rules of the market: they break away from monastery, native village, and traditional crafts and occupations in order to experience life on their own. They all come back, however, having internalized the rules, and they then begin to create images that are identifiably their own and yet commonly recognizable. The cult and exhibition value of an art object happily come together in the work of a national artist.

Chapter Six

The Predicament of Influence:
Rilke and Tolstoy

TOLSTOY AS EXPERIENCE

As Rainer Maria Rilke approached his fiftieth birthday, he was frequently asked to comment on the literary influences on his career and personal life. In a 1924 letter to Alfred Schaer, a Swiss literary historian, he mentioned the names of Russian authors who had become important to him: Alexander Pushkin, Mikhail Lermontov, Nikolai Nekrasov, Ivan Turgenev, and Afanasij Fet. Leo Tolstoy was conspicuously missing from his list. Several months later, Rilke explicitly denied that his visits with Tolstoy had had any literary impact on him whatsoever. He insisted in response to Hermann Pongs's biographical questionnaire that Tolstoy's role was cultural and had served solely to confirm his personal discovery of Russia. But Lou Andreas-Salomé recalled that, at the time of their travels in Russia, the image of the bearded Russian sage served them, so to speak, as a point of entry into Russia: "If at an earlier point Dostoyevsky had opened up to them the depths of the human soul in the Russians, it was to be Tolstoy who personified the Russians as such . . . in all his portrayals."[1]

Besides his role as an "eternal Russian," Tolstoy intrigued Rilke as an artist who stubbornly resisted the powerful drives of his genius—while nonetheless allowing his nature to renew itself from within. At the time of Rilke's Russian journeys, Tolstoy's antiaesthetic pronouncements seemed both heretical and saintly. Rilke privately spoke about his "Russian master" in reverential tones. By the time Rilke eventually overcame his inhibiting inability to describe Tolstoy, the psychological urgency of confronting "the master" in writing was gone.

TOLSTOY AS PROVOCATEUR

Rilke had been familiar with Tolstoy's work since his student days in Prague. In an early letter of 1894, he referred to Tolstoy, Zola, and Turgenev as prophets who for a long time had promised the coming of a new and happier age.[2] His ambitions at the time, however, were directed westward from Prague, toward German cultural centers in Berlin and Munich; the turn toward Russia and Tolstoy came later, in 1898. Just as Rilke began preparing for his first Russian journey with Andreas-Salomé, Tolstoy published his treatise on aesthetics, "What Is Art?" The celebration of Tolstoy's seventieth birthday in the same year was largely overshadowed by the heated debate over this controversial treatise, which scandalized the European intellectual and artistic community.[3] Both Rilke and Andreas-Salomé responded to Tolstoy in print: Rilke with the essay "About Art" ("Über Kunst"), and Andreas-Salomé with an article entitled "Leo Tolstoy, Our Contemporary" ("Leo Tolstoi, Unser Zeitgenosse").

In his provocative denunciation of almost everything called "upper-class art" over the last two centuries, Tolstoy took it upon himself to redefine his relationship to culture and to explain to his contemporaries what had gone wrong with art and its institutions in the modern age. Tolstoy's project consisted in developing a view of art whose overriding concern would be ethical rather than aesthetic. In the fifteen years of study preceding his weighty formulations, Tolstoy had come to the conclusion that the art he had served for years represented a temptation leading his readers into moral weakness. His ethical duty thus required him to forsake literature and to reconsider the basic concepts of God, beauty, and art in the light of his new philosophy of life.

Tolstoy focused his argument on the vital relationship between the artist, the community, and God. Unlike the majority of his contemporaries, he was not much concerned with either God's personality or God's creation, but with the essence of life, as he understood it, and with representing it in a simple and adequate way. Art appeared to him unconvincing and immoral in its claims to reflect both God and life singlehandedly. Moreover, the life of the modern artist had become too narrow and self-centered to deliver a moral message with the appropriate authority. Only those artists who concerned themselves with the people's daily lives were in a position to make a constructive contribution toward the progress and well-being of mankind.

In Tolstoy's grandiose schema of the world, religious experience subsumed the aesthetic, and all of art's functions were subservient to a totalizing utilitarian goal. Tolstoy's was a self-styled religion, coming as it did from the world's leading novelist. "What is God?" the aging Tolstoy asked himself in his diary. "God is an X. . . . Yet although the meaning of this X is unknown to us, without it, it is impossible not only to solve but even to formulate any equation."[4] As the prophet of a new age, he introduced a set of new moral rules to guide humankind through life; even if there were no God, Tolstoy "might not have invented him but would have formulated a set of commandments and interpreted them as religion."[5]

As far as contemporary art movements and artists were concerned, Tolstoy pronounced them "godless" and morally offensive. He spared neither Baudelaire nor Wagner, neither Nietzsche nor Manet. The "antiaesthetic" system he offered as a substitute for the cacophony of competing theories of art was aimed at correcting the "warped" relationship between modern art and its institutions. Tolstoy knew how to stir up the debate by putting the weight of his personal charisma behind his denunciations. The announcement of his defection from literature drew public attention more than the actual logic of his argument. Tolstoy portrayed himself as one of those few individuals who were endowed with "the highest comprehension of life available to the best and most advanced men at a given time and in a given society—a comprehension toward which all the rest of that society [has to] advance inevitably and irresistibly."[6] Although such shock therapy occasionally reached its goal with individual readers, Tolstoy miscalculated the overall effectiveness of his moralizing tone. His arrogant and derisive evaluations sounded to Western ears like a sectarian chant. Most European readers were offended or repelled by this megalomaniac tone and overlooked the importance of his cultural message.

European responses to Tolstoy's challenge were distributed across a broad spectrum, from outright rebuttals of his "preposterous claims" to logically argued critiques of his philosophical imprecisions. Opposing voices overwhelmed the debate. There was no shortage of psychological studies of Tolstoy's frustrations or of the physiological causes of his supposed senility. Views of Tolstoy as a victim of local Russian mores and social and cultural conditions were just as widespread. But a small and notably heterogeneous band of supporters enthusiastically seconded his claims. Writers as diverse as Maeterlinck and George Bernard Shaw granted their Russian colleague the accuracy of his social critique.[7] Tolstoy's fellow iconoclast George Bernard Shaw—himself known for "an antiaesthetic fissure as deep and as wide as Tolstoy's"—welcomed "What Is Art?" as "a most effective boobytrap."[8] The large majority of European intellectuals and artists, however, did not find Tolstoy's moralistic pronouncements quite so amusing. Tolstoy's drily utilitarian outlook (and what an impoverished view of use!), his ascetic denial of all aesthetic pleasure, his emphasis on communal rather than individual experience, and, not least, his outright rejection of all contemporary Western art—everything became the subject of heated criticism. Tolstoy's personal attacks on individual artists made it difficult for his Western reviewers to focus on the underlying issues.

Rilke and Andreas-Salomé joined a vocal group of Tolstoy's supporters who believed in him as an artist but criticized the moralist. Andreas-Salomé's study "Leo Tolstoy, Our Contemporary" was published in late 1898 by the Berlin naturalists in *Neue deutsche rundschau,* and Rilke's essay "About Art" followed shortly thereafter in the Viennese secessionist journal *Ver sacrum.*[9] When Tolstoy's last novel, *Resurrection,* appeared in the spring of 1899, shortly before their first Russian trip, Rilke received it as a promising gesture of a long awaited compromise.[10] In *Resurrection,* he believed, Tolstoy's moral goal to reform humanity came together with his natural desire to create fictional lives. In a letter to the artist and art historian Alexander Benois, Rilke wrote: "Tolstoy's thousand contradictions are the sign of an incomparably great artist who is only now beginning to break painfully through the organic stone wall of his personal worldview, just as that wonderful spring grass does in the beginning of *Voskresenie* [*Resurrection*]."[11]

"LEO TOLSTOY, OUR CONTEMPORARY" AND "ABOUT ART"

In 1924, recalling the stir created by "What Is Art?" Rilke remembered that Tolstoy's "slanderous and foolish brochure" had made him appreciate the sheer force of the Russian writer's argumentation. Most amazing for Rilke was Tolstoy's non-Western capacity for self-abnegation: the writer's public announcement of his personal crises put him ahead of the majority of Western artists who spent most of their lives desperately trying to conceal through counterfeit art their embarrassing artistic barrenness.[12] The underlying connecting theme between Andreas-Salomé's and Rilke's very different essays was their sense of an almost missionary responsibility for salvaging Tolstoy's reputation from cynical Western opinion. Neither of them was ready to offer any reconciliation with Tolstoy's disabused aesthetic; the best they could do as Westerners was to ask the right questions of him.

Andreas-Salomé's usual approach was to analyze the careers of philosophers, writers, and whole cultures in terms of the individual psychology of the people involved. For her, Tolstoy's predicament represented a profoundly strange and most interesting human phenomenon. Why, she asked, would a great writer like Tolstoy decide to publish a disclaimer of his whole career? Why would he make himself vulnerable to the most unsophisticated criticism? To understand Tolstoy correctly, she felt, one had to locate him in the Russian cultural context; one had to place him at the intersection of nature and culture. "It is at this point that we can rightly understand the paradoxically gigantic personality of Tolstoy," Andreas-Salomé argued, and "we can grasp and appreciate his close connection with Russian cultural development."[13] Tolstoy reminded her of a Nietzschean superman, the likes of Zarathustra, who failed as an artist because he internalized the guilt of his social class to the point of self-destruction. Even Tolstoy, with all his creative potential and dedication, was unable to mediate between Russia's illiterate peasant majority and its European educated elite. Andreas-Salomé argued that, in the Russian circumstances, to turn toward the people by no means meant to retrieve one's lost origins but to acquire a wholly new faith through conversion. The elite's move to reduce itself to the level of uneducated folk was motivated by the desire to regain their unique Russianness, which Western culture could not give them. Thus, paradoxically, the Russian elite's zealous devotion to its "folk" only appears to have been self-sacrificial, whereas in fact it was the same old egotistic search for self-fulfillment. According to Andreas-Salomé, the gigantic scope of Tolstoy's paradoxes could best be grasped in terms of the Russian dialectic of loss and gain. "As if the worlds were to break apart and come together again for the sake of a single man's soul," Andreas-Salomé concluded.

The problem that Andreas-Salomé identified as central for any fair evaluation of Tolstoy's message was to decide whether his call for a purely pragmatic aesthetic was equally valid when addressed to the West. She answered in the negative. Even if Tolstoy's utilitarian approach to art elicited intense self-examination on the part of the West, it would be inappropriate, naive, and unconvincing as a program for action. Tolstoy could "never recognize us completely," she announced. "He could never understand us fully when we wanted to reveal through our most personal art and our most private longings the deepest religiosity of our way of living" (1155; 142).

Having dismissed the relevance of Tolstoy's attacks on the West as mere cultural misunderstanding, Andreas-Salomé proposed her own set of aesthetic criteria and her own definition of art. Arguing from a "Western" point of view, she insisted that art should always originate in the artist's inner impulse to create, and it should never be constrained by an ethically calculated response to a social order. The artist "creates not to influence others by suggestion, not to 'infect,'—it would be as if ulterior motives were at work here,—but he lets out his deepest desires often in contradiction with the reality surrounding him. Creation is the artist's modus vivendi, his way 'to live, win, and celebrate life'"(1154; 141).

Andreas-Salomé's intention in this essay was not to expose Tolstoy's theoretical inconsistencies but rather to save him from the biased evaluations of his shortsighted Western critics. She called on Tolstoy's Western readers to reach beyond cultural limitations and to keep the novelist's unique artistic talent in perspective. "We should respect, love, and recognize him as powerful in his convictions when he strides through our ranks in his homespun Russian garments. An artist by the grace of God even if he wanted to be a thinker, he remains a priest of the unnamed God whom we all serve" (1155; 142). Personally, she remained unswayed by Tolstoy's remonstrations against her argument when they met. His stubborn refusal to consider her point of view with due seriousness for the simple reason that it was "Western" confirmed her initial suspicion that the Russian side of his character struggled to suppress his Western sensibility.

Rilke took the occasion of Tolstoy's essay to clarify his own aesthetic position vis-à-vis Andreas-Salomé's. In his essay "About Art," he was concerned least of all with either developing a consistent argument against Tolstoy's thesis or commenting directly on his character. Tolstoy's name is mentioned only at the beginning of the essay, as a lead into Rilke's own views regardless of his opponent's. As Rilke would comment many years later, he was just beginning to learn observation without personal involvement.[14]

Rilke opposed Tolstoy on three specific issues: on the nature of art, on the artist's relationship with God, and on the autonomy of the art object. He shared Tolstoy's expectations that "true" art would become "the worldview of the final goal" ("die Weltanschauung des letzten Zieles," *SW* 5:426). In contrast to Tolstoy, however, art for Rilke was an ideology in its own right, distinguished from religion, science, and socialism in its pursuit of a perspective beyond the immediate one. Art resembled God in its ability to rejuvenate the world in times of death and destruction. If the world were to fall apart, Rilke argued, "art would be capable of standing alone and would beget new worlds and times" (*SW* 5:427). Tolstoy's most tragic miscalculation, Rilke continued, was his demand for artists to bind themselves within the fleeting present. Rilke's artists choose their craft freely in full awareness of the high psychological costs of their vocation; true artists do not demand rewards in the present, but commit themselves instead to "patient and aimless work" for the future.

The second area of disagreement arose from Tolstoy's belief that art justified itself only as ethical or religious practice; for Rilke, art was the most viable religion, and Tolstoy fatally erred by sacrificing the artist's infinitely re-creatable God for the ready tailored finite deity. Tolstoy's inability to recognize and accept the weighty responsibility for his own private God led him into temptation, and he shortchanged his incomparable novelistic skills for writing political pamphlets like "What Is Art?" "The minority needs God because they have everything else; the majority, because they have nothing," Tolstoy once wrote when he decided to give up his personal God, that of the minority, for the commonly shared God of the majority.[15] For Rilke, God was above possession, he was always the greater personal Unknown that had to be desired and achieved but never inherited, learned, or handed down by others.

Rilke's third disagreement with Tolstoy concerned the latter's claim that a work of art depended for its intrinsic value solely on a set of collectively shared feelings. Rilke did not believe in the artist's control over the creative process and its products. To him, art objects were autonomous; they immediately parted from the artist at the moment of creation and entered the timeless cycle of other people's experiences. By refusing to accept the autonomy of art objects, Tolstoy turned them into empty and meaningless vessels, thus allowing the ideological abuse of art.

It could be argued that Rilke's ambition to become a writer, to try out his own voice and to be heard and accepted for his own work, prevented him from grasping the essence of Tolstoy's quarrel with art. Later in life he acknowledged that his shortsightedness was due to a "failure of distance": his view of life then was "totally determined by what *I* needed to learn and experience from the master."[16] Rilke often recalled how much more difficult it was for him to justify his aesthetic when he finally confronted Tolstoy in person (the description of that meeting will follow in the next chapter). Before Russia, his attempt at formulating a theoretical program of his own had been unsuccessful: it lacked substance and did not come to much until he "began to work at it and make it real" ("an ihr Arbeit zu tun und sie zu verwirklichen," *SW* 6:944). The most important lessons Rilke learned from Tolstoy were that he should ask his own questions and that the world could be adequately represented only in its own image: everything—creatures, plants, things, and natural phenomena—has to speak through art in its own separate language.[17]

THREE "RAGING ELDERS": TOLSTOY, RODIN, AND CÉZANNE

When the opportunity to write a book about Auguste Rodin offered itself in 1902, Rilke readily accepted the offer, hoping to continue in Paris the work he had begun in Russia.[18] It soon became clear that Paris not Moscow would become his real home, but he was still reluctant to abandon all hope of returning to Russia. "In Paris, I have not come any closer to Russia," he complained to Andreas-Salomé, "but nonetheless I think that somehow . . . I have been preparing myself to return there."[19] In the beginning, he judged Paris through the Russian prism, and his first move was to find a mentor.

Just as Tolstoy had been Rilke's entry point to Russia, so Rodin was his introduction to Paris. Rilke's description of his first visit with Rodin parallels his earlier accounts of his meetings with Tolstoy. The two old men appeared to Rilke to be "smaller but stronger, kinder, and more noble" than he had anticipated. The Frenchman's "powerfully restrained, form-giving gestures" were just as telling as Tolstoy's picking up forget-me-nots in the fields of Yasnaya Polyana. Despite their imposing appearance, neither of the two artists disguised his human vulnerability. They both looked to Rilke like two gifted but "spoiled" children who had tasted the original sin of creation.[20] "And now I saw his hair . . . ," Rilke's Malte recorded his impressions of

Tolstoy. "It was somewhat shy and touching, it was house hair grown indoors, and spoiled by the warmth of cushions."[21] Of Rodin, Rilke reported to his wife that his "mouth had a language whose sound was close and full of youth. And so was his smile, that spoiled and at the same time the joyous smile of a beautifully endowed child."[22]

The physical similarity between Tolstoy and Rodin belied their radical differences as artists. Rilke considered Tolstoy to be his contemporary but he thought of Rodin as a man "without contemporaries,"[23] a master of the future. Tolstoy divested himself of literature, declaring it to be an exploitative and shameful luxury; Rodin participated in the "world of objects," working with his hands freely, happily, and without reflection.[24] Rilke identified Tolstoy's self-imposed artistic infertility with the sparse spring grass slowly making its way toward the sun in the pages of his novel *Resurrection*; Rodin's productivity approached nature's potency itself. He was happy only when he was working. "To work as nature works, not as men, that was his determination" ("Zu arbeiten wie die Natur arbeitet, nich wie Menschen, das war seine Bestimmung," *SW* 5:226). "The body is the soul to him" ("Der Körper . . . is für ihn die Seele," ibid, 277), Rilke concluded, looking at Rodin's sculpture.

Rilke turned to Rodin partly because Tolstoy had failed him as a teacher: "It was not solely with the purpose of writing a study that I came to you, but to ask you how I should live," Rilke wrote in one of his first letters to the *maître*. Rodin's answer was definitive and simple: "one has to work, nothing but work. And one has to have patience" ("il faut travailler, rien que travailler. Et il faut avoir patience").[25]

To compare Tolstoy with Rodin was for Rilke like comparing Russia with the West: in Tolstoy, the artist lived in discord with the peasant; in Rodin, the sculptor got along with the artisan splendidly.[26] Tolstoy lived in constant self-refusal and squandered his unique natural gift on meaningless occupations; the stubborn artisan Rodin was too busy to pause for reflection, "his hands [were] bound up in work." The Russian novelist denounced his novels as "bad art"; the Frenchman "wanted nothing from life but to express himself wholeheartedly and totally through his models."[27] Contrasted with Tolstoy, Rodin's personal example was so contagious that Rilke adopted for himself the sculptor's artistic credo: "one has to work, nothing but work." Thus Rilke's overall experience of Rodin was liberating after the imposing authority of Tolstoy, and in Rodin's studio, he witnessed a living example of Tolstoyan "infection" of art.

Rilke completed his conversion from the Russian model of "art for life's sake" to the French "life for art's sake" after experiencing Paul Cézanne's paintings at the Salon d'automne in Paris in 1907. He described the impact of Cézanne's art on him as the "last temptation to exercise in writing his capacity for admiration and portrayal."[28] In a series of twenty letters to his

wife he described the artist as the "greatest event in painting." Those frag-
mented letters connect thematically to make up a lyrical diary of reflections
on the problematic interdependence between life and art, *Letters about
Cézanne (Lettres sur Cézanne)* (1907).[29]

The story of Cézanne as told by Rilke is one of a sick and lonely man
who lived in total oblivion of his surroundings. Misunderstood by his family,
ostracized by the good burgers of his native village, and jeered at by the
neighborhood children, Cézanne's spent his life in unremitting work. His
monastic self-denial in art, his fanatical striving for complete fulfillment
(*réalisation*) in art, appealed to Rilke more than all of Tolstoy's moralizing
and Rodin's unreflecting craftsmanship.[30] Cézanne's example made Rilke
question the sincerity of his own commitment to art.[31] It was Cézanne who
finally helped Rilke find the model for an artist's coexistence with the world.
Only in continuity with these two remarkable artists did Rilke begin to
understand the significance of Tolstoy as a starting point for his career.

Rilke never completed a monograph or an essay about Tolstoy, as he did
about Rodin (*Auguste Rodin,* 1902). Nor did he collect his scattered
thoughts and impressions of Tolstoy into a separate publication, as he did in
Letters about Cézanne. Rather, he made Tolstoy into a fictional hero, a character in his only novel.

Rilke expressed his general feelings about Tolstoy in a discussion of a
German translation of Tolstoy's correspondence with his aunt Countess
Alexandrine Tolstaya.[32] In 1914, Tolstoy seemed to him a saintly figure who
could not reconcile in himself two conflicting kinds of righteousness: worldly sainthood and authorship.[33]

TOLSTOY AS "MAN-ORCHESTRA"

The event that marked Rilke's final reconciliation with the "raging" Russian
elder was the publication in 1920 of the German translation of Maxim
Gorky's justly praised memoir, *Erinnerungen an Tolstoi.*[34] Gorky's essay
helped him finally to identify the right language with which to speak about
Tolstoy without painful omissions, silences, or embarrassing inhibitions.
Gorky alone, as far as Rilke was concerned, was able to articulate the feelings he had experienced as a guest and observer at Tolstoy's house two
decades earlier: "Als ich . . . zu Tolstoi reiste, war mein inneres zu-ihm-
Bezogensein ebenso kontrasthaft in seinen Betonungen, ebenso unverein-
lich" [On my way to Tolstoy, my inner attraction to him was so full of contrasts, so irreconcilable].[35] No one before Gorky had been able to sketch
Tolstoy's portrait with a complexity that expressed admiration and awe as
well as secret suspicions and doubts, and in a tone that did not require apolo-
gies or explanations. "Maxim Gorki hat es hier zustande gebracht, ein Zeug-

nis größter Liebe und Bewunderung für den Alten Tolstoi abzulegen; . . . er hat sich niergends das Leiden erspart, abträgliche Einsichten und Verdachte . . . genau und rücksichtslos aufzuzeichnen" [Maxim Gorky has succeeded here in bearing witness to love and admiration for the old Tolstoy . . . he has nowhere spared himself the pain of recording derogatory observations and suspicions, precisely and without reservations].[36] Rilke became convinced that only a true Russian with Gorky's sensitivity could venture into the depths of Tolstoy's psyche with insight and understanding. Moreover, Rilke felt affinity with Gorky's hesitation before giving Tolstoy's character its final literary shape. Behind Rilke's sympathy for most of Gorky's probing was the latter's ability to combine an almost filial affection for the old man with a recognition, and an often unflattering portrayal, of unpleasant aspects of Tolstoy's character.

For Rilke, Gorky's memoir served as an occasion for reexamining his own attitude toward Tolstoy at a time when he was himself rapidly becoming the object of a growing literary cult. The shift in perspective from that of an apprentice to being Tolstoy's fellow writer might have accounted for the heightened awareness and interest with which Rilke reacted to Gorky's biographical venture. "Ich sagte oben: Interesse," he wrote, responding to Gorky's memoirs, "aber ich habe weit mehr für diese Aufzeichnungen Gorki's, ich kann es wohl Einsehen nennen" [I have said it above: interest. But I feel much more about these notes of Gorky's. I can call them insight].[37]

The paradoxical effect of Gorky's presentation was that he, an atheist, could best identify the three fundamental concerns that had dominated Rilke's own views of Tolstoy: God, art, and the artist in their mutual responsibilities and interactions. Gorky succeeded in dramatizing these three Tolstoyan themes in vivid episodes from the writer's life. His method of fleshing out ideas with images cast in "real-life" scenes appealed to Rilke's aesthetic sensibility; he himself kept such visualized concepts in his active repertoire of artistic devices.

Gorky opened his memoir with the pronouncement that Tolstoy was a "God-seeker" who had lost his way. The idea of God, Gorky wrote, disturbed Tolstoy's peace of mind more frequently than any other.[38] Rilke's Russian admirers, similarly, saw in Rilke a German pilgrim, a *Gottsucher* in their land, who impressed them as a pious and sensitive young man, a visitor to Russia from the world of higher spiritual harmony. Rilke, indeed, came to Russia determined to replace his lost Western God with a Russian deity of artists.[39] Tolstoy could have become the embodiment of such a new god; not a god from Olympus or the Lord of Sabbath, but some Russian fairy-tale god "seated on a throne of maple wood beneath a golden linden tree."[40] Instead, he became for Rilke someone who betrayed his ideal of the Russian god of artists. As Gorky put it, he was "more cunning than all the other gods together" and therefore more human, vulnerable to delusions, and open to interrogation. The image of the unholy elder treading the vast Russian fields thus took a far from majestic place in the pantheon of Rilke's artistic models. He was destined to bear an uncanny resemblance to the bearded God-*muzhik,* the hero in Rilke's *Stories of God.* The main protagonist of the Russian tale "How Treachery Came to Russia" lived in the world and, much like Tolstoy, occupied himself with building houses. Unlike Tolstoy, however, he turned out to be the genuine Russian god.

Another of Gorky's central images suggested a connection between Tolstoy and the rebellious protagonist of "The Book of Monkish Life," the wayward icon painter who confronted his God as an equal:

Was wirst du tun, Gott, wenn ich sterbe?
. . . .
Nach mir hast du kein Haus, darin
dich Worte, nah und warm, begrüßen.
Es fällt von deinen müden Füßen
die Samtsandale, die ich bin.
. . . .
Was wirst du tun, Gott? Ich bin bange. (*SW* 1:275–76)

What will you do, God, when I die? . . .
Homeless without me, you will be
robbed of your welcome, warm and sweet.
I am your sandals: your tired feet
will wander bare for want of me. . . .
What will you do, God? I am afraid.

In Gorky's presentation, Tolstoy was an irreverent pilgrim and an iconoclast, much like Rilke's monk. He paced the earth his whole life, staff in hand, covering thousands of miles from monastery to monastery, from shrine to shrine, terribly homeless, alien to everyone and everything. "The world was not for him—nor God, either. He prayed to him from habit but in his secret heart, he hated Him. The question he asked was why did He have to drive him over the world, to the ends of the earth—why."[41] Rilke's own homelessness, his cosmopolitan wanderings from country to country, from city to city, from hotel rooms and attics to castles and villas, recalled Tolstoy's spiritual pilgrimage.

After years of anxiety and resistance, after rejection and condemnation of Tolstoy's defection from literature, Rilke finally discovered in Gorky's literary portrait a sympathetic character with whom he felt empathy and compassion. Gorky's description of Tolstoy as a "wonderful one-man orchestra, endowed with the ability to play several instruments simultaneously—a trumpet, a drum, an accordion, and a flute,"[42] corresponded to Rilke's idea of the ultimate artist. But this was only after he himself had tasted the fruits of high accomplishment and fame. Thus at the end of his life, Rilke experienced a rare moment of reconciliation with the erring elder, and the shadow of Tolstoy no longer haunted his art.

Chapter Seven

Fictionalizing Tolstoy

THE MAKING OF THE MYTH

On their first trip to Russia, in 1899, there was nothing unusual in the desire of the three German travelers—Rilke, Andreas-Salomé, and her husband—to solicit an invitation to Leo Tolstoy's. The writer's Moscow home in Khamovniki had long been a regular meeting place for local literati, artists, intellectuals, and foreign celebrities.[1] Most foreign visitors sought out Tolstoy as a local curiosity, a tourist stop recommended by Baedeker; others came looking for spiritual counsel, and a third group, the "pilgrims" like Rilke and his companions, expected an introduction to the "true" Russia. Any sophisticated Westerner could not help noticing the striking self-consciousness with which Tolstoy, confronted by this steady stream, engaged in his mythmaking. Rilke and Andreas-Salomé were intrigued by his peculiar admixture of communal "Russian soul" and extreme elitism, and their primary interest in visiting the writer was aesthetic. As Andreas-Salomé wrote in her essay "Leo Tolstoy, Our Contemporary," "The great fascination that Tolstoy's image holds is therefore partly of an artistic nature: he who had stopped working as an artist embodies in himself a powerful living artwork which finds no equal in its original energy and its enormous capacity for self-reconciliation."[2]

Tolstoy's public announcement of his resignation from literature in the 1880s was partly responsible for the torrent of publications examining his life and career. Russian and Western interpretations of the Tolstoy myth fell into two distinct categories. In the eyes of his compatriots, Count Tolstoy was a popular dissident, important primarily for his spiritual and moral opposition to the autocratic Russian state and official religion. A. S. Suvorin, the influential editor of the Petersburg journal *Novoye vremia,* explained the nature of his countrymen's feelings about Tolstoy in a statement that became proverbial: "There are two tsars in Russia: Nicholas II and Leo Tolstoy. . . . Which one is stronger? Nicholas II can do nothing about Tolstoy; he cannot shake his throne. Whereas Tolstoy, undoubtedly, is shaking his and his dynasty's."[3] Ideological exploitation of Tolstoy's image continued in Russia well after Suvorin's time. Lenin's essay "Leo Tolstoy as a Mirror of the Russian Revolution" (1908) established the parameters for explaining the Tolstoy phenomenon for the next seventy years of the socialist state.

In the West, however, Tolstoy was generally perceived to be a confused spirit, full of inner contradictions, an enfant terrible. His Russian spirituality came in conflict with his Western rationality, and his Russian need to serve offset his Western will to power. What made him great and unique, however, was the sheer force with which his genius undertook to resolve the enormity of his human predicament.[4]

The making of the Tolstoy myth had become a veritable industry, expertly managed from Yasnaya Polyana by family members and their rivals from Tolstoy's immediate cohort. The first tentative Western publications about Tolstoy appeared in the late 1880s. Twenty years later, every conceivable aspect of his life and work was being packaged and presented for public consumption: his appearance, his vegetarian diet, his daily routine of work and exercise, along with the most intimate details of his family life were reported to the public. The stooping figure of the bearded prophet of Yasnaya Polyana became a familiar image in the early twentieth century. By 1910 the Tolstoy vogue had reached its climax in Europe with the French Ethnographic Society's award of an honorary membership and the founding of an International Tolstoy Society in Breslau to propagate Tolstoy's teachings. A German journalist commented wryly in 1899 on the un-Russian sensationalism and commercialism surrounding Tolstoy's public persona in the West.

> It is hard to understand why it still has not occurred to one of the American impresarios to persuade Count Tolstoy to undertake a tour through the capitals of Europe and the USA. One can imagine the writer, as we had seen him in Moscow, in the afternoon on Unter den Linden or on Broadway in New York and then, in the evening in a spacious concert hall delivering a lecture and in the meantime exposing himself to thousands of stares. He must, of course, wear his usual peasant clothes.[5]

In the last years of his life, the most advanced technology and media were put to use producing, reproducing, and circulating Tolstoy's image. Thomas Edison presented a phonograph to record Tolstoy's voice; Kodak's first personal photo and movie cameras were delivered to Tolstoy's house as soon as they became commercially available. Russia's best artists, sculptors, and photographers competed for his sitting time.[6] The first colored photograph in Russia and the first photograph endorsed with an autograph were both portraits of Tolstoy. Sofia Andreevna Tolstaya was in charge of compiling a photohistory of her husband's life. After his death, she waged a legal battle with Vladimir Chertkov, Tolstoy's self-appointed factotum and later trustee, for legal rights to the films documenting Tolstoy's daily life. Chertkov initiated the printing of postcards in a series of eight to ten pictures documenting Tolstoy's last years. Each photograph was supplied with an appropriate quotation from Tolstoy's teachings. The tradition was familiar to any Russian from folk woodcuts, *lubki,* and popular marketplace portrayals of scenes from saints' lives. Thousands of these images were sold in newspaper kiosks, train stations, and bookshops at affordable prices. Tolstoy himself was in charge of supervising illustrations of his books, particularly those for children and for illiterate peasants.

Those who found themselves outside Tolstoy's inner circle, and who thus could not contribute directly to his hagiography by drawing, photographing, or making movies of the master, left a trail of memoirs recording their impressions. Many leading European journals and newspapers sent special correspondents to Russia with the primary assignment of visiting Tolstoy's estate and reporting their impressions in a form accessible to their readers. Foreign reporters often then reworked their articles into books.

Tolstoy's was perhaps the best media-covered death the world had ever known. Reporters and photographers converhed on the obscure provincial train station, Astapovo, where the writer had fled. Russia's imperial railroad could not accommodate the thousands of mourners who flocked to Astapovo to witness the end of Tolstoy's last journey. Reports from his bedside were published daily, and telegraph and telephone lines were jammed with hourly announcements.

It was Rodin who brought to Rilke the newspaper clipping announcing Tolstoy's death in November 1910.[7] Rilke immediately wrote to his wife, Clara Westhoff Rilke, telling her that the eighty-two-year-old writer had fled from his home to seek a free and meaningful death. The thought of the magnitude of Tolstoy's existential project made everything else in his own life appear insignificant. What impressed Rilke most in Tolstoy's staging of his own death was the tenacity with which the Russian writer clung to his image of moral rebel: "How much room to act we still have in our time; how many ways remain for us to leave this life," he wrote. Rilke realized that Tolstoy's death completed a lifetime of mythmaking: "He became his own ultimate image in the loftiest meaning of the word." With death, "the inner life of this man rendered itself visible and immediately transformable into its own legend."[8] In 1915, when he found himself trapped in wartime Munich, Rilke again remembered Tolstoy's portrayals of death: "This man had observed in himself and in others different types of anxiety about death," Rilke wrote. "His own attitude to death remained until the end a grandiose and all penetrating *angst,* a fugue of fear, an enormous construction, a tower of fear, an *Angst-Turm,* so to speak."[9]

PARTICIPATING IN THE MYTH: TEA AT TOLSTOY'S

Rilke and Andreas-Salomé decided to make one exception to their rule to avoid Moscow's elite circles. "If we are lucky, we will visit Leo Tolstoy," Rilke had written to von Bülow before departing for Moscow.[10] Upon arrival, he promptly called on the painter Leonid Pasternak, the head of the life-drawing section at the Moscow School of Painting, to ask him to mediate on their behalf. Pasternak saw Tolstoy almost daily while working with the writer on illustrations for the novel *Resurrection*, and, with his help, a tea at Tolstoy's house was promptly arranged.[11]

The story of Rilke's two visits with Tolstoy belongs to the genre of similar tales about meetings between famous people. The further into the past, the more anecdotal their tone, and each detail is subject to the teller's imaginative tampering with facts. It is interesting to note that this much-anticipated event was hardly mentioned in Rilke's and Andreas-Salomé's Russian journals—one of those eloquent moments of self-censure which are always more interesting to unravel than the actual story. Fortunately, when it comes to Tolstoy, there is never a lack of memoirs to fill in the remaining gaps. After all, receptions at Tolstoy's house in Moscow and at Yasnaya Polyana were world-renowned, and their format varied only slightly from one visitor to the next. The recollections of André Beaunier, reporter for the French newspaper *Le temps*, Maxim Gorky, and Sophie Nikolaevna Schill provide important details that are missing from Rilke's and Andreas-Salomé's record. Taken together, these reports display two diverging trends: Westerners tended to explain Tolstoy's behavior in psychological terms, while Russians identified the social causes and effects of his actions.

André Beaunier came to Yasnaya Polyana on a special assignment from *Le temps* to observe and send back to Paris "human interest" stories about Tolstoy's daily habits and personal idiosyncrasies. Beaunier's reports were serialized in weekly installments in January 1898, generating considerable attention for their lively description of Tolstoy's household.

Beaunier opened his series with the description of Tolstoy's daily routine: the writer's mornings and afternoons were devoted to work, while visitors and friends were customarily received at tea and dinner. These family meals frequently turned into embarrassing occasions for the guests. The host's modest vegetarian fare, especially in contrast with the elaborate main meal, made his conscientious visitors uncomfortable. Adding to this unease were frequent arguments between Tolstoy and his wife which, like brush-fire, could spread to other family members. The role of involuntary witnesses to family fracases compounded the vistors' unease.

A private conversation with Tolstoy after the meal always came as a long-awaited relief. Tolstoy's personal charisma was so overwhelming that his visitors later often forgot the nature of their discussion and the subject matter of their conversation. Beaunier's frankness in laying open his ambivalent feelings about Tolstoy is particularly valuable in comparison with others' reverential mystification. "What struck one immediately when meeting Tolstoy was the certainty with which he manifestedly knew the Truth," the journalist recorded. "He was sure of not being mistaken, of speaking the purest truth, impersonal and endowed with characteristic evidence that he did not defend with the jealousy and passion with which one would have defended an opinion. He had no patience with doubts. Everything that had to be known, he knew, and what he did not know, held no interest for him." Tolstoy's personal authority compelled those who came to him doubting his course to turn into willing participants in his mythmaking—if only for the duration of their visit. As Beaunier observed, in the end the sincerity of his intentions could not be doubted: "If, at times, his eyes were clouded and if he did not always have the absolute serenity of the sage, it was because . . . it grieved him not to be able to give his confidence to others and because they did not want to surrender themselves to his evidence."[12] Tolstoy was often portrayed as a lonely man who, in Gorky's testimony, was "seeking God not for himself but for others so that he . . . may be left in peace in the desert he has chosen."[13]

Tolstoy's aristocratic origins became an issue with members of the Russian intelligentsia. It was common knowledge in Moscow that there were two entrances to Tolstoy's house in Khamovniki. People who were comme il faut or those with some position in society entered by the front door, while simple folk, the threadbare seekers after truth and bread, were admitted by a rear flight of steps, through the so-called black entrance. The proletarian writer Maxim Gorky recalled how in 1889 Sofia Andreevna mistook him for a simple peasant, told him that her husband was ill, sent to the kitchen for a treat of coffee and bread, and never stopped lecturing her humiliated guest about the hordes of visitors who disturbed her husband.[14] "Perhaps the muzhik is simply a bad smell for him, which he can never forget and feels compelled to talk about," Gorky concluded afterward.[15]

By coincidence, Sophie Schill attended a dinner at Tolstoy's house within a few days of Rilke's and Andreas-Salomé's tea reception and reported feeling similar discomfort at the Tolstoys' double standard of hospitality. Schill remembered how she was ushered by a lackey in white gloves into the living room filled with guests and then left at the periphery of a crowd consisting of nobility, celebrities, and members of Tolstoy's family. Tatyana, Tolstoy's favorite daughter, kept a special black tablecloth on which, according to the fashion of the time, distinguished visitors and family members were requested to leave their signatures. Tolstoy was the first one to sign, to be followed by others with either "Prince" or "Count" before their names. Schill was not invited to sign her name. That night, Sergei Diaghilev and Dmitrii Filosofov arrived from Petersburg to solicit Tolstoy's support for a special Pushkin anniversary issue of their journal *Mir iskusstva*. Their arrival immediately aroused Tolstoy's anger and interrupted the smooth flow of the evening. After a brief but brilliant pronouncement of what he liked and disliked about Pushkin's work, Tolstoy refused to have anything to do with the official celebration. Homage of any kind, he declared, was vain and superfluous for a writer, for there was no immortality and one had to live only in one's own time. Diaghilev and Filosofov departed, obviously offended by Tolstoy's exhibition of temper.[16] The remaining guests were left to listen to their host's remonstrations against the Pushkin cult. Even though Tolstoy himself seemed well on the way to having a cult of his own, this outburst against "immortality for artists" did have a certain consistency; Rilke had noticed it in his essay "About Art" when he noted that Tolstoy wanted art to have an immediate effect—that, for him, was infection—and any future goal or blossoming was illegitimate and idolatrous.

These witness accounts make it easier to recapture the atmosphere in Tolstoy's tea parlor during Rilke's and Andreas-Salomé's visit on Easter eve in 1899. There is enough circumstantial evidence to indicate that in the course of their conversation the host strongly objected to Andreas-Salomé's views that there was a need for a synthesis between Western rationality and Russian spirituality. Tolstoy disapproved of Andreas-Salomé's idealized view of Russian religiosity as a manifestation of the nation's primordial closeness to God, and he cautioned his foreign visitors against romanticizing Russian national traits of servility, humility, and ignorance. Andreas-Salomé and her companions remained just as obstinately unwavering as their host; the party would have broken up in total discord were it not for Friedrich Karl Andreas. Andreas's research on the Babists, a Persian sect, engaged Tolstoy's interest. His own studies of sectarian religious movements worldwide had led to a growing realization of their intellectual and theological importance for understanding the world's major religions.

Rilke stayed out of that evening's lively controversy altogether. In the account to his mother sent on the following day, he was long on metaphors but short on actual commentary: the experience, he wrote, was "beyond all words and descriptions"; they were all touched by the count's "generosity and humanity," moved by his simplicity and kindness, and surprised at his "youthfully good and angry" disposition.[17] At this age, Rilke frequently resorted to clichés to cover up his confusion. The passing reference to Tolstoy's "anger" speaks of an underlying tension between the four interlocutors. Another revealing detail about that night surfaced twenty years later. Rilke remembered overhearing Tolstoy's son, who came in later, exclaim after seeing their coats in the hallway: "What! all the world is still here!" The loud comment sent a signal that it was time for the guests to depart.[18] As soon as they stepped out of the house, the sound of the Easter bells drowned out Tolstoy's warnings about the dangers of indulging in superstitious folk practices.

Later, Rilke wrote Tolstoy that he wished for nothing more than to "enter Tolstoy's house again, imaginatively . . . in [his] books."[19] Shortly after his return to Germany, he selected three books to be sent to Tolstoy's house: his own *Two Prague Stories* (*Zwei prager Geschichten*), Andreas's *Babists in Persia: Their History and Teaching* (*Babi's in Persien, ihre Geschichte und Lehre*), and Andreas-Salomé's collection of stories *Children of Man* (*Menschenkinder*). Tolstoy treated the three volumes just as he treated his visitors: he thoroughly perused Andreas's study, looked over the first three stories in Andreas-Salomé's collection, and cut Rilke's book only through page ninety-eight.[20]

VISITING THE SACRED SITE: RILKE AT YASNAYA POLYANA

In contrast to their tea at Tolstoy's in Moscow, Rilke's and Andreas-Salomé's visit to Yasnaya Polyana in May 1900 is a well-documented event. There exist at least eight individual accounts describing this meeting: Rilke's letters to Sophie Schill and his mother written the day after the visit, his two entries in the *Worpswede Diary*, a draft of the letter to Andreas-Salomé, a letter to the Russian editor A. S. Suvorin, a series of lectures given in Switzerland, and his reflections recorded in private by Maurice Betz and Charles Du Bos in 1925.[21]

The obvious inconsistencies between the various accounts constitute something of a problem for keepers of Rilke's chronologies.[22] Biographers and critics have long wondered whether Rilke misrepresented the actual event; for that matter, did he even have to have met with Tolstoy at all in order to have created the image of the old man he did?[23] From the start, Rilke viewed Tolstoy as an inalienable part of his own biography, and his image of the Russian writer evolved along with his own career. The actual record of his attitude toward Tolstoy is a palimpsest, an open-ended text that evolved gradually from the first letter to the last, all accounts reflecting and commenting on one another and always open to a new, improvisational entry.[24]

On their way to Kiev on 31 May 1900, Rilke and Andreas-Salomé unexpectedly encountered Leonid Pasternak and his family at a Moscow train station.[25] Pasternak once again offered his mediation in arranging a visit to Yasnaya Polyana. From Pavel Boulanger, a railway official traveling in their train, Pasternak had earlier learned that the Tolstoys had just returned to their Tula estate. Rilke and Andreas-Salomé decided to take their chances and call on Tolstoy without a formal invitation. They sent a wire to the Tolstoys announcing their arrival and set off, the spirit of the adventure adding a special excitement to their trip.

The route from Moscow to Yasnaya Polyana was a well-trodden one. At Pasternak's suggestion, they took a freight train to Kozlovka, the station nearest to Tolstoy's estate, and from there hired a peasant cart to take them to the village of Yasnaya Polyana. They dismissed the carriage at the gates to the old park and walked through the overgrown ancestral park to the famous white house. Tolstoy himself opened the door when they rang and let the unexpected visitors in, promising to spend more time with them in the afternoon. When Countess Sofia Andreevna discovered the intruders, she almost turned them out of the house under the pretext of Tolstoy's ill health. After they explained that they had already agreed with Tolstoy to see him after his work, she abruptly left for the adjacent library and began talking loudly about the loafers who would never give her husband time to unpack.

While waiting for Tolstoy, Rilke and Andreas-Salomé were escorted through the house and around the park by Lev L'vovich, the eldest son at home. During the tour of the estate Rilke occupied himself with identifying individual signs of Tolstoy's presence. The overgrown central alley and the moss-covered boulders in the park, the silver Russian samovar on the dining room table, and the faded seventeenth-century portrait in the family gallery gave him, he felt, special insight into Tolstoy's genius. In this connection, Andreas-Salomé later claimed that the distinctive tendency of Rilke's art toward a "realism of objects" represented the unmistakable "Russian" quality of his perception. Tolstoy's house, and not Tolstoy himself, was to become the hero in the scene of the prodigal son's return in *The Notebooks of Malte Laurids Brigge*.

When Tolstoy finally emerged from his study, he offered his guests a choice of either a walk in the fields with him or a luncheon with the rest of the family. Rilke and Andreas-Salomé unhesitatingly chose the walk, having already suffered the discomfort of a family meal at Tolstoy's house. At seventy, Tolstoy still presented an arresting sight: his stooping gait, his gesture of picking up forget-me-nots, and his manner of greeting peasants who came to receive his blessing.[26] The conversation which followed was an embarrassing experience for Rilke: Tolstoy's only question to him was: "Womit befassen Sie sich?" ("What do you occupy yourself with?") and Rilke humbly responded, "Mit Lyrik" ("With lyrical poetry"). The young man's answer provoked a diatribe from Tolstoy against poetry; he quickly switched from German and French into Russian, making it difficult for his listeners to follow his argument. As a result, Rilke's and Andreas-Salomé's eyes rather than their ears were engaged, and Tolstoy's words had an altogether different effect on them than had his remonstrations against Russian religiosity a year before. After the meeting, Rilke and Andreas-Salomé decided to forgo the carriage and walked back to the station talking about what had just passed between them and the great man.

ADJUSTING THE RECORD: RILKE'S LETTERS ABOUT TOLSTOY

Rilke's letters about Tolstoy are heterogeneous in presentation and do not belong to the same genre of semiliterary meditations on life and art as his better known and stylistically perfect *Letters about Cézanne*. Each Tolstoy letter is an involved dialogue with his correspondent, finely attuned to the correspondent's unique personality.

Rilke's first report about his impressions of Tolstoy was addressed to his mother. He knew that the mere fact that her son had been received by a world-renowned celebrity, a novelist and a count, would flatter Phia Rilke's ambitions.[27] Rilke's letters to his mother had never been the place to discuss the matter-of-fact particulars and small details of his life; from his youth, he had established in his correspondence with her a grandiloquent language full of superlatives such as "famous," "great," "rich," and "important." Now he wrote, "He received us and we walked slowly with him in the big wild park which surrounded the famous white house where this great life was passing. He is now old and ill but the rich stirrings of his soul have become even more transparent!"[28] Having listed objects and events he gave no direct indication of his real feelings and impressions.

Rilke's report to Sophie Schill, in contrast to his letter to his mother, betrays his eagerness to demonstrate to his liberal Russian friend that on his visit he had finally caught sight of "Russia's true face." He knew that Schill could relate to his feeling of shock when they arrived in the village of Yasnaya after an exhilaratingly reckless drive through the countryside. Rilke's letter to Schill is almost deliberately naturalistic, marking the incongruity between the merry bells of their cart and the grey impoverished Russian landscape: "The poor huts of Yasnaya were clustered together but disconnected from each other like an animal herd which sadly idled around on a barren meadow." Even the Russian peasants in this description were worlds away from his fairy-tale *muzhiks:* "Groups of women and children were mere red and sunny spots in the monotonous grayness which lay over ground, roofs, and walls like luxuriant mosses which had been overgrowing everywhere, undisturbed for hundreds of years."[29]

Schill, he knew, could easily relate to their embarrassment at walking into a family quarrel between the Tolstoys: Sofia Andreevna was "unapproachable and inhospitable," portrayed as angrily throwing books around and complaining about the intruders. Rilke noted one victim of Sofia Andreevna's anger: a weeping young woman who briefly emerged from the back rooms and was later consoled by Tolstoy himself. One noticeable omission in Rilke's report to Schill was Tolstoy's oration against poetry, which Rilke ignored, noting only in passing "certain" differences between himself and the host.

TOLSTOY AND THE LEGEND OF THE PRODIGAL SON

Only in 1962, when the drafts of Rilke's novel were made public, did it become known that the present ending of *The Notebooks of Malte Laurids Brigge* was the third of three alternatives that Rilke was considering in the final stages of editing the novel: the two so-called *Tolstoi-Schlüße* (Tolstoy-Conclusions) and the present "parable of the prodigal son."[30] This belatedly uncovered textual connection between the real Tolstoy and the fictional Malte sheds new light on the autobiographical undercurrents in Rilke's fiction.

In his novel, Rilke describes the fate of a young Dane, Malte Laurids Brigge, who leaves home, family, and country to come to Paris in order to dedicate himself to art. Malte's decision costs him his life; he is fighting a losing battle against the city and dies an unknown and destitute death.[31] At the end of the novel, and in contrast with Malte's lot, Rilke drafts a portrait of the famous apostate from literature: Tolstoy. The author's allegiances are not difficult to detect; he favors Malte's unconditional faith above Tolstoy's apostasy and desertion. His Malte goes on an imaginary journey to visit Tolstoy and confronts him with a question about the nature of artistic commitment. The two *Tolstoi-Schlüße* dramatize the tragedy of Tolstoy's doubt as seen through Malte's eyes.

The first draft represents a meditation on the artist's relationship with God. "Wenn Gott *ist*," reads the opening line, "so ist alles getan und wir sind triste, überzählige Überlebende, für die es gleichgültich ist, mit welcher Scheinhandlung sie sich hinbringen" [If God exists then everything is already accomplished and we are melancholy, superfluous survivors for whom it makes no difference in which accidental way they will perish] (*SW* 6:967). If God were indeed "dead," the artist alone would be in the position to mediate between the world and the eternal Divine. Tolstoy, unlike Malte, was anxiously seeking to compromise his art for the sake of life, for which purpose he had to strike a Faustian pact with the Tempter (*Versucher*). The Tempter succeeded in convincing him that inventing fictional lives was immoral as long as real lives had to be reckoned with. Yielding to the Tempter's seductive call, Tolstoy abandoned his art and dissipated his talent with trifling manual trades.[32] His betrayal of his genius resulted in a painful struggle against the natural creative force and brought about the fear of dying an "unachieved" death. Malte finds Tolstoy at the end of his life, when the old man is restlessly trying to upset the entire world to find his own peace of mind.³³ Tolstoy's internal turmoil contrasts with Malte's composure; the difference between the two artistic temperaments serves as an instructive reminder of the importance of faith in one's vocation in the face of the adversities of fate.

The second draft takes up where the first one left off; it continues to develop the theme of Malte's visit to Yasnaya Polyana, adding to it an autobiographical dimension. The ending's opening question invites further reevaluation of the past: "Wozu fällt mir aufeinmal jener fremde Maimorgen ein? Soll ich ihn jetzt verstehen nach soviel Jahren?" [Why, all of a sudden should that strange May morning occur to me? Must I understand it now, after so many years?] (*SW* 6:971). Descriptive details accentuate the Russian setting of the scene: a long *telega* cart ride through nearby villages, poor peasant huts gathered on the slopes of the hill, blue fields of forget-me-nots, a walk to the famous white house through the old park, and then, finally, a long and patient wait for the host.

The story's allegorical center is the scene of Malte's contemplation of a forgotten ancestral portrait hidden in the dark corners of Tolstoy's family gallery. As old paintings often do, the portrait contains a clue to the tragic secret of the house. It portrays a nun, a seventeenth-century abbess of a convent of a strict canonical order. Her disproportionately large hands capture the observer's eye; they grow out of the picture and become too real, too live to conform to the conventions of seventeenth-century portraiture. The grotesque awkwardness of those hands symbolizes for the onlooker the artist's unconscious refusal to follow canonical prescriptions. It is precisely such experience of sudden inspiration that has been consistently suppressed in this house, Malte observes. There is not a single corner of the house that does not remind one of this suffering. When the host finally appears, Malte cannot help asking himself: "War er nun ruhig? Man stand vor ihm, man zwang sich aufzusehen, man wußte es nicht. . . . Wie, wenn die ungeheuer angewachsene Forderung seines Werkes sich noch einmal in ihm erhübe?" [Was he now content? One stood in front of him and forced oneself to look, one could not tell. . . . How could he be, if the enormous ever growing demands of his works surged in him once again?] (*SW* 6:975–76). The elder's authority is exposed, made vulnerable and open to questioning. Never again will Malte experience such fear and compassion (*SW* 6:973). The Tolstoy of the second draft acquires an Aristotelian tragic stature: he is guilty and at the same time innocent in his suffering. It is precisely this internal "overcoming" of the faltering father and the return of filial compassion that the novel's third and final ending—by then emancipated from Tolstoy's image—succeeds in projecting.

Perhaps to resolve his anxiety about Tolstoy, Rilke omits him altogether from his parable of the prodigal son. In his retelling, the biblical legend becomes the story of the returning son rather than of the forgiving father.

Rilke's opening line reads: "Man wird mich schwer davon überzeugen, daß die Geschichte des verlorenen Sohnes nicht die Legende dessen ist, der nicht geliebt werden wollte" [It will be difficult to persuade me that the story of the Prodigal Son is not the legend of him who did not want to be loved] (*SW* 6:938).[34] The son who returns home is now different; he has not come to seek love or forgiveness. On the contrary, he comes to confirm his independence and to set himself free from memory, finally and irrevocably. As the son becomes more central in Rilke's story, the father (a Tolstoyan character) anonymously retreats into the household crowd, unmentioned, invisible and inconsequential.[35] The decision whether to stay or go is no longer the father's or the family's but the son's own. The prodigal's world is beyond their influence, and Rilke leaves his decision uncertain: "Wir wissen nicht, ob er blieb; wir wissen nur, daß er wiederkam" [We do not know, whether he stayed; we only know that he came back] (*SW* 6:945).

Rilke's preference for the legend of the prodigal son over the two earlier Tolstoy endings suggests an answer to the predicament of Tolstoy's influence. The Russian writer had failed him as a model on several counts. Tolstoy's primary transgression consisted in his refusal to take art as seriously as his religious faith. He was too vain and too impatient to wait for the slow results of the artist's "still and aimless work." Left without the difficult faith of the artist, Tolstoy blindly attached himself to those who were incapable of creating their own god and yet, out of their need, were willing to accept a ready-made substitute.[36] Rilke, as did his Malte, always believed that art was faith in its own right, higher than religion, and that it was the only worthwhile path to follow. Tolstoy's dissipation of his genius and the suffering he inflicted on himself and others by his conversion reaffirmed Rilke in this conviction. Tolstoy's Yasnaya Polyana offered no shelter to a young artist; rather, it served as a reminder of the tragic disillusionment of life without art. To paraphrase the present ending of *The Notebooks of Malte Laurids Brigge:* to take all this once more, and this time really, upon himself—this was the reason why Rilke, the estranged and mature artist, returned to the puzzling experience of his youth.[37]

Chapter Eight

Russia Revisited: Gorky and Pasternak

AESTHETICS AS POLITICS: MAXIM GORKY

Leonid Pasternak's greetings on Rilke's fiftieth birthday in December 1925 and Rilke's prompt reply set the stage for his final Russian encounter: correspondence with members of Boris Pasternak's family and Marina Tsvetae-va-Efron.[1] "Do you remember the old, enchanting, now legendary Moscow? . . . Tolstoy, his house, Yasnaya Polyana?" Pasternak nostalgically recalled from his exile in Berlin. Rilke reassured Pasternak that he had always remained loyal to the "unforgettable and unfathomable *skazka* (fairy tale)" of his youth. Even though he could no longer reply to him in Russian, Russia had remained forever embedded in the foundations of his art.[2]

To turn to Russian culture in the transitional 1920s from his place in the secluded Swiss castle Muzot required from Rilke not just a declaration of faith in the old Russian myth but a sense of responsibility and a determined resolve. "Dear old Russia," Europe's last hope for spiritual renewal, had since disappeared from the world map. Its ancient name was lost in the awkward acronym RSFSR, and subsequently dissolved altogether in the anonymous USSR. Those Russian citizens who rejected the Bolshevik regime had emigrated or been expelled, resettling in other countries and establishing for themselves a new identity in exile. Their principal bonds with the homeland were linguistic rather than legal, and they perpetuated cultural values while rejecting ethnic and national ties. The émigrés' life continued to be distinctly Russian and for the most part unaffected by the laws and mores of their host countries.[3] For Westerners, manifest Slavophilism became more of a liability than a fashionable exoticism, and it was equivalent to making a political decision in an atmosphere of growing chauvinism and militarism.[4]

It was courageous of Rilke to renew his active interest in Russia's historical destiny just when the rest of Europe was turning away from it. He was convinced—and, as it now appears, not without cause—that the Communist state was only a detour in Russia's cultural development. The events of the Revolution and the civil war reminded him of the Golden Horde, which had invaded Russia in the thirteenth century and for three hundred years halted the country's indigenous cultural development.[5] Having witnessed Russia's belated renaissance at the close of the nineteenth century, Rilke always remembered the feeling of rejuvenation and convinced himself that it would return. He was optimistic to the end that "the profound, the real, the surviving other Russia had only fallen back on her secret root system." Under the Bolsheviks, Rilke wrote to Leonid Pasternak, Russia once again "hid itself underground, inside the earth," gathering its forces in that darkness, "invisible to its own children."[6] He never doubted that his Russia was still there, even if he did not live long enough to see its rebirth.

Although Rilke had always disapproved of radical extremes in Russian political life, he made it his project to accept Russia's cultural paradoxes. Guided by his faith, he shared neither the blind utopian optimism of radical intellectuals nor the apocalyptic prophecies of inveterate Russophobes, and in his judgments he appealed to the fundamental Russian values that he upheld with a handful of his contemporaries. He continued to insist that the Russians were a deeply religious, patient people inclined to inward contemplation; in short, anything but destructive revolutionaries. "A revolutionary is the Russian's direct adversary," Rilke commented upon hearing the reports of the social unrest in Russia in 1907.[7] As late as 1921, he chose not to accept evidence of the violence and destruction caused by the Bolshevik Revolution and continued to make ill-advised statements, such as "Only a Russian can show how the will to be truthful can do no harm."[8] Rilke never came even remotely close to deserving the label of political artist; nonetheless, his opposition to politics, staunch defense of aesthetics, and belief in Russia against all historical and political odds made him a deeply engaged writer. Art, not religion or ideology, was Rilke's path to the new century: "How the future worlds will ripen to God I do not know, but for us, art is the way."[9]

No other Russian writer better embodied for Rilke the ambivalence of the country's political extremes than did Maxim Gorky. Rilke met Gorky briefly in April 1907 at Gorky's villa on Capri and described their conversation in several letters to friends. Gorky's manner convinced Rilke that the proletarian literary guru had little in common with the ideal Russian artist he had imagined. For the world, Gorky cultivated the image of a flamboyant hobo writer, publicly announcing his loyalty to the revolutionary cause; yet at the same time he spent most of his life in the West and exploited his literary fame to generate a substantial income. Most surprising for Rilke was to hear Gorky discuss art. He spoke like a politician, Rilke reported, a "man of the people" who was unable to disengage himself from political commitments and ideological biases. In a letter to Leonid Pasternak Rilke described Gorky as an "unsatisfied and angry person" who expressed his opinions in a straightforward manner that was meant to make clear all possible ambiguities and to allow no room for doubts and questions.[10] Such political egalitarianism, quick and categorical judgment, and disregard for nuances and subtle meanings were hard for Rilke to accept from an artist of Gorky's stature. "Is he still a truly Russian person?" Rilke inquired of Pasternak. "I am afraid that he is a Westerner who has been corrupted by fame and international socialism."[11] Rilke's intuitive distrust of Gorky's dangerous linking of art and ideology proved prophetic. A decade later, in 1934, Gorky finally surrendered his responsibility as an artist to endorse the totalitarian state and become its faithful functionary. As chairman of the newly organized Union of Soviet Writers, Gorky presided over the literary creation of a "New Soviet Man" who "possessed faith in the organizing power of reason" and had no grounds for pessimism—in other words, the exact opposite of Rilke's ideal of a creative, individual Russian.[12]

Rilke's initial enthusiasm for the Bolshevik Revolution was similarly short-lived. When the text of Trotsky's manifesto "To All the Toiling, Oppressed, and Deceived Peoples of Europe" reached him amid the devastations of World War I, he mistook the dramatic turn of events for the fulfillment of Russia's messianic promise. "I would have had nothing to celebrate in my hotel room if it were not for the thought of wonderful Russia," he wrote, believing that the universal brotherhood of all people had arrived.[13] He soon recognized that the Bolsheviks' blatant disregard for cultural continuity and for the centuries-old traditions of their country swept away not only the abuses of the old regime but also the difficult historical achievements of previous generations. The promised "brotherhood of all peoples" did not materialize, as history soon demonstrated, but Russia's own fragile spiritual legacy was seriously endangered. "The old lack of principles worked here under the pretext of the great upheaval; it grew even bigger under the red flags," Rilke concluded bitterly.[14]

In the meantime, the temporary revitalization of cultural life in the interwar 1920s renewed Rilke's interest in the emerging forms of the Russian messianic idea among members of the intellectual émigré community. In 1921 he came across Alexander Blok's poem "The Scythians" (January 1918), which had become a virtual manifesto of the Eurasian movement.[15] Written in the aftermath of the Bolshevik Revolution, Blok's poem portrayed Russia as mired in humiliation but rising from the depths of its own dark history to reaffirm its creative spirit.

O, staryi mir! Poka ty ne pogib,
Poka tomishs'a mykoi sladkoi,
Ostanovis' premudryi kak Edip,
Pred Sfinksom s drevneiu zagadkoi!

105

Rossia—sfinks. Likuiaiskorbia,
i oblivaias' chernoi kroviu
ona gl'adit gl'acit gl'aditvteb'a
i-s-nenavis't'u isl'ubov'u.

V poslednii raz—opomnis', staryi mir!
Na bratskii pir truda i mira,
V poslednii raz—na svetlyi bratskii pir
Szyvaet varvarskaia lira!

O, ancient world! . . .
Halt, wise as Oedipus, and seek to solve
The riddle of the Sphinx.

The Sphinx is Russia. Now exulting through her tears,
As black blood from a thousand gashes flows
It is at you, at you she stares
With hatred—and with love.

For the last time, old world, we bid you come,
Come to the feast of labor and peace,
For the last time to a happy feast
The barbarian lyre is calling you to come.

Blok's theme of his country's proud reincarnation in its new twentieth-century image reaffirmed Rilke's faith in Russia's second coming. In the 1920s it was impossible to predict what would come next, and Russia continued to be Europe's cultural unknown.

THE RUSSIAN PARIS

In January 1925, Rilke left his seclusion in Muzot for the last time, heading for Paris in hopes of finding distraction from his illness in the city's boisterous social life. He also had plans to finally shape his Russian memories into a book.[16] There could not have been a better place to renew his prerevolutionary Russian contacts than Paris. In the mid-1920s the cultural capital of the Russian diaspora had moved from Berlin to Paris, and Europe's most cosmopolitan city was bustling with Russian intellectual and cultural life.[17] Soon after his arrival, Rilke was able to resume some of his former Russian friendships, but most of those reunions only reminded him of his major loss. His former Petersburg acquaintance Helene Voronina, whom Rilke had always associated with Russia's future, lived with her husband among the refugees, without any hope for the future ("sans avenir aucun").[18] But once the circle of his acquaintances expanded beyond his former friends, Rilke found himself drawn into the dynamic cultural life of Russian Paris. Even though he met such eminent émigrés as the Nobel Prize winner Ivan Bunin,[19] the literary critic Lev Struve, and the translator Mikhail Zeitlin, Rilke preferred to skirt the émigré center looking for unconventional and "unpolitical" friends. The ballet dancers Alexander and Clotilde Sakharoff, the artist Alexander Volkov-Muromzev, and the puppeteer Julia Sazonova were among his new Russian acquaintances.[20]

Rilke visited Sazonova's Parisian atelier frequently. He had always been attracted to the uninhibited atmosphere of puppet theater, and the unusually animated quality of Sazonova's performances reawakened in him his old fascination with dolls, puppets, and marionettes—a fascination that was to leave its creative trace. Sets and costumes for Sazonova's theater were executed by the Russian avant-garde artist Natalia Goncharova, who combined Russian designs and foreign folk motifs. The happy meeting among different folk types—the Russian marketplace hero Petrushka, the traditional characters of the Italian commedia dell'arte, and the Turkish folk marionettes—all served to transcend, if largely symbolically, current Russian uprootedness and loss.

For his part, Rilke discerned in the marionettes' obliviousness to the tragic fate of their human prototypes a subtle reminder of the precariousness of the human condition. Mythic but mindless dolls loved without loving and suffered without suffering, ignorant of the significance of their performance. Rilke saw in Sazonova's presentation a challenge to humanity: "Are they happy, they who ignore the essentials of human nature while impersonating it?"[21] On the stage, love and suffering turned into grotesque parody.

Rilke had arrived at a similar realization some fifteen years earlier in an essay entitled "The Puppets" ("Puppen") (1914). There he recalled his visit to the estate of a provincial Russian landlord; in the house, there was an old family doll that uncannily resembled every member of the household for several generations at once. The doll took on everyone's face without having one of its own. Every incoming generation left an imprint on the doll's ageless face.[22]

Rilke continued to develop his thoughts on dolls, angels, and masks in his *Duino Elegies* (*Duineser Elegien*) (1912–22). The Fourth Elegy (1915) evokes the image of a puppet play, which absorbs in one powerful metaphor the poet's earlier reflections on the relationship between life, art, and theater: "Who's not sat tense before his own heart's curtain?" Rilke asks the angels. By means of art, the artist frees himself to live with emotional vitality behind his multiple masks.

Ich will nicht diese halbgefüllten Masken,
lieber die Puppe. Die ist voll. Ich will
den Balg aushalten und den Draht und ihr
Gesicht aus Aussehen. Hier. Ich bin davor.
Wenn auch die Lampen ausgehen, wenn mir auch
gesagt wird: Nichts mehr—, wenn auch von der Bühne
das Leere herkommt mit dem grauen Luftzug,
wenn auch von meinen stillen Vorfahrn keiner
mehr mit mir dasitzt, keine Frau, sogar
der Knabe nicht mehr mit dem braunen Schielaug:
Ich bleibe dennoch. Es giebt immer Zuschaun. (*SW* 1:697–98)

I don't want these half-filled masks, no, rather the doll.
It's full. I'll put up with the skin and the wires
and the face that's only appearance. I'm out here
in front.
Even if the footlights go out and I'm told: That's all—
if emptiness from the stage blows in gray drafts,
if none of my silent forefathers sits beside me,
no woman, not even the boy with brown squint eyes:
I'll stay, in spite of it. One can always look on.[23]

Rilke concluded that the theater was ultimately more honest in representing life than life itself. For him, ever the advocate of art, a truly creative person protected himself from being engulfed into life's uncontrollable flow by holding up a work of art as a mask. Hiding from himself, the artist became so powerful that his captivated audience would break into applause, "as though . . . to ward off something that would force them to change their life."[24] To let himself be entertained by Sazonova's deliberately artificial merrymaking amid the unfolding revolutionary drama served Rilke as an occasion for reflection on Russia's historical fate. Rilke realized that the closer he approached Russia aesthetically, the more distant he grew from it existentially: "the more calmly he reflected, the more unachieved did it seem to him."[25] He realized that to continue to worship Russia as "poetry embodied" he had to exit from history into art.

In August 1925 Rilke's general weariness of the city's new tempo compounded by his deteriorating health compelled him to leave Paris, after having spent eight months there. He sensed that the city's unique cultural diversity was threatened by intolerance, as well as by the rising influence of two novel presences: Americanism and Bolshevism.[26] Had he remained until November, he might have met the poet Marina Tsvetaeva-Efron when she arrived in Paris from Prague. In the following year, Tsvetaeva would play a major role in Rilke's last, and, perhaps, most dramatic encounter with Rus-

sia; between March and November 1926 he became the occasion for and a participant in an exchange of approximately fifty letters among members of the Pasternak family and Tsvetaeva. For Rilke, the unexpected opportunity to correspond with two younger Russian poets offered the chance he had been waiting for to retrieve his "unachieved" Russian memories.

THE RUSSIAN RILKE: BORIS PASTERNAK

While in Paris, Rilke chanced upon two of Boris Pasternak's poems in Paul Valéry's literary almanac *Commerce*. He was impressed with the distinctly Russian stanzas whose French translation had a Baudelairian absence of rhyme. Rilke recognized in the two melancholy poems a rising literary talent and shared his impressions with Leonid Pasternak. The elder Pasternak informed his son in Moscow of Rilke's favorable notice.[27]

The news that Rainer Maria Rilke thought highly of his poetry arrived, as Pasternak put it, as an "electrical short circuit of the soul." He did not expect that a medium as prosaic as the postal service could be a link to Rilke, whom he considered his teacher. Boris had remembered Rilke since their single meeting at a Moscow train station in early summer 1900. Later, he had found in his father's library two autographed volumes: *In Celebration of Myself* (*Mir zur Feier*) and *The Book of Hours*.[28] Rilke's *Book of Hours* sounded to Pasternak's ear particularly familiar: its themes were mystical and yet earthly, religious and at the same time irreverent. Most important, they promised the continuation of life despite all evidence to the contrary.

Und doch, obwohl ein jeder von sich strebt
wie aus dem Kerker, der ihn haßt und hält,—
es ist ein großes Wunder in der Welt:
ich fühle: *alles Leben wird gelebt.*

Wer lebt es denn? Sind das die Dinge, die
wie eine ungespielte Melodie
im Abend wie in einer Harfe stehn?
Sind das die Winde, die von Wassern wehn,
sind das die Zweige, die sich Zeichen geben,
sind das die Blumen, die die Düfte weben,
sind das die langen alternden Alleen?
Sind das die warmen Tiere, welche gehen,
sind das die Vögel, die sich fremd erheben?

Wer lebt es denn? Lebst du es, Gott,—das Leben? (*SW* 1:317)

109

Although, as from a prison walled with hate,
each from his own self labors to be free,
the world yet holds a wonder, and how great!
All life is lived: now this comes home to me.
But who, then, lives it? Things that patiently
stand there, like some unfingered melody
that sleeps within a harp as day is going?
Is it the winds across the waters blowing,
is it the branches beckoning each to each,
is it the flowers weaving fragrances,
the ageing alleys stretching endlessly?
Is it the warm beasts moving to and fro,
the birds in alien flight that sail from view?
This life—who lives it really? God, do you?[29]

Pasternak had introduced Rilke's poetry to members of the bohemian literary group Serdada, who used to gather at Yulian Anisimov's house in Moscow in 1908–9. Anisimov, the group's versatile leader and himself a poet, completed in 1913 the first Russian translation of *The Book of Hours*. Thus chance and Pasternak's personal predilection for Rilke's early poetry were responsible for *The Book of Hours* becoming the best known and better understood of Rilke's works in Russia.

When in 1926 Pasternak received from Rilke a gift of his two most celebrated works, *The Duino Elegies* and *Sonnets to Orpheus,* he became aware of how much he had changed since he had last read Rilke. Initially, Pasternak had elevated Rilke to the ranks of his seer-saints, Aeschylus or Pushkin.[30] Later, Rilke became for him a teacher and an older contemporary with whom he had much in common, both as a poet and as a person. In his letter of 12 April 1926, Pasternak addressed Rilke in his highly exalted idiosyncratic German with protestations of love and gratitude lasting over two decades. Pasternak also used the occasion of this letter to share his concern over the miscarriage of the Russian Revolution and its effects on the writer.

There is one lesson which life here teaches everyone who is willing to learn: a great event is most contradictory when it takes an *active* form, for in reality it is *inconsequential* and proceeds at a sluggish pace. Such is our revolution, a contradiction in its very appearance, a fragment of shifting time in the form of a fearful, motionless spectacle. And such are our own fates also—the *static* temporal *subjects* of this sinister, noble historical curiosity, tragic even in their smallest, most ridiculous aspects.[31]

Pasternak's view of the revolution as a blatant perversion of Russia's traditional values echoed Rilke's own. The two poets agreed that, on the one hand, the revolution seemed to have called for an active participation in life's creation; on the other, it arrested life's inception in embryo. The artist, unlike the politician, had to observe laws of culture rather than alter them; he had to allow for time-bound daily experiences to coalesce into timeless aesthetic values. Since his travels in Russia, Rilke had thought of the artist's position in life as a condition of pure receptivity characterized by humility, unpretentious piety, and patience. For both Rilke and Pasternak, art represented a circular return to life's basic fundamentals: things and creatures provided the poets with immediate material for writing, and their sense of the sublime was permanently burdened with the concern for the real and earthly. The language of their most exalted verse reverberated with autobiographical echoes. Rilke led Pasternak to a discovery of God, not in his transcendental form, but embodied in the objects of the real world, and his Orphic "Song is existence" resonated in Pasternak's "The live, real world is the only plot for the imagination."[32]

Boris Pasternak's confessional letter to Rilke was the only letter he ever wrote him, leaving his puzzled biographers to ponder the mystery of his silence. Four possible reasons have been advanced: the lack of a direct postal connection between Russia and Switzerland; Pasternak's unwillingness to include his father and his sisters as mediators between him and Rilke; that Tsvetaeva either deliberately delayed or belatedly summarized Rilke's letters for him; and Pasternak's reluctance to make claims on Rilke's attention.[33] None of these arguments is persuasive by itself, and I see the situation quite differently. Pasternak was only six when he met Rilke, and as he was growing up, his memory of the Austrian poet had become increasingly private. He did not feel that he had to meet Rilke personally to equal him as a poet, while a chance personal encounter might jeopardize the sanctity of Rilke's image.[34] Pasternak had transformed and internalized Rilke's message that the poet's primary responsibility was to his art, and, most likely, he saw no need for direct contact. Distance and independence were as crucial to Pasternak's ability to create as they were to Rilke's: "My voice can ring out pure and clear only when absolutely solitary," he explained in a letter to his father. "I do not dedicate my reflections to the memory of Rilke, I myself received them from him as gifts," he wrote in his autobiographical *Vozdushnye puti* (Airways).[35]

Pasternak once proposed, speaking of Rilke, that the individuality of a genius was collective; that even though he might be unaware of the origin of his art, it absorbed the richness of his future readers' experiences.[36] The life of the poet never belonged to himself, Pasternak concluded, but had to be constructed from the biographies of those who came after him. These words were prophetic: Rilke entered twentieth-century Russian literary history through Boris Pasternak's and Marina Tsvetaeva's biographies and in their works.

111

Pasternak took it upon himself to represent Rilke for his Russian contemporaries from within his own experience, based on his own understanding of Rilke's poetry. He explained that Rilke's work had been misunderstood in Russia precisely because the translators had tried unsuccessfully to reproduce the content of his poems rather than follow their tone. In Rilke everything depended on the tone, which needed to be rendered into the corresponding Russian mood.[37] To Western taste, Pasternak's selections for translation were idiosyncratic and perhaps not the best choices.[38] For Russian readers, Rilke remained the neoromantic author of his early books: *The Book of Hours* and *The Book of Pictures*, and *The Life of the Virgin Mary* (*Das Marienleben*). These readers were much less interested in Rilke's later efforts to master his emotional world and to subject his art to the rigorous discipline of language. His later philosophical cycles, *The Duino Elegies* and *Sonnets to Orpheus*, interested them least of all.[39] Slavic readers invariably responded to Rilke's emotional, mystical messages, and his dictum "Resignation takes us further than resistance" could not find a more receptive audience than in the land of Tolstoy and Dostoyevsky. If Rilke had conjured up a Russia of mysticism and simple communal faith to sustain himself, then perhaps that sort of Russian reader was preordained.

Chapter Nine

Beyond Rilke: Marina Tsvetaeva

RILKE AS TSVETAEVA'S CORRESPONDENT

Marina Tsvetaeva's "Poem of the End" ("Poema kontsa") reached Boris
Pasternak in Moscow on the same day in 1926 as Leonid Pasternak's news of
Rilke's praise, and Boris hastened to interpret this coincidence as destiny's
intercession. To get the two poets personally acquainted, he asked Rilke to
write to Tsvetaeva in Paris and to send her an autographed volume of his latest poetry.[1] Thirty years later, Pasternak explained his mediation as a
courtship "gift" to Tsvetaeva; he confessed that his love for Marina at that
time was as strong as if not stronger than his love for Rilke.[2] As a gesture of
friendship to Pasternak, Rilke wrote a letter to Tsvetaeva within an hour of
receiving Pasternak's request: "But why, why, must I ask myself now, it was
not granted to me to meet you, Marina Ivanovna Tsvetaeva? . . . Can it still
be made up for some day?"[3]

Ironically, Pasternak's self-effacing remark that he was not good enough
to match Tsvetaeva in correspondence (and that she could easily replace him)
turned out to be a self-fulfilling prophecy.[4] Tsvetaeva understood Rilke's letter as his personal recognition of her as a poet and as an invitation to a relationship. She thus decided to continue writing to him whether he wanted it or
not. "Why did I not come to you?" she asked in her last letter. "Because I love
you of all things most. It is very simple."[5] Even though Tsvetaeva considered
both Rilke and Pasternak to be her poetic equals, Rilke still ranked for her the
greater of the two, and she decided to leave Pasternak out of the exchange.
She ignored Pasternak's polite reminders of the originally planned union: "I
have a vague feeling that you are gently pushing me away from him [Rilke].
And since I see the three of us as a unity, held in a single embrace, that means
you are pushing me away from you, too, without openly acknowledging it."[6]
Tsvetaeva was uncompromising when it came to sharing Rilke with Pasternak
and insisted that for her Germany, she needed all of Rilke. As she later
explained, it was still *this* world—and not the world of poetry—in which the

geography of her immaterial possessions knew no boundaries: "Listen so that you know: In Rainer-land I alone represent Russia."[7]

There is no doubt of an affinity between Rilke, Tsvetaeva, and Pasternak as poets, one that set them apart as exemplars of the lyricism of their troubled age. We cannot assume, however, that the poets' correspondence was as spontaneous and disinterested as they hoped at the outset; three poetic temperaments, three lyrical styles, commingled and nearly canceled each other out in the course of this exchange. For inspiration, they looked in different directions: at the end of his life, Rilke turned eastward toward his lost Russia; Tsvetaeva reached westward to Germany and Europe; and Pasternak searched for difficult answers within himself. Understandably, most critical readings of this correspondence have been guided by the personal interests of the interpreter and have reflected the discrepant levels of personal involvement of each of the three participants: Tsvetaeva was totally absorbed in her new role, Pasternak withdrew after writing his first letter, and Rilke kept at a secure distance in his Swiss retreat.[8]

Whether or not one approaches Rilke's epistolary legacy as the best of his prose, and whether or not one considers Tsvetaeva's letters as mirror images of her "naked soul," one must carefully distinguish between the literary significance of these writings and the realities of their authors' lives.[9] Letters are a boundary genre, bridging prose and biography and thus giving rise to special problems of interpretation.[10] More specifically, the two poets' long-distance relationship evolved from a personal conflict between Rilke's anxiety about the dangers of intimacy and Tsvetaeva's desire for an uplifting affiliation. If their letters chronicle a miscarried personal relationship, their poetry reveals an accord in art. The two poets could maintain an artistic union only if they remained separate in life.

Rilke wrote to Tsvetaeva not because she was a great poet but primarily because he felt an almost messianic sense of obligation to all writers and artists in distress. As a matter of professional duty, Rilke took it upon himself to write to poets, regardless of their status, fame, or talent. He once remarked that all poets shared a common lot: "The Poet, here where the great name no longer matters. One can say Dante or Spitteler—it is the same, it is the Poet, for in the last resort there is only one—undying, manifesting himself here and there down through the ages, in this or that genius."[11] In addition, at the end of his life, Rilke pledged to support exiled Russians in every possible way. He helped Julia Sazonova, the Russian puppeteer; met and exchanged letters with the ballet dancers the Sakharoffs; and hired a Russian secretary, Evgenia Tchernosvitova, to read to him in Russian.[12] Tsvetaeva was not aware of the extent of Rilke's participation in the fates of the women writers and artists who turned to him for help and advice, some of them single mothers living on meager literary earnings.[13] Having had Malte's experiences early in his career, Rilke believed that a suc-

114

cessful poet owed it to his less fortunate contemporaries to share his accidental fortune generously. "There are many people who expect from me I do not know what: an extension of help, a piece of advice," Rilke wrote to a friend. "Malte's experience often forces me to answer calls from people whom I do not know. He would have done it. . . . He left me with a challenging legacy and I cannot deflect from his charitable course [*une destination charitable*]."[14]

Rilke located Tsvetaeva "on the inner map of his soul" "somewhere between Moscow and Toledo."[15] She belonged in his larger existential project of art-as-existence. At the time when he started writing to Tsvetaeva, Rilke had already received international acclaim for the *Duino Elegies* and *Sonnets to Orpheus* and was carefully guarding against intrusions on his privacy in secluded Muzot. The solitary man and poet that he was, Rilke wore a mask of intimacy in his letters that enabled him to veil and protect his inner life from his admirers, who, he felt, were constantly draining his limited vitality and creative energy.[16] To describe his suspension between solitude and the need for a dialogue, Rilke coined the word *Hinaussüchtigkeit*, "craving to get out."[17] His initial enthusiasm for Tsvetaeva was due primarily to nostalgia for his youth, for his lost health, and for his vanished Russia. But Tsvetaeva's insistence on being his last woman, his only Russia, and his sole connection with the outside world quickly dampened Rilke's enthusiasm. Her almost surreal play with words fatigued him, and he began to resent the burdensome role of demiurge that she had thrust on him. In the end, as Rilke explained in his final letter to Tsvetaeva, her discourteous treatment of Pasternak was the last straw in his decision to stop writing to her: "I find you too strict, almost too hard on him [Pasternak] (and too strict toward me if you wish that Russia should be never and nowhere else except in you!). If I rebel against any exclusion (which grows out of the love root but hardens into wood): would you then recognize me, like this, too?"[18]

All of his life, Rilke was wary of idolatry in any form and preferred to live at a "distance from success."[19] He was never afraid to appear vulnerable and human in his letters.[20] In response to Tsvetaeva's "I love the poet, not the person," he cautioned that the separation between his body and his soul had become too real for him in the confines of a sanatorium: "And now dis-cord, doubly cored, soul clad one way, body mummed another, different."[21]

Tsvetaeva scholars often speculate whether Rilke could fully appreciate Tsvetaeva's poetic talent solely from her letters. Even though he admired her almost native command of German, he admitted that he could not understand her poetry: "Your books, despite your help in difficult places, are difficult for me." Tsvetaeva's experimental play with the German language appeared somewhat "heavy" and "uneven" to him: "Your German—no, it doesn't 'stumble,' it just takes heavier steps now and then, like the steps of someone who is going down a stone staircase with steps of unequal size and

115

thus cannot estimate when his foot is going to come to rest, right now or suddenly farther down than he thought."[22]

Rilke was not condescending in his comments, as Tsvetaeva suspected, but merely seeking to clarify for himself the evasiveness of her metaphors. In the better known *Letters to a Young Poet* (*Briefe an einen jungen Dichter*), he used similar language to urge his unnamed addressee to be patient, to accept all that might come, to learn to love the questions that bothered him more than the answers, and, most importantly, not to burden others with the responsibility for his private doubts and joys.

Tsvetaeva did not share Rilke's egalitarianism: "Her voice always knew above what it was elevated, knew what was there, down below (or, more precisely, what—there below—was lacking)."[23] She ranked her fellow poets according to their poetic "height" (*rost*) and "force" (*sila*), and "accidental outsiders," like Evgenia Tchernosvitova, were considered unworthy intruders for carrying on with their insignificant lives after the poet's death.[24]

Tsvetaeva wrote to Rilke because he was "poetry itself," an embodied timeless "phenomenon of nature":

> Wars, slaughterhouses, flesh shredded by discord—and Rilke. The earth will be absolved for our time because Rilke lived in it. He could have been born only in our time because he is its opposite, because he is necessary, because he is its antidote. That is what makes him our contemporary. Our time did not commission him, it called him forth. . . . Rilke is as ineluctably necessary to our times as a priest is to the battlefield: to pray for these and for those, for them and for us: to pray— for the enlightenment of the still living and for the farewell to the already fallen.[25]

Tsvetaeva's praise of Rilke demonstrated that it was not the exotic quality of his style that attracted Russian poets to Rilke but something more central to their uniquely poetic experience of the world: their desire for wholeness and belonging. In her first letter to Rilke, Tsvetaeva remarked on their different perspectives: "You will always feel me as a Russian; I—You—as a purely human (Godlike) phenomenon." "This is the difficulty of our too individualized nationality. Everything that is for us an 'I' is for the Europeans—Russian."[26] Thus in the name of Russia, the three poets set out to win for poetry some of the ground that had been lost to politics and history.

RILKE'S ANXIETY OF AUTHORSHIP AS THE ANXIETY OF LOVE

Rilke's correspondence with Tsvetaeva was one of his last attempts to come to terms with the self-imposed isolation demanded by his art and his illness. With the brief exception of his Russian experience, Rilke lived his life in the constant anxiety of being taken over by others, smothered, possessed, and fixed in clichés and formulas. He exposed his fears to the world in the pages of his autobiographical novel, *Malte Laurids Brigge*. In the last pages of the novel he wrote:

> Not until long afterward was it to become clear to him how much he had then intended never to love, in order not to put anyone in the terrible position of being loved. It occurred to him years later and, like other projects, this too had been impossible. For he had loved and loved again in his solitude; each time with waste of his whole nature and with unspeakable fear for the liberty of the other. Slowly he learned to penetrate the beloved object with the rays of his feeling, instead of consuming it in them. [27]

To protect himself from the demands of intimacy, Rilke resorted to letter writing as the most beautiful and productive means of social intercourse, a dialogue among friends and lovers. For many years, Rilke's entire production consisted in writing such letters, which he would often collect and present as self-contained works. As one of his biographers suggests, Rilke's social persona, manners, and clothes were often a protective mechanism developed by the poet to defend his inner freedom against intrusions from the outside.[28] In his letters, Rilke invariably attuned himself to the epistolary style of his addressees.[29] It is not surprising, therefore, that a sensitive reader can discern fluctuations of Tsvetaeva's mood and tone in the lines of Rilke's letters: "I'm writing like you and I descend like you the few steps down from the sentence into the mezzanine of parentheses. . . . Marina, how I have inhabited your letter." Rilke himself seems to have encouraged her displays of emotion: "You are right, Marina (isn't it a rare thing for a woman?) such Being-right in the most effective, the most lighthearted sense? This Being-right *not for some purpose,* hardly coming from anywhere; but such *pure lack of need,* out of fullness and completeness and, through it all, always right into eternity."[30] Rilke's dialogical style unsuspectingly "kindled the fire" of Tsvetaeva's emotions, inviting the "hurricane" of her letters.

Tsvetaeva was not the only woman who was misled by Rilke's manner of holding a mirror to their emotional world, and she was not the only one who took his empathy for an invitation to an intimacy beyond the purely poetic.[31] Claire Goll, Rilke's former lover, remarked in this connection that "he received many proofs; collections of letters . . . filled his drawers." "Many women, who did not know to which saint they should devote themselves, chose Rilke as the guide of their conscience."[32] An advocate of women's artistic self-expression, Rilke considered Tsvetaeva's intoxication with control over him in letters to be a mere gender reversal of the old masculine ways, a transitional stage on her path to genuine independence: "It will

117

become apparent that women were only going through the profusion and the vicissitudes of those (often ridiculous) disguises in order to cleanse their own most characteristic nature of the distorting influences of the other sex." Rilke concluded that eventually "there will be girls and women whose names will no longer signify merely opposites of the masculine but human beings whole in themselves, something that would make one think not of a complement to or a limit of, but of life and existence: the feminine human being."[33]

Rilke had spent much of his life cultivating the aesthetics of femininity: he became an astute reader of women's writings in order to nurture in himself the traits of sensitivity, receptivity, and intuition traditionally attributed to women.[34] He translated collections of women's letters and poetry and enriched German literature with the writings of Marianna Alcoforado, Mechtild von Magdeburg, Louise Labé, and Elizabeth Browning. When women artists, writers, and poets turned to him for help and advice, he spoke on their behalf, wrote prefaces to their works, and extended financial assistance whenever he could.

Tsvetaeva was not the only woman who sensed an ally in Rilke; his undisguised preference for feminine creativity was well known. "The woman who loves always transcends the man she loves," Rilke wrote, "because life is greater than fate. Her devotion wants to be immeasurable; that is her good fortune. But the nameless suffering of her love has always been this: that she is required to restrict her devotion." He likened the creative moment to "an impregnating and birth-giving experience transmuted into the spiritual sphere." Despite his gender, Rilke refused to be excluded from the female life-giving experience: "Even in a man there is motherhood, physical and spiritual; his procreating is also a kind of giving birth, and giving birth it is when he creates out of inmost fullness." Rilke was well aware of creativity's darkest side: violation. To Princess Marie von Thurn und Taxis, he described the moment of inspiration at Duino castle in explicitly gendered terms: "The spirit rushes in and out so brusquely, comes so wildly, and absents itself so suddenly that I feel as if I am being physically torn to pieces."[35]

In her memoir, the princess recorded how essential it had become for Rilke to live within a woman's sphere, but as soon as his independence was threatened by demands for physical closeness, he took flight and withdrew into his old pain and sorrow.[36] Rilke was aware of his psychological need for monasticism and cautioned every woman at the outset of a new relationship: "Never forget that solitude is my lot, that I must not have a need for anyone, that all my strength, in fact, comes from this detachment. . . . I implore those who love me to love my solitude."[37] Within this distance and solitude, Rilke fashioned a philosophy of "unpossessive" or "intransitive" love that renounced union with the beloved. He refused to speak of "love" in the abstract but reflected at length on the predicament of those who were

118

"lovers." For Rilke, lovers were of two types: those who loved (*Die Liebende*) and those who were loved (*Die Geliebte*). Traditionally, women received love unconditionally, without reservation, as a life task (*eine Aufgabe*); men understood love as a challenge, an accomplishment (*eine Leistung*) to be achieved and a victory to be celebrated. Feminine renunciation of love's immediate pleasures, according to Rilke, increased one's inner strength and gave form to the anarchy of intense emotions that, in return, produced great art. For Rilke, only women and artists could be called "great lovers" in the true sense of the word.[38] Love was a companionship that strengthened two neighboring solitudes; relationships that depended on merging, giving, or taking were destructively uncreative.

RILKE'S LAST MESSAGE

In his letters, Rilke never directly elucidated for Tsvetaeva his philosophy of love and art, but he did inscribe the terms for their relationship when he sent her a copy of the *Duino Elegies* with the following dedication:

> Für Marina Zwetajewa
> Wir rühren uns. Womit? Mit Flügelschlägen,
> mit Fernen selber rühren wir uns an?
> *Ein* Dichter einzig lebt, und dann und wenn
> kommt, der ihn trägt, dem, der ihn trug entgegen.

> For Marina Tsvetaeva
> We touch each other. With what? With beat of wings,
> with distances themselves we touch and meet?
> Alone *one* poet dwells, and now and then
> comes one who bears him now to meet the one who has borne him.[39]

The *Elegies* illuminate Rilke's main message to all artists regardless of gender: "We *are* solitary." His metaphors for the poets' lonely fate range from a hopelessness "beyond description" in the First Elegy: "Wer, wenn ich schriee, hörte mich denn aus der Engel / Ordnungen?" (*SW* 1:685) [Who, if I shouted, among the hierarchy of angels / would hear me? (3)][40] to a tentative affirmation of imperfect human existence in the Tenth Elegy:

> Und wir, die an *steigendes* Glück
> denken, empfänden die Rührung,
> die uns beinah bestürzt,
> wenn ein Glückliches *fällt*. (*SW* 1:726)

Then we, who think of *rising* happiness,
would feel the emotion
that almost confounds us
when a happy Thing *falls*.

Rilke appeals to lovers to dissolve their imaginary unions in the name of love:

> . . . Ist es nich Zeit, daß wir liebend
> uns vom Geliebten befrein und es bebend bestehn:
> wie der Pfeil die Sehne besteht, um gesammelt im Absprung
> *mehr* zu sein als er selbst. Denn Bleiben ist nirgends. (*SW* 1:687)

> Isn't it time that we lovingly free ourselves
> from the beloved and stand it, although we tremble,
> as the arrow stands the bowstring, tense to be *more* than itself?
> For abiding is nowhere. (7)

Lovers' feelings are never eternal:

> Liebende, euch, ihr in einander Genügten,
> frag ich nach uns. Ihr greift euch. Habt ihr Beweise? (*SW* 1:691)

> You lovers, self-sufficient, I ask you
> about us. You hold each other. Have you proof? (15)

Rilke contrasts man's love, controlled by compulsive, irrational passions to woman's spiritual selflessness. In his highly pessimistic Eighth Elegy, he portrays the lovers' predicament: two people come close to seeing the unknown but they then obstruct each other's view by seeking self-reflection in the face of the beloved.

> Liebende, wäre nicht der andre, der
> die Sicht verstellt, sind nah daran und staunen . . .
> Wie aus Versehn is ihnen aufgetan
> hinter dem andern . . . Aber über ihn
> kommt keiner fort, und wieder wird ihm Welt.
> Der Schöpfung immer zugewendet, sehn
> wir nur auf ihr die Spiegelung des Frein,
> von uns verdunkelt . . . .
> . . . .
> Dieses heißt Schicksal: gegenüber sein
> und nichts als das und immer gegenüber. (*SW* 1:714–15)

Lovers, were it not for the other who blocks the view,
are close to it and marvel . . .
as if by carelessness it is open to them
behind each other . . . but neither gets past, and again
it's world. Always turned to creation, we see there
only the reflection of the free,
darkened by us. . . . .
. . . .
That's what Destiny is: to be face to face
and nothing but that and always opposite. (63)

Rilke concludes that people should perpetually wander and constantly take
leave of one another:

. . . . in jener Haltung sind
von einem, welcher fortgeht? Wie er auf
dem letzten Hügel, der ihm ganz sein Tal
noch einmal ziegt, sich wendet, anhält, weilt—,
so leben wir und nehmen immer Abschied. (SW 1:716)

. . . . —we have the bearing
of a man going away? As on the last hill
that shows him all his valley, for the last time,
he turns, stands still, and lingers, so we live,
forever saying farewell. (67)

In the Ninth Elegy, Rilke urges his readers to praise the world of real things
while we live among them and not to count on compensations for life in
future realms and in imaginary relationships:

Preise dem Engel die Welt, nicht die unsägliche, *ihm*
kannst du nicht großtun mit herrlich Erfühltem; im Weltall,
wo er fühlender fühlt, bist du ein Neuling. Drum zeig
ihm das Einfache, das, von Geschlecht zu Geschlechtern gestaltet,
als ein Unsriges lebt, neben der Hand und im Blick.
Sag ihm die Dinge. Er wird staunender stehn; wie du standest
bei dem Seiler in Rom, oder beim Töpfer am Nil. (SW 1:719)

Praise the world to the angel, not the unutterable world;
you cannot astonish him with your glorious feelings;
in the universe, where he feels more sensitively,
you are just a beginner. Therefore, show him the simple
thing that is shaped in passing from father to son,

that lives near our hands and eyes as our very own.
Tell him about Things. He'll stand more amazed,
as you stood
beside the rope-maker in Rome, or the potter on the Nile. (71)

Rilke's tribute to life as a commitment to the world of things and his praise of a solitary condition of creative artist reach an emotional peak in the *Sonnets to Orpheus*, whose theme directly anticipates the message of the Marina elegy. Orpheus, the "singing god," travels between the kingdoms of life and death delivering his message to the artists, "Song is existence" (*"Gesang ist Dasein"*):

Zu dem gebrauchten sowohl, wie zum dumpfen und stummen
Vorrat der vollen Natur, den unsäglichen Summen,
zähle dich jubelnd hinzu und vernichte die Zahl. (*SW* 1:759–60)

To the consumed, as well as to the muffled, damp, and dumb
storehouse of full Nature, the unspeakable, the immense sums,
add yourself, count yourself among them, jubilantly, and
cancel the count.[41]

When Tsvetaeva turned to Rilke to consummate her imaginary union with an idealized poet, she found him retreating into the privacy of his own world; as was his habit, he donned the protective cloak of poetry, a forewarning of the approaching end of his correspondence with her.[42] One may see in the elegy to Marina (*SW* 2:271–73) Rilke's attempt to communicate with Tsvetaeva via poetry, the language she understood best. The Marina elegy not only allowed Rilke to distance himself from Tsvetaeva's demands for intimacy but also helped him to elevate their relationship to the poetic level. Poetry, for him, was no man's land and no woman's private property; poetry was neutral ground, shared equally. The Marina elegy begins with a warning about the disappointment, pain, and despair that result from unconditional emotional dependence on people and things; unless one accepts life's losses with gratitude one can never join the natural cycle of life.

O die Verluste ins All, Marina, die stürzenden Sterne!
Wir vermehren es nicht, wohin wir uns werfen, zu welchem
Sterne hinzu! Im Ganzen ist immer schon alles gezählt.
So auch, wer fällt, vermindert die heilige Zahl nicht.
Jeder verzichtende Sturz stürzt in den Ursprung und heilt.
Wäre denn alles ein Spiel, Wechsel des Gleichen, Verschiebung,
nirgends ein Name und kaum irgendwo heimisch Gewinn?

O the losses into the All, Marina, the plunging stars!
We do not augment it wherever we fling ourselves, towards whatever star!
In Entirety, everything is already counted.
So, whoever falls does not diminish the holy count.
Every relinquishing plunge plunges into the Source and heals.
Would it then all be a game, exchange, displacement,
nowhere a name, and scarcely anywhere familiar gain?[43]

Human weaknesses are a part of life. No one, not even the gods, is exempt
from vanity and self-indulgence: "Auch die unteren Götter wollen gelobt
sein, Marina. / So unschuldig sind Götter, sie warten auf Lob wie die
Schüler." [Even the lower gods want to be praised, Marina / So blameless
are gods, they await praise like schoolchildren.] Gods only appear to be
"powerful" and "forceful"; in fact, they are mere "blueprints" of reality waiting to be completed in somebody's imagination. Rilke's mocking of fallible
"gods"[44] demonstrates that he does not count himself among them; he
belongs to a more difficult profession: the poets. The poets bear the responsibility for completing the world in their imagination; they must recognize,
resist, and transform desire into art, a task that may ultimately be too overwhelming for individuals to fulfill. Human desire to possess, control, or
reproduce the world in harmony is an illusion, and the temptation to interpret the world as one's own ideal is difficult to overcome. Hence the poet's
eternal sadness and solitude: "Wir beginnens als Jubel, schon übertrifft es
uns völlig; / plötzlich, unser Gewicht dreht zur Klage abwärts den Sang."
[We begin it as jubilation, already it wholly exceeds us / suddenly, our weight
tips the song down to lament.] The only solution for all living creatures is to
recognize and submit to life's uncontrollable flow:

Wellen, Marina, wir Meer! Tiefen, Marina, wir Himmel.
Erde, Marina, wir Erde, wir tausendmal Frühling, wie Lerchen,
die ein ausbrechendes Lied in die Unsichtbarkeit wirft.

Waves, Marina, we are sea! Depths, Marina, we are heaven!
Earth, Marina, we are Earth, we are a thousand times spring, like larks
that a bursting song flings into invisibility.

Rilke wishes Tsvetaeva to reconcile herself to life's eternal contradictions
and not be possessive:

Loben, du Liebe, laß uns verschwenden mit Lob.
Nichts gehört uns. Wir legen ein wenig die Hand um die Hälse
ungebrochener Blumen. Ich sah es am Nil in Kôm-Ombo.
So, Marina, die Spende, selber verzichtend, opfern die Könige.

Praising, Love, let us be lavish with praise
Nothing belongs to us. We lay our hands lightly around the throats
of unbroken flowers. I saw it on the Nile, in Kôm-Ombo
Just so, Marina, the kings, self-renouncing, offer bounty.

A metaphor of the moon's continual return to its fullness is Rilke's last
bequest to Tsvetaeva. The symbol helps organize and transform the chaos of
her contradictory emotions into the symbolic order of words:

. . . . Wir in das Kreisen bezogen
füllten zum Ganzen uns an wie die Scheibe des Monds.
auch in abnehmender Frist, auch in den Wochen der Wendung
niemand verhälfe uns je wieder zum Vollsein, als der
einsame eigene Gang über der schlaflosen Landschaft.

We, drawn into the circle
filled ourselves out to the Whole like the Moon's discs.
Even in waning phases, even in the weeks of turning
no one would ever help us again to Fullness,
except for our own
solitary course over the sleepless landscape.[45]

The elegy to Marina Tsvetaeva stands apart from the elegies in the *Duino*
cycle in its primary use of an advisory tone: it does not ask questions, it gives
answers; it adjures and entreats Tsvetaeva to stop setting up mirrors and
seek self-reflection in counterfeit idols. Through it, Rilke urges Tsvetaeva
not to challenge others but to listen to the rhythms of her own destiny. Only
by coming to terms with her inner being can she achieve the fullness of life.[46]

Shortly before his death, Rilke composed the epitaph to be inscribed on
his gravestone: "Rose, oh pure contradiction, desire, / To be no one's sleep
under so many / Lids."[47] The epitaph may be read as his farewell to Tsvetaeva. It talks of the union between the inner and the outer, of sleeping and
waking, of nothing and being, and of life and death. Sleep is no one's treasure, desire is pure contradiction, and the rose is not a desire for another,
but a desiring being.

Tsvetaeva entered Rilke's life when his image of Russia was already
completed, and he was in no physical condition to maintain the intense personal relationship demanded by her letters. Her forceful "knocking, crying,
pleading" her way into Rilke's life ("dostuchats'a, dokrichats'a, dozvats'a")[48]
violated his ideal of an unpossessive self-sacrificing lover the likes of Eury-
dice and Luoise Labé, Sappho and Tolstoy's aunt Tatyana Ergolskaya. Those
women were capable of loving without asking for love in return. Besides,
Tsvetaeva's desire to be Rilke's only correspondent, his only woman, and his

only Russia were tragically belated. That exclusive place in his life had been taken forever by Lou Andreas-Salomé. It was Andreas-Salomé who received Rilke's last words written in Cyrillic: "Proschai dorogaia moia," Farewell, my dear one.

RILKE AS A MYTH

Rilke's poetic farewell to Tsvetaeva had a strangely helpful, almost healing effect on her. Her reply was conciliatory, and she readily confessed her transgressions against Pasternak: "Ugly enough. And painful enough for him." She even agreed not to insist on calling their relationship "love": "We did not even love each other, never had loved. He speaks about our 'non-love' in his last (Marina)-Elegy."[49] Although Tsvetaeva conceded some ground to Rilke as correspondent, she never yielded her sovereignty as an artist: the laws of poets' lives were different, she insisted, and it did not really matter how false she might have appeared to him in life as long as she remained true to herself in poetry. "So the deed and the poem are on my side. What is between us accuses me. The between is mendacious, not I," she explained. The key to Tsvetaeva's painful quandary lay in her realization that Rilke did not and could not have fully known her as a poet. Furthermore, writing letters to Rilke meant competing with a poet of mythic stature, which overwhelmed her, drained her emotionally, and left her feeling barren and infertile. "Do you think it is easy to cope with the treasure of the Nebelungs [Niebelungenhort]?," Tsvetaeva wrote, sharing her predicament with Pasternak.[50]

Tsvetaeva's triumphant ascent to the poetic heights of Olympus arrived with the news of Rilke's death. With Rilke gone, she could move freely in the ideal world of poetry and unburden herself of the responsibility of answering the living poet. Her creativity was finally unleashed. "Just finished a letter to Rilke—a poem. Now I am writing the 'prose'. . . of his death," Tsvetaeva reported to Anna Tesková, adding, "His death will yet move me to much more (internally)."[51]

Not only did Tsvetaeva mold a mythic persona for Rilke throughout her correspondence with him and with her chosen "Rilke circle of friends" (Boris Pasternak, Anna Tesková, Evgenia Tchernosvitova, Nanny Wunderly-Volkart, and Ruth Sieber-Rilke, Rilke's daughter), but she created an "otherworldly" image of him in an impressive body of her writings. Tsvetaeva's texts dedicated to Rilke include, among others, her poems "New Year's" ("Novogodnee," 1927), "Attempt at a Room" ("Popytka Komnaty," 1927), "The Poem of the Air" ("Poema Vozdukha," 1927), and her essays "Your Death" ("Tvoja smert'," 1927) and "Some Letters of Rainer Maria Rilke" ("Neskol'ko pisem Rainera Marii Rilke," 1929). She also addressed the subject of Rilke and his poetry in her critical writings on art and artists.[52]

As Elena Korkina has shown, Tsvetaeva's posthumous writings on Rilke belong in a trilogy of her lyrical cycles of "de-personalization" (*liricheskaia trilogiia raschelovecheniia*); her entire oeuvre unfolds as a unitary progression toward one main theme: death and nonbeing.[53] Marina Tsvetaeva was a poet who put her trust in the eternal and unchanging world (*bytie*) and the poet's death compensated her for the vagaries of daily existence (*byt*).[54] She understood Rilke's death as "his personal order" (*sobstvennoruchnyi prikaz*) to revive her relationship with Pasternak. But as long as Rilke was alive she had refused to admit anyone into their union: "I was so lonely with him," she later complained to Wunderly-Volkart.[55]

"New Year's," Tsvetaeva's posthumous letter to Rilke, crowns her rite of passage from being Pasternak's protégé to Rilke's chosen Russian heiress. According to her mythopoetic logic, the "German Orpheus" could not have had any legitimate male successors in this world,[56] while she would have secured a place among recognized literary hierarchs through Rilke's symbolic patronage: "Today I want Rilke to speak—through me. . . . Today, I bring Rilke into the Russian tongue as he would someday bring me to the other world."[57]

"New Year's" chronicles Tsvetaeva's tumultuous relationship with the godlike Rilke, the larger than life friendship interrupted by death itself. But even though they have failed to come together in life, poetry will unite them in the other world: "I am not sure we could have met, but I am confident we will sing together." The poem's key scene is the finale, in which Tsvetaeva portrays herself delivering sacrificial offerings at Rilke's altar; her gifts are exchanged for his forgiveness, recognition, and acceptance.

> Vnese lestnitsa, ponei s Darami
> Snovym rukopolozheniem, Rainer
> Chtob nezalili derzhu ladon'u
> Poverkh Rony i poverkh Rarogn'a
> Poverkh javnoii sploshnoi razluki
> Rainer—Maria—Rilke Vruki.

> Up the stairway in the sky I climb with Gifts,
> with the new laying on of hands, Rainer!
> I am holding my palms over Rhône and over Rarogne
> so that they do not spill over,
> Over obvious and unintermittent separation
> to Rainer—Maria—Rilke—into his hands.

Critical readings of Tsvetaeva's allegory frequently cite biblical imagery as her source.[58] It is more likely, however, that she was performing a pre-Christian pagan rite of obligatory gift giving, like a potlatch. Ritualistic potlatches were enacted at turning points in the spiritual lives of communities, particularly when the death of a chief and the subsequent elevation of his successor had to be acknowledged in a festive ceremony.[59] Tsvetaeva waited for the opportune moment to respond to Rilke's gift of poetry with one of her own, and in the true spirit of Germanic lore, "she revenged herself" (*sich revanchieren*) with a gift equal to "the treasure of the Nibelungs." In addition to her dedications, she conceived of an ambitious publishing project, a collection of Rilke's works, notes, and letters on the Russian theme entitled "R. M. Rilke et la Russie" or "La Russie de R. M. Rilke." After Rilke, death and Russia formed a close-knit unity in Tsvetaeva's mythic world: "His Russia like his death: everything that belonged only to him, no one else," she insisted. Tsvetaeva emerged from this epistolary relationship as a reincarnated Russian Orpheus: "Never: Rilke about Russia, not Rilke and Russia— but Russia in Rilke. This is how I live it."[60]

Conclusion

      RILKE FOUND IN Russian culture the native intuitiveness and unproblematic accessibility to God for which he had long been searching. Coming from a borderland between the Germanic and Slavic worlds, he was particularly susceptible to the intangible qualities of Russian life: its atmosphere, latitude, landscape, and mythology. Whether his ideas about Russia were independent or simply adopted from the Pan-Slavic Russophilia, they were undoubtedly sincere; he refused to be put into any nationalist straight-jacket and had none of the inhibitions of his class-minded contemporaries. Service of art was the only law that he recognized and religiously followed. Genuineness alone mattered to him and he used to say of the Russian people that they helped him see Divine Providence at work behind all human destiny and suffering. The Russian poet M. A. Voloshin best described the healing effect of Russian art on Rilke's generation: "In the days of deepest artistic disintegration, in years full of disorder, aspiration, and purpose, old Russian art unveils itself to give a lesson of harmonious balance between tragedy and individuality, method and intent, line and color."[1] Thus Rilke experienced a unique moment of cultural rapprochement between Russia and the West, and Russia was attractive precisely because it could offer the displaced and disenchanted Western poet the lost notion of the genuine and the awe of tradition.

      In an apt assessment of his life as a poet, Rilke described his career as a connection that linked things and animals with the angels, skipping the stage of "worldly" life.[2] Rilke envisioned his life's progression as a series of circular returns to his earlier themes, and described it thus in his *Book of Hours*:

Ich lebe mein Leben in wachsenden Ringen,
die sich über die Dinge ziehn.
Ich werde den letzten vielleicht nicht vollbringen,
aber versuchen will ich ihn.

Ich kreise um Gott, um den uralten Turm,

129

und ich kreise jahrtausendelang;
und ich weiß noch nicht: bin ich ein Falke, ein Sturm
oder ein großer Gesang. (*SW* 1:253)

I live my life in ever widening circles, which circle around Things. And even though I may not accomplish my last one, nonetheless I will try.

I circle around God, the ancient Tower, as I have circled for a thousand years; and I cannot yet tell: whether I am a falcon, a storm, or a long song.

After Russia, Rilke abandoned the mystical style of writing that characterized his early "Book of Monkish Life" and developed the object-centered aesthetic of the austere *Ding-Gedicht*. Furthermore, his detachment in later works (the *Duino Elegies* and *Sonnets to Orpheus*) was a far cry from the oceanic feeling of oneness conveyed in his early Russian writings. At the end of his life, he merged his worlds into a new kind of mysticism called by Erich Kahler "a piercing analysis of the texture of sensory appearance."[3]

Marina Tsvetaeva's failure to become Rilke's Russia was a consequence of his singular interiorization of Russian culture. For him, Russia belonged in the realm of the elemental and the universal, protected from the vicissitudes of history and intrusions from the outside. He achieved his vision of Russia by freeing its unexploited aesthetic and religious potential out of the bedrock of accepted cultural preconceptions.

Gide once described the psychology of a literary creator who seeks himself. A genius, Gide wrote of Dostoyevsky, runs a great risk—the risk of finding himself: "From then onwards, he writes coldly, deliberately, in keeping with the self he has found. He imitates himself. . . . His great dread is no longer insincerity but inconsistency."[4] Rilke's almost religious aesthetic vision of the "Russian soul" was overrun by a competing ideology of soulless "class consciousness." But once again, at the close of the twentieth century, his hope has been revived, having proved to the world that his faith in Russia, as in his art, was prophetic.

Leo Tolstoy, Our Contemporary:
A Study by Lou Andreas-Salomé

THROUGH ALMOST THE entire course of Russian history and literature runs a uniquely eruptive energy that appears to those who carefully follow it to be indigenous to the Russian character: it is an outburst, a violent takeover by powerful initiatives and far-reaching impulses playing themselves out against the broad background of a dull stagnation. In every sphere of life the gap between the leading personalities and everyone else appears to be particularly enormous and particularly unexpected. Therefore, so much in Russia's cultural development impresses us not as having sprouted from slowly cultivated organic soil but as having been created spontaneously and only afterward artificially emplanting itself. Political as well as literary life leads us to the same somewhat paradoxical conclusion: Peter the Great accomplished in politics what Pushkin the Great did in literature. They did not simply wake up their people but carried their self-contained work through to the end, bringing it to a one-sided and bewildering perfection that was not easily repeatable.

I name these two together because of two diametrically opposed tendencies that in them gained momentum and encompassed the main conflict in Russia's development to the present day. Peter the Great opened Russia to the West and Western culture and fertilized it with a thousand new ideas, bringing about its immediate phenomenal cultural growth. The poet Pushkin, on the other hand, virtually created Russian letters, as he turned from mere unfruitful imitations of the West homeward to Russian ideals. This opposition becomes even more significant, since not only Pushkin himself but writers before and after him came from the same upper orders, in which their entire social grounding had been fashioned by Western European culture. All of them belonged to the aristocracy or were close to it, and as a result Russian literature was shaped originally by their attempts to translate foreign models into the Russian language.

Peter's sister, the Regent Tsarevna Sofia, herself almost started the trend when she ordered Molière's *Médecin malgré lui* to be translated and performed in her private quarters. This took place after a German theater troupe led by the jolly Lutheran priest Gottfried Gregori infused the Kremlin court with an enthusiasm for theatrical entertainment. Even before this, Peter the Great's mother, the foster daughter of Bojar Artamon Matveev, had come to the Russian throne from a house in which everything German—theatrical, artistic, and educational—was loved and promoted.

The first original Russian comedy, "The Prodigal Son," is still available in an illustrated edition; it was written by a learned monk, a court poet and tutor to Tsarevna Sofia and young Tsarevich Fjodor. The first Russian verses were composed by a count, Kantemir, a man of foreign education and an ambassador to London and Paris. Kantemir's satires aimed at deriding everything that opposed the innovations and improvements of the Petrine and post-Petrine reforms. Finally, Lomonosov, whom Pushkin called "the first Russian university," studied in Germany and devoted his life to the task of transplanting West European science to Russia. At the same time, he set out to cleanse foreign elements from his native speech and to lay down laws and rules in order to train it, so to speak, in native poetic art. But even though two writers with him at the court of Tsarina Elizabeth, Trediakovsky and Sumarokov, produced a host of tragedies and dramas in that language, and even though a truly gifted court poet, Catherine the Great's eulogist, Derzhavin, followed in their footsteps, original Russian poetry remained a terra incognita. And even after pseudoclassicism in Russia was superseded by a Russian form of romanticism, Zhukovsky still sang his melancholy tunes, and Karamzin, the famous Russian historian, wrote his sentimental tale about a poor peasant maiden, "Poor Liza"; nothing more significant had happened than a preparation for the poet of the future, Alexander Pushkin. Only with him and at his behest did Russian speech begin to resound with its native poetry; it no longer strained in an effort to prove itself capable of literary creation but sang in a wonderful and unsurpassed harmony of simple and artless daily expression and superior glamour of poetic suggestion. Those who read Pushkin will involuntarily remember Lomonosov's declaration: "The Holy Roman Emperor Charles V used to say that it is best to speak Spanish with God, French with friends, German with enemies, and Italian with women, but had he known Russian, he would have added that it was suited for speaking with everyone, because it had at its disposal the solemnity of Spanish, the liveliness of French, the strength of German, the softness of Italian, and, besides, the richness and the resolute conciseness of expression of Greek and Latin!"

By origin and upbringing, Pushkin himself belonged to his country's aristocracy, and had he not displeased the authorities with some pranks during his youth in St. Petersburg's high-society circles, and had he not had to endure long years of exile to the Crimea, his genius might have wandered worldly paths for much longer. Within that short period of time he was granted to live, his stay in the Crimea, in the Caucasus, and at his familial estate near Pskov proved to be immensely valuable and creatively rich. "Till midday, I write in my diary," Pushkin wrote from the Pskov estate to his brother, "dine late, then ride after dinner. In the evenings, however, I listen to folk tales, thus filling in the gaps of my wretched education." He had his old nurse, Arina Rodionovna, tell him those tales and was introduced by her to the world of songs and legends, over which he never tired of roaming, as if it were some unknown, rich paradise. What Pushkin did as he sat in the evenings reverently listening to the unpretentious stories of this guardian of his youth, blissfully forgetting everything he had been taught by "Europe's varnished politeness"—all of Russian literature after him did precisely the same. From the cultural heights of Western Europe, in which for the most part they had been raised and lived, the representatives of Russian literature descended to the Russian people with all the dreams and longings of their poetry. In Russia, the deeper the gap between the almost completely uncultivated and overwhelmingly vast folk population and the relatively small, highly educated, and spiritually refined elite, the more significant this fact. To cite a political analogue: when Alexander II abolished serfdom, something liberating and uplifting happened to the peasant, something he could not yet comprehend, desire, or aspire to get what he received as a gift or directive for his future action. Poetry took control of the people in the same way, passing far above their heads and not taking root in their still unripe national character.

Remarkably characteristic in this connection is the anecdote recorded by Leo Tolstoy from personal experience in his brochure "Against Modern Art." It tells how not long ago a petit bourgeois from Saratov—"an educated man, incidentally," Tolstoy adds—came to Moscow with the sole purpose of reprimanding church authorities for allowing the Pushkin monument to be built. "He tried to find out who Pushkin was, and when he learned that Pushkin was neither a hero nor even a general but quite simply a writer, he concluded then that Pushkin surely ought to have been a holy man or a charitable educator. One can imagine his dismay when he discovered that Pushkin was a man of a more than frivolous mind, that he died in a duel—that is, while trying to kill another man—and that his entire accomplishment consisted in writing verses about love." I deliberately cite Tolstoy's words literally, for—as we have recently heard him confirm once again—he completely takes the side of the indignant peasant and not at all Pushkin's. It is at this point that we can rightly understand the paradoxically gigantic personality of Tolstoy and we can grasp and appreciate his close connection with Russian cultural development. Tolstoy is merely the culmination point of a development started in literature by Pushkin as he sat at the feet of

Arina Rodionovna listening to her tales. To understand the problem of Tolstoy—one of the most interesting and unusual human problems that has
ever existed—to solve it, we must continue to examine how this propensity
toward the common people among the Western-educated Russian elite
gradually spread and deepened. In other lands, a similar process would have
evolved naturally from within, because the educated classes are not brought
in from elsewhere and are not to such a degree strangers to folk life, and
because the intellectual aristocracy, which wants to meld with the folk spiritually, cannot help feeling their own educational superiority. There is something wholly unique as well as humanly deeply touching in this longing of
the culturally privileged to lower themselves to the level of as yet uneducated folk, not so much to teach them but to receive and to learn from them
what a foreign culture could not give the Russians as Russians. And this is
neither a Rousseauian rapture over nature nor abstract reasoning, but an
instinctive insight that lies buried in the depths of the Russian folk, an
almost entirely untouched treasure, an authentic, individual culture impa-
tiently waiting for its hour and its master. The noble egoism of individuals
satisfies itself in this passionate love for the folk; their longing for individual
human self-fulfillment makes them behave in a way that only seems to be
self-denial but instead deprives them of much of their achievement and
makes them equal with the most deprived among their people.

This tendency did not begin to manifest itself immediately as a painful
contradiction or a violent split of the soul, nor did it immediately lead to
those external consequences at which Tolstoy's life and work would arrive.
For those developments to take effect, more time was needed, in the course
of which the tendency toward the Slavophile ideal and primitive populism,
on the one hand, and the entire complicated refinement of the modern soul,
on the other, further deepened among educated Russian circles, until finally the contradictions intensified almost tragically. In the immense personality of Leo Tolstoy, the count in a worker's blouse, this tragic intensity led, so
to speak, to a personal rupture. It was his fate to embody this whole typical
split, and what made him great, what made him unique, was the force with
which his genius took it upon itself to resolve this conflict—as if the worlds
were to break apart and come together again for the sake of a single man's
soul. Not without reason, Pushkin appeared to him insignificant next to his
own struggle, a mere entertaining author of charming love poems. Pushkin's
is a much simpler soul; it exists in a harmonious simplicity that easily and joy-
fully finds its balance. Pushkin's is an infinitely Russian soul, more Russian,
perhaps, than Tolstoy's, shaken by West European fever and doubt. Pushkin
also found peace only when he dared to flee from his life in society to nature
and folk art. He did it like a child, however, listening to fairy tales and forgetting them in his practical life, as immediately as would a child, as soon as
Petersburg life surrounded him again and drew him back in into its love

affairs and honor games. That enchanting grace that so often emanates from the unpretentious charm of his works is possible, perhaps, only outside the bitter and confusing struggle of a contemporary person troubled by refined internal contradictions. That is why it was natural for Pushkin to bring into his writings characters and situations primarily of a general, and precisely therefore of an eternal, human type; it is not that his intention was the same as Tolstoy's—to represent something that was effortlessly obtained as being healthier—but that nothing else lay within Pushkin's emotional sphere. One becomes particularly aware of this when one compares Pushkin with his famous successors. Even the brilliant officer and society man Lermontov, who did not measure up to Pushkin either in scope or in depth and who perished in a duel like Pushkin at an even younger age, even Lermontov possessed a more modern, sensitive soul than Pushkin; he possessed nuances that strike us as more relevant and, to a certain degree, more contemporary.

Then Gogol sprang up with the satirical realism of his *Taras Bulba, The Inspector General,* and *Dead Souls.* Having started as a light-hearted pastoral writer celebrating the lives of Ukrainian peasants, he continued to write with ever more bitter anger against the abuses of the ruling caste, until he eventually perished, seized by maniacal religious ideas and bewildering doubts about the negative spirit of his creations, the picture of a lamentable split within himself. His realistic portrayal of the land and the people gave literary expression to a whole emerging generation, which represented a stronger and increasingly more self-conscious reaction by Russians against the intellectual movement of *zapadniki,* that is, the so-called adherents of West European culture. Gradually, Gogol's satire against the ruling elite turned into the glorification of the seemingly underprivileged—the poor, the uncultured, the artless and deceived—just as they would be represented in Dostoyevsky's genius.

Dostoyevsky is not as tendentious as Gogol; he simply portrays what he passionately loves; he loves these people and is able to bring out precious human material from what others consider the scum of the earth. There is no sickness or crime in which his love could not unearth vestiges of spiritual beauty. It is not a doctrine, therefore, but an instinctive flow of feeling when he says that it would be good to abandon himself, to let himself lie at the feet of these people—poor, and yet so rich in their divine simplicity. In the midst of life's evil, he found peculiar comfort and the best relief in his art, which knows how to represent it all. He was an epileptic, himself suffering from nervous illness and full of internal unrest after returning home from many years of prison labor. In every sense and in every connection he lacked healthy harmony, both in his existence and in his character. It was from him that we received poignant portrayals of spiritual conditions that closely border on insanity and breakdown, and those deep insights into the darkest mysteries of man's inner world which made his name so famous abroad.

135

Despite all this and regardless of modernity, fermenting and agitating more in Dostoyevsky than in Tolstoy, it was not ultimately in Dostoyevsky that the growing contradiction between cultural life and the primitive life of the Russian soul came to confront itself. It may sound paradoxical in view of Dostoyevsky's way of life, but he is more at one with himself and in essence less internally disturbed than Tolstoy. Dostoyevsky reveals himself entirely in his art, by bringing out everything contradictory and sinister that he carries inside. Thus his impassioned enthusiasm for the humble simplicity of the underprivileged and for the instinctive proto-Christianity of those who think not and know not becomes an integral part of his inner being. He does not draw from it for the selfish purpose of personal healing, consolation, or self-improvement; rather, it becomes an integral part of him—the way he is and the way he represents himself in his works.

When after a difficult struggle Tolstoy arrived at the idea of saying *farewell* to art—because it belonged neither to the highest nor to the noblest of his occupations (and one might imagine what art's inexpressible pleasures meant to a genius of Tolstoy's magnitude!)—something else expressed itself in his decision other than simply a changing religious and moral value system. It was a loud declaration of an ultimate disunity with himself that was too deeply, too dreadfully concerned "with the one thing that was needed" in order to have any time left for creative work alone. It was an expression of an urgent and deadly need to secure for himself, first and foremost, enough room and air for survival and for the soul, so that literally everything, including the most refined high art, had to withdraw in the face of this frightened helplessness as if it were some idle play. All genuine art demands a complete retreat into oneself, and no masterpiece can emerge in flight from oneself. Whenever art arises, the artist must already have some ground under his feet—consciously or unconsciously, just for a single moment or constantly—upon which he can stand in the moment of creative rapture. Tolstoy saw this ground opening so widely that he completely lost his footing. Although the ground was also shaky for Dostoyevsky, it oscillated in harmony with everything that was unstable around him—as if there were in everything some mindless swinging and lulling to which modern man has become so surprisingly well-adjusted that he could artistically savor it in Dostoyevsky's work. Tolstoy, by contrast, grimly drove modern man to the edge of doubt and there confronted him with less menacing existential questions, it may seem; those questions that we today are able to look square in the face only in two rare moods: in the hour of personal doubt or in the hour of heavenly peace of the soul.

For this reason, much of what does not in the least disturb the pleasure of our reading Dostoyevsky interferes with our aesthetic appreciation of Tolstoy. This is what happens, for example, with the religious-scriptural and moralizing aesthetic emphasis that is common to both writers. It is precisely through Dostoyevsky, who accomplishes the same goals artistically rather than pedagogically, that we realize more clearly how unjust we occasionally are to Tolstoy; and it is from Dostoyevsky that we learn precisely to what high degree these manifestations of humility in writing actually conceal Russian nature itself. Glorification of the Russian national character expresses itself much more in the works of these two writers than in the religion of Jesus of Nazareth. And this art is extremely important. Deeply trusting, unquestioning artlessness and humane passivity lie deep in the Russian being, providing a profound source of religiosity corresponding to certain aspects of Western Protestantism. A warm living force took shape precisely among the folk, emerging out of the chaos of superstitions and mindlessly inherited dogmatic assumptions in which the Russian people worship their own ancient Russian ideals. Byzantine form covers it up, pressed like golden and jewel-encrusted armor; beneath it, however, beats the childish Russian heart.

I cannot help mentioning at this point a short story that I cited elsewhere, in my discussion of one of Russia's most talented writers, the teller of legends, Leskov. The story is about a highly educated bishop who travels to the north of Siberia to convert the local pagan tribes to Christianity. He and his pagan coachman lose their way. At the point of starving and freezing to death, the coachman saves the bishop by making his way on snowshoes with great effort to an empty bear's lair with a dead bear in it, and bringing a piece of his booty to his master. Even though the lair is empty, the pagan coachman disregards the danger of freezing and leaves his fur hat to the bear as compensation for the stolen portion: "God watches him" and does not want him to harm a man, he explains. This experience convinces the bishop that even without the scripture a Russian person is "close to God."

Such stories by Leskov illustrate better than any sentimental or amusing evidence how indeed the Russian feels childishly confident of being "close to God." The Russian God is by himself nothing but Goodness and Simplicity, and not an exceptionally mighty ruler. He can be forgetful, after all, and quite a few things can escape his attention. But when a child is fearful, when a woman cries, or when a man loses his way in the night, then God becomes omniscient. As a result, and insofar as they remain consistent with themselves, the people who look up to him as their ideal develop a strong resentment of certain features of Christianity. The surest way for the Russian people to enlighten themselves would be to shake off Byzantine trappings and to acknowledge everything that represents religion in the Russian tradition. Insofar as Tolstoy relied on these religious feelings, he fostered in the hearts of his peasants more of the future culture than West European educational reforms could achieve. When we read him we must always translate his designations of "religious" as "ideal-Russian" and thus explain to ourselves why we invariably arrive at a dead end when examining his religious judgment, a definite limit from which no logical thinking can lift him. Nonetheless, he freely modifies or repudiates existing religious teachings and high-handedly dismisses most complex theological arguments. He is a Russian, after all, and his entire being, not his thinking, sets his limit—the most intimate desire which strives and yearns for its free spiritual fulfillment. Stripping himself of everything he had been taught, of all the highly praised richness that culture claims to have bestowed on him, he turned away from the pinnacle of life, education, and high society to return home to the peasants, who know better how to exist without doubt and inner conflict. And as someone who learned from them, he went on single-handedly spreading the blessings of his teachings, which are so incredible to us: he took in so thoroughly what they had to tell him, he pressed so deeply into the naked grimmness of their lives, that through him, through his works and words, the Russian ideal of life revealed its most authentic features as if in a transfigured image; it became clear to every one of them amid their gloomy and raw everyday routine.

This is no longer the case of the Russian writer who enhances his foreign upbringing by intoxicating himself with folk tales and songs; rather, he is himself that person who eagerly sets out to make real this internal meltdown from the top to the bottom. And in the process of building stoves and mending fences with his peasants, Tolstoy embodies in himself the human type that has been straining toward the light throughout the entire development of Russian history; and it is highly unlikely that this is a personal whim or a mere mood swing, as one often hears it called. One could add much more here; he has become an innocent, suffering stage for those struggles and contradictions that for several centuries have been seeking an appropriately rich and deep human soul in order to play themselves out. The great fascination that Tolstoy's image holds is therefore partly of an artistic nature: he who had stopped working as an artist embodies in himself a powerful living artwork which finds no equal in its original energy and its enormous capacity for self-reconciliation. One must not forget in this connection that we should not generalize in such abstract terms about what appears to us to be a leveling of all culture and a fruitless, an almost narrow-minded retreat to an earlier cultural stage. We first must situate it in the intimate context of his personality and his life—only then does it become his own creation, a truly remarkable living artwork and no longer a mere pedagogical treatise hardly worthy of serious refutation. He is a person who carries in himself everything of the culture that lives inside all of us and that he no longer is able to shake off either by changing his mind or through extra effort; this person speaks to us through all his secrets and public pronouncements, which strangely charm us and draw us to him. No matter how low Tolstoy prostrates himself before his peasants, he cannot help hovering above them as a mountaintop: as he learns from them, he teaches, and, while learning, he continues to create. He creates art whose splendid features illuminate his immediate surroundings and help him write and explain his life; we, in the meantime, have to settle for the pale traces of this art in his writings.

Russian youth perceives him in the same way. Even those who do not share his political, social, artistic, or other ideas, feel that he is first and foremost one of their own, one of their own in the highest degree, perhaps, but nonetheless a contemporary and a fellow sufferer in everything that may be of concern to men of their time. And every struggle or conflict significant in any sense that passes through the life of every Russian finds in him everlasting words, celebrates everlasting victory, and springs open the everlasting sources of reconciliation. Those who do not live in Russia can hardly imagine how much the mere fact of Count Tolstoy's existence matters by itself: "He is still here and therefore compassion is still here. A shelter, a shield and security! With him, one can empty out one's soul, one can speak up, one can pull oneself together when everything goes wrong." These are generally the feelings of Russia's best youth toward Tolstoy. And even if it might reach us in outwardly weakened form, we can still grasp its significance as soon as we open one of Tolstoy's works, even if it belongs to those latest writings most vulnerable to our criticism. They all have one thing in common which could perhaps be expressed in the following words: "how unconvincing, but how appealing nonetheless."

And now, just when all eyes have been directed at Tolstoy on the occasion of his seventieth birthday, he publishes a work that is, in this respect, extraordinarily interesting and characteristic of him: a work about art produced after fifteen years of brooding over the subject. It is worth noting that it exists in German only in a mediocre translation, full of annoying misprints and arbitrarily ripped apart into two books. If one were to read endless discussions of this work without prior knowledge of Tolstoy, one would wonder why this book had been at all successful in having an effect on people, since it is so unbelievably easy and so unbelievably effortless to refute and to criticize it, especially in a journalistic tone! If, on the other hand, one knew more about the author's spiritual quest, then even those parts of his latest book would appear significant which, to our West European way of thinking, should be read with a smile. And one would only be surprised if he were to let himself be prevented from entering into the beautiful and sacred nature of this work, like some casual reader who would stumble over a couple of crude paradoxes that appear on the surface as absurdities. The artistically interesting meaning of this work arises, not from mere abstract pronouncements of disputable worth, but from the fact that Tolstoy, a person of our culture and our cultural outlook, dreams about art like a Russian laborer who rests on his hoe while working in the middle of his wide native fields and dreams of an art that could ripen to fulfill his and his people's highest potential. Naturally, even if one were to assume that all people are Russian,

139

and that all find themselves at the same stage of development as the majority of the Russian folk, even then there would remain in Tolstoy's aesthetic theory much that is redundant and that can justifiably be disputed. But one must imagine the kind of person who could dream in such a way, and how the extremes of his bitter and ascetically one-sided thought are justified because he has to deal with the opposite extreme: with the pupils of all shades and sins of our contemporary secular culture who are dissipating their precious energy in superficial pleasures. If while reading one assumes the place of a person portrayed in a novelistic work, then one gets a rare overview of our entire civilized artistic life: from very far away and very high up. Then one recognizes to his embarrassment that much of it is only too true, and that one has always known it but has not visualized it in immediate proximity.

The artist's innermost longing will loudly cry out "Yes!" to Tolstoy's harsh picture of the universally sanctioned circumstances under which art and money closely depend on each other and art has become a "profession" in its external meaning. And would not many artists, at least to themselves, dream of an art that would accompany an outwardly quiet and primitive existence, an existence full of simple labor and the experiences of peasants and workers, instead of our life of artificial denial and excitement, taken to the extreme? And would not the best of them long for a deep, quiet, and stable background in life for everything that wants to live out and shape itself from tender and changing colors and lines? And don't many of them already feel that in this withdrawal from the conflicting emotions to which they are most intensely driven in their creative hours, they must retain space, first and foremost, for rare, eternal, and fundamental feelings of human existence—in other words, for those feelings that somehow touch upon the life of the majority—if they do not want to turn themselves from lonely eccentrics into hypocrites? Every once in a while, our contemporary literature makes it seem as if the latter process does not happen. The situation about which Tolstoy so loudly and so unfairly complains, without making any exceptions for his allies, indeed appears to be of this nature: the isolation of an individual from others which drives him to the edge of the incomprehensible and to a desire to remain incomprehensible, focusing on his own feelings and experiences. On this point, the central thought of Tolstoy's writing has met with particular indignation, as if the "others" played any role at all in artistic achievement, and as if creation was indeed accomplished for others' sake. Without a doubt, Tolstoy is as blatantly wrong about the motivations and the psychological grounds for artistic achievement—when he says that an artist is a person who knows how to represent his feelings in such a way that they would infect his fellow humans—as only he could possibly be. But what is wrong with respect to the spiritual motives of an artist remains true as a distinguishing mark of all art. The artist creates not to influence others by suggestion, not to "infect,"—it would be as if ulterior motives were at work here,—but he lets out his deepest desires often in contradiction with the reality surrounding him. Creation is the artist's modus vivendi, his way "to live, win, and celebrate life." He can prove himself to be an artist, however, only as long as and insofar as his work can be suggestive. One can think of an abnormal situation whereby the artist would rise so high above or sink so below every other living person that he proves himself powerless, and only the long past world and the distanced afterworld would still recognize him. Furthermore, one experiences daily the situations with which only certain groups and certain artists among us, complicated and individualistic people, are able to understand and sympathize completely. One will have to admit in such cases that a great artist is someone through whose special individuality sounds quite distinctly the deepest undertone of universal human values, thus giving to those eminent and idiosyncratic individuals a powerful language to speak. The more one is an artist, the more isolated his work makes him; the more artist he is, the more suggestive and human the forms in which his creativity speaks from within his loneliness and makes everything that has had value for him alone valuable to others, proportionate with their appreciation of and affinity with him.

Insofar as Tolstoy starts off with a false reason for creative activity, he succeeds (in one daring leap of logic) in pronouncing all art to be the means to achieve brotherhood among people. Art must serve this goal partly indirectly, through its suggestive character, and partly directly, through its choice of material. He thus denounces outright his own great artistic works and claims that only a couple of his works still matter: those that preach brotherhood among people, as happens beautifully, for example, in his late short masterwork "Master and Man." Insofar as this short story unpretentiously affects everyone who reads it, it warns us urgently not to let our pleasure in reading Tolstoy diminish because we take him more philosophically than he is. It also shows clearly that everything that swelled in him to become his teaching—erroneous, abstractly speaking—becomes for him personally his justified longing and his way of life: he sees, he feels things as true and beautiful only once, only in *this* light; they reveal themselves to him in this artistic illumination only by virtue of his distinct personality. It is something specifically Tolstoyan; furthermore, it is somewhat sharpened and one-sidedly fixed, his Russian view of things. The fact that he attributes to it such enormous universal importance and that he wants to make it into the worldview of all people, meanwhile falling from literary creation into empty and pure abstraction—this fact should be deplored as well as admired. It would seem to me that at least a certain process has been underway here that could explain for the first time what it was that attracted us so unconditionally and so unreservedly to Tolstoy, regardless of all his faults and misunderstandings and despite our regrets about the great artist that has been lost in him. The force that has almost brutally split apart every existing vessel of art is here the power of humanity itself, resulting from Tolstoy's inharmonious and painful development; it raises itself before us naked and enormous and warns us that in the long run the energy for everything, including art, comes from it alone. The manner in which Tolstoy's instructive discussions persistently connect aesthetic arguments with morality and religion should not blind us. What constitutes morality and religion for him or for the Russian peasantry is not relevant to us: what concerns us is the true fact that all these words are merely meant to point the way to the depths of life and the soul. When we reject the binding power of morality and religion we do so in order to oppose their institutional forms in history. We can also understand them in their rather simple internal meaning, relevant to each of us within the historical framework of Tolstoy's words. We can also understand the intensity with which one man's soul calls on him to account for the meaning of life and organize his life from within itself. Like everything else, all our life experience—be it joy or sorrow—has its deepest roots in this phenomenon alone: we cannot be truly happy, truly miserable, truly strong or truly calm without comprehending our lives as wholes. Artistic activity is no exception: in every artist and in every artwork there exists a living essence that makes both into living organisms and expresses the artists' instinctive attitude toward the meaning of life: something, in a sense, of their religious and moral being taken together. We are justly terrified at the rigidly fixed forms that morality and religion assume in Tolstoy's mind. After all, we stride toward our own life goals in clothes quite different from those he wants to throw over our souls in his lordly fashion. He could never recognize us completely, he could never understand us fully when we wanted to reveal through our most personal art and our most private longings the deepest religiosity of our way of living. We should respect, love, and recognize him as powerful in his convictions when he strides through our ranks in his homespun Russian garments. An artist by the grace of God even if he wanted to be a thinker, he remains a priest of the unnamed God whom we all serve.

142

Notes

The following abbreviations and short titles have been used throughout the notes. For complete publication information, see Bibliography.

Briefe u. Tagebücher	Rilke, *Briefe und Tagebücher der Frühzeit*
GB	Rilke, *Gesammelte Briefe*
R–AS Briefwechsel	*Rainer Maria Rilke, Lou Andreas-Salomé: Briefwechsel*
R–Z–P Briefwechsel	*Rainer Maria Rilke, Marina Zwetajewa, Boris Pasternak: Briefwechsel*
Rilke und Rußland	*Rilke und Rußland*, the collection edited by Konstantin Azadovsky
Schnack, *Chronik*	Ingeborg Schnack, *Rainer Maria Rilke: Chronik seines Lebens und seines Werkes*
SW	Rilke, *Sämtliche Werke*
Tagebücher	Rilke, *Tagebücher aus der Frühzeit*

INTRODUCTION

1. Rilke to Helene Voronina, 27 July 1899, in *Rilke und Rußland*, 105–6. Nietzsche's ideas were still relatively novel in Europe at the close of the nineteenth century and much less known in Russia. In this same letter to Voronina, Rilke expresses his concern about her reading Nietsche: "Read little German, dear Helene, leave Nietzsche alone." Rilke was concerned that Nietzsche would not be understood in Russia and that his ideas would only be harmful. On the development of Russian attitudes toward Nietzsche, see *Nietzsche in Russia*, ed. Bernice Glazer Rosenthal (Princeton, N.J., 1986).

143

2. Rilke to Ilse Sadee, 13 March 1912, quoted in Carl Sieber, *Réne Rilke: Der Jugend Rainer Maria Rilke* (Leipzig, 1932).

3. Ruth Benedict, *Patterns of Culture* (Boston, 1959), 23.

4. Hayden White argues that fascination with the "wild" or primitive people or elements within one's culture occurs in times of sociocultural stress. "The Noble Savage Theme as Fetish," in *Topics of Discourse: Essays in Cultural Criticism* (Baltimore, 1978), 183–96.

5. Edith W. Clowes, Samuel D. Kassow, and James L. West, eds., *Between Tsar and People: Educated Society and the Quest for Public Identity in Late Imperial Russia* (Princeton, N.J., 1991). This collection of essays covers a broad range of topics concerned with Russia's social and cultural environment after the Emancipation. As in previous stages in Russia's historical development, the post-Emancipation Russian society found itself torn between two binary opposites: nostalgic nationalism and modernist experimentation. This exaggerated sense of new beginnings was all pervasive, and an atmosphere of expectancy and disturbing uncertainty prevailed. See Iu. M. Lotman and B. A. Uspensky, "Binary Models in the Dynamics of Russian Culture (to the End of the Eighteenth Century)," in *The Semiotics of Russian Culture,* ed. Alexander D. Nakhimovsky and Alice Stone Nakhimovsky (Ithaca, N.Y., 1985).

6. Quoted by Robert Heinz Heygrodt, "Rilke und Russland," *Berliner Tageblatt,* 22 November 1921, 7.

7. Rilke to Voronina, 28 May 1899, *Rilke und Rußland,* 97.

8. Erich Kahler's term, which he explains as "a piercing analysis of the texture of sensory appearance." In his *Tower and Abyss: An Inquiry into the Transformation of Man* (New York, 1957), 154, 98.

9. *Duino Elegies,* trans. C. F. MacIntyre (Berkeley and Los Angeles, 1965), 55, 57.

10. Sophie Brutzer, "Rilkes russische Reisen."

11. E. M. Butler, *Rainer Maria Rilke,* 60.

12. See, e.g., Demetz: "Those works that now belong to the enduring achievements of contemporary literature emerged from need rather than abundance." *René Rilkes Prager Jahre,* 202.

13. Joachim W. Storck, ed., *Rainer Maria Rilke: Ausstellung des deutschen Literaturarchivs im Schiller-Nationalmuseum.*

14. Rilke, *Briefe über Politik,* ed. Joachim W. Storck (Frankfurt am Main, 1992), 682.

15. See Bibliography for full bibliographical information.

16. Azadovsky's "R. M. Ril'ke i A. N. Benois," his "R. M. Ril'ke i L. N. Tolstoi," and Azadovsky and Chertkov's "Russkie Vstrechi."

17. Patricia Pollock Brodsky, *Russia in the Works of Rainer Maria Rilke;* and Daria Reshetylo-Rothe, *Rilke and Russia: A Reevaluation.*

CHAPTER ONE

1. Walter Benjamin, "The Storyteller," in *Illuminations,* ed. Hannah Arendt (New York, 1969), 84.

2. ". . . daß uns nicht fremdes Wiederfahre, sonder nur das was uns seit langer gehört." "Letters to a Young Poet," Rilke to Franz Xaver Kappus, 2 August 1904, *Briefe,* 3 vols. Insel Taschenbuch (1987), I: 96.

3. See Foreword to *Two Prague Stories* (*SW* 4:98).

4. Demetz, *Rilkes Prager Jahre,* 205.

5. Letter to A. S. Suvorin, 5 March 1902, *Rilke und Rußland,* 337.

6. Moritz Hartmann and Alfred Meißner went to Saxony, Franz Werfel to Hamburg, and Franz Kafka to Berlin.

7. Andrzej Walicki, *The Slavophile Controversy: History of a Conservative Utopia in Nineteenth-Century Russian Thought,* trans. Hilda Andrews-Rusiecka (Notre Dame, Ind., 1980). A distinction should be made between the uses of Pan-Slavic ideology in Russia and in other Slavic states. In Russia, Pan-Slavism more often assumed the form of thinly veiled Pan-Russianism, nationalism, and a romanticized conception of Slavdom combined with the expansionist political aims of many conservatives. Frank Fadner, *Seventy Years of Pan-Slavism in Russia: Karamzin to Danilevskii, 1800–1870* (Washington, D.C., 1962), 10.

8. Hans Kohn, *Pan-Slavism: Its History and Ideology* (New York, 1960). Liah Greenfeld analyzes Russian nationalism as an ideology based on *ressentiment*: a direct reversal of the original hierarchy and the adoption of values directly antithetical to those of the West. Liah Greenfeld, "Introduction" to her *Nationalism: Five Roads to Modernity* (Cambridge, Mass., 1992), 14–17.

9. Among the first consistent articulations of Pan-Slavic ideology in Russia was Nikolai Danilevsky's *Russia and Europe: An Inquiry into the Cultural and Political Relations of the Slav to the Germano-Latin World* (1869), which Dostoyevsky pronounced to be the obligatory daily reading of every Russian (Dostoyevsky to S. A. Ivanova-Khmyrova, 20 March 1869, in *Complete Letters,* trans. David Lowe [Ann Arbor, Mich., 1990], 3:144–45), and Strakhov called "the most complete catechism of Slavophilism" (qtd. in Linda Gerstein, *Nikolai Strakhov* [Cambridge, Mass., 1971], 106). For a comparative study of constructions of the national "soul" in the African-American and Russian tradition, see Dale Peterson, "Justifying the Margin: The Construction of 'Soul' in Russian and African-American Texts," *Slavic Review* 51, no. 4 (1992): 749–57.

10. Even at its most liberal, as in the thought of Herder, the Slavic essence was defined by the Germans as "far from proportionate to the extent of country they occupied. . . . They were liberal, hospitable to excess, lovers of pastoral freedom, but submissive and obedient. . . . Is it to be wondered

that, after this nation had borne the yoke for centuries . . . its gentle character should have sunk into artful, cruel indolence of the slave?" In Johanne Gottfried von Herder, *Outlines of a Philosophy of the History of Man,* trans. T. Churchill (New York, 1969), 482–83.

11. Even though there always existed a distrust of Russian imperial aggrandizement, particularly after Russia's suppression of the Polish uprisings of 1831 and 1863, the idea of Slavic solidarity was too attractive to be abandoned altogether. The combination of the reactionary politics of the Austrian Bach government and the outbreak of the Russo-Turkish war in 1877 was the decisive breaking point.

12. *Pokrok,* 3 March 1870; *Národní listy* quoted in William E. Harkins, *Russian Folk Epos in Czech Literature, 1800–1900* (New York, 1951), 141.

13. "The Revival of the Czech Nation" (*Obrození naroda*), Arné Novák's term, is to be distinguished from the earlier nationalist stage, the "National Revival" (*Na'rodni obrození*). In the earlier period, only a small group of patriotic intellectuals had been active; after 1860, the entire Czech people joined in the cause of nationalism.

14. Jungmann, Palacky, Safarik, Linda, and Langer were all under the influence of Herder's *Stimmen der Volker in Liedern* (1788–89), as well as his *Ideas on the History of Mankind* (1784–87).

15. František Palacky later pointed out in his *Gedenkblätter* (Prague, 1874) how unfortunate it was that the Czech tradition had nothing that could be compared to the Russian or Serb folk songs. Quoted in Harkins, *Russian Folk Epos,* 245n.

16. Folklore has been used by politicians and intellectuals at least since the seventeenth century to promote the concept of ethnic identity. Identification with the "folk" serves as part of a group's revitalization attempts in resistance to the acculturation pressures of another, politically dominant, group. See Anthony F. C. Wallace, "Revitalization Movements," *American Anthropologist* 58 (1956): 264–81. The unprecedented interest in the Slavic folk tradition in the nineteenth century had been anticipated by Rousseau's elevation of the "noble savage," Herder's discovery of language and song as the "heart and soul" of the nation, and Carlyle's anti-industrial criticism of men with "soul extinct but stomach well alive." Robert C. Williams, "The Russian Soul: A Study in European Thought and Non-European Nationalism," *Journal of the History of Ideas* 31, no. 4 (1970): 573–88.

17. The rise of the so-called diffusionist school in folklore studies in the second half of the nineteenth century erased the earlier distinction between the scholar and the artist made by the Brothers Grimm.

18. Julius Dolansky, *Záhada Ossiana v Rukopisech kralovedvorskeém a zelenohorském* (Prague, 1975).

19. Ernst Denis, *La Bohême dépuis la Montagne-Blanche* (Paris, 1902–3), quoted in Kohn, *Pan-Slavism,* 336.

20. An argument has been made by later historians that the group did not really exist as a conspiratorial organization. The government trumped up the charges because it did not like the association between intellectuals and workers in the Progressive movement. See L. Pernes, *Spiklenci proti jeho veličenstvo* (Prague, 1988).

21. Oskar Wiener, *Deutsche Dichter aus Prague* (Leipzig, 1918), quoted in Demetz, *Rilkes Prager Jahre*, 141.

22. Heinz Politzer, "Prague and the Origins of Rainer Maria Rilke, Franz Kafka, and Franz Werfel," *Modern Language Quarterly* 16, no. 1 (1955): 49–62. Quotation from Hermann Bahr, *Frana Sramek: Das bunte Buch* (Leipzig, 1914), 109–10.

23. Bahr, *Sramek: Das bunte Buch,* 109–10.

24. It has been argued that Rilke's political sympathies toward the Czechs went far beyond what was socially permissible for a liberal German. When Czechoslovakia declared its independence in 1918, Rilke accepted citizenship from the republic rather than from Austria. It is unclear, however, how much Rilke's decision was motivated by his resentment of any association with Germany and German imperialist politics, particularly during and after World War I.

25. Klaus Wagenbach, "Prag um die Jahrhundertwende," in *Franz Kafka: Eine Biographie seiner Jugend, 1883–1912* (Bern, 1958).

26. Egon Erwin Kisch, *Die Abenteuer in Prague* (Vienna, 1920), 69.

27. Rilke, "Die Letzten," *SW,* 4:247.

28. Rilke, *Tagebücher,* 115.

29. Oskar Wiener, *Im Prager Dunstkreis* (Vienna, 1919), 104; Ernst Wodak, *Prague von gestern und vorgestern* (Tel Aviv, 1948), 16.

30. Paul Leppin, "Prague," *Witiko II* (1929): 115; Rilke's "wegen der Straßenunruhen," quoted in Reshetylo-Rothe, *Rilke and Russia,* 16. Statistics of the time show that in the 1840s the ratio between the German-speaking and Czech-speaking population of Prague was 66,046 to 36,687; in 1910 only 7.3% of German-speaking population remained. Pavel Petr, "Franz Kafkas Böhmen: Tschechen, Deutsche, Juden," *Germano-Slavica* 3, no. 6 (1981): 377.

31. Heinrich Teweles, *Der Kampf um die Sprache* (Leipzig, 1884), 12; Franz Kafka, *Letters to Milena,* ed. Willy Haas, trans. Tania Stern and James Stern (New York, 1982), 24.

32. Fritz Mauthner, "Erinnerungen I," in *Prager Jugendjahre* (Munich, 1918), 29; see also Demetz, *Rilkes Prager Jahre,* 152–53.

33. Heinz Politzer, "Problematik und Probleme der Kafka-Forschung," *Monatshefte* 42, no. 6 (1950): 280.

34. Rilke to Alfred Sauer, quoted in Demetz, *Rilkes Prager Jahre,* 202.

35. Demetz, *Rilkes Prager Jahre,* 89–112; Mauthner, "Erinnerungen I," 29.

36. Rilke to Marie von Mutius, 15 January 1918, quoted in Maurice Betz, *Rilke in Frankreich* (Vienna, 1938), 53–54.

37. One of Rilke's last stylistic visitations of his Slavic home occurred in his responses to the effusive style of Marina Tsvetaeva-Efron's Russian letters. See chap. 9.

38. Václav Černý, *Rainer Maria Rilke, Prag, Böhmen und die Tschechen* (Brno, 1966).

39. According to Carl Sieber, Phia Rilke did not allow her son to learn Czech and taught him French, demanding that he answer in French at school and ignore Czech altogether. Sieber, *René Rilke*, 10.

The phenomenal ease with which Rilke learned to read and understand the Russian language, for example, can be attributed to his early exposure and willingness to absorb, if not learn, the Czech language. Conversely, his "shadow knowledge" of Czech could have been the obstacle in his ability to master conversational Russian. Hence the conflicting accounts of Rilke's level of competence in speaking Russian. "Erstaunlich mit welcher Kenntnis er . . . über die besonderen Schönheiten der altrussischen Volksdichtung 'Slowo o polku Igoreve' sprach, die er in Original, in der Altslavische Sprache zu lesen vermochte." Leonid Pasternak, cited in André von Gronicka, "Rainer Maria Rilke's Translation of the 'Igor' Song (Slovo)," 182–83, and in a slightly different form in Azadovsky, *Rilke und Rußland*, 457.

40. Rilke to Pavel D. Ettinger, 4 January 1901, *Rilke und Rußland*, 245.

41. In March/April 1904, Rilke filled out a questionnaire from Ellen Key in which he discussed his possible Slavic ancestry. Schnack, *Chronik* 1:181.

42. 29 January, 1896; quoted in Donald Prater, *A Ringing Glass: The Life of Rainer Maria Rilke*, 18. Rilke makes the connection between the folk soul and the folk music he identifies with the Dionysian spirit in "Marginalien zu Friedrich Nietzsche: *Die Geburt der Tragödie*," SW 6:1163–77.

43. Numerous editions of Old Czech tales and legends were being published in Rilke's time in Prague. For the version of the folk myth that Rilke may have known, see *Staré Pověsti České*, ed. Alois Jirásek (Prague, 1933), 185–89.

44. Rilke, "Marginalien zu Friedrich Nietzsche."

45. "Rilke's letter to Svatopluk Czech," in *Slovo a slovesnost*, no. 1 (1935): 44; see also Schnack, *Chronik* 1:42.

46. According to Peter Demetz, the exhibition was boycotted by the German part of Prague's population, and Rilke clearly violated the ban by visiting and writing about it. In his poem, Rilke described with meticulous naturalism the characteristic simplicity of Týl's room, admiring the poet's self-sacrificing dedication to the cause. See Demetz, *Rilkes Prager Jahre*, 144–45.

47. Čech's songs proclaimed Russia as the sole alternative to a decaying

Europe. "Hej Slovane" was written for and performed at an 1891 Prague fair. The reference in the song is to the signing of the Franco-Russian alliance against Germany.

48. J. Patejdlová-Janícková, "Znali se Rilke se Zeyerem osobně?" in *Sborník Narodnogo muzea v Praze,* series C, vol. 8 (Prague), 86–96.

49. See, among others, Černý, *Rilke, Prag, Böhmen und die Tschechen,* 29–36.

50. Arne Novák, *Die tchechische Literatur* (Potsdam, 1931), 76.

51. Zeyer to Professor Kašpar, 6 March 1872, quoted in Harkins, *Russian Folk Epos,* 186. The religious associations in Zeyer's letters from and about Russia are strikingly similar to Rilke's accounts. Rilke wrote to Helene Voronina in anticipation of his first Russian trip: "Der neue Norden, seine Sitten und Geselligkeiten, seine Kämpfe und Künste, die Wunder und Weiten des russischen Reiches: das alles mutet mich an wie eine neue Schönheit, die mir noch geschenkt werden soll zu jenem bestsen Besitz." [The new North, its customs and mores, its struggles and arts, the wonders and expanses of the Russian empire: it all charms me like a new beauty that still has to be given to me to make the best use of it.] 9 March 1899, *Rilke und Rußland,* 85. If in Zeyer's life religion played an increasingly more important role, for Rilke, by contrast, the original religious character of his interest in Russia subsided, giving way to more secular interests.

52. Quoted in Harkins, *Russian Folk Epos,* 188.

53. Zeyer to Kašpar, 6 March 1872, quoted in ibid., 187.

54. Rilke's own collecting was a gesture of "gathering" around himself the Russian world. In his Worpswede house, he kept a Russian corner in one of his rooms decorated with mementos from his trips. On collecting as a self-affirming strategy, see Jacques Hainard and Rolland Kaehr, *Temps perdu, temps retrouvé: Voir les choses du passé au present* (Neuchâtel, 1985).

55. At the time of his meeting with Rilke, Zeyer was researching Russian religious epic poems, and his late stories "Aleksei, Man of God" and "Song of the Woe of the Good Youth, Roman Vasilic" were adaptations from the Russian (*ohlas velkorusky*).

56. First published in the modernist journal *Lumír* (1882).

57. In response to von Gronicka's accusation that Rilke's "modern Russian sources misled him" in his translation of the poem, Caryl Emerson offers a possible justification in Rilke's defense: as a true artist, he was merely making an aesthetic choice among the multiplicity of circulating versions of the poem. In the end, his German version was the product of his initial selection, enhanced by his own creative rendition. See Gronicka, "Rilke's Translation of the 'Igor' Song (Slovo)," and Caryl Emerson, "Rilke, Russia and the Igor Tale."

58. "Ich fühlte mich überreich belohnt, einerseits durch den aufrichtigen warmen Beifall, den er mir mit Stimme und Blick zollte, anderseits

durch Episoden und Erzählungen, die seine weiten Reisen ihm eingegeben haben und die er in schlichter Weise wiederzugeben versteht." [I feel that I have been generously rewarded, on the one hand by the sincere and warm approval which he showed in his voice and expression, on the other hand by the scenes and tales which his extensive travels have given him and which he knew how to convey in a simple way.] Schnack, *Chronik* 1:36.

59. E.g., Demetz, *Rilkes Prager Jahre,* 150–51.

60. The manifesto "Ceská moderna" was published in October 1895 and called for the cultivation of individuality within unity in both art and politics.

61. Rilke to Jenny Oltersdorf, 28 July 1911, and Nora Goudstikker, 4 April 1897; quoted in Prater, *Ringing Glass,* 19.

62. Rilke to Tolstoy, 8 September 1899, *Rilke und Rußland,* 109.

63. *Duino Elegies,* MacIntyre trans., 65.

64. Letter to Phia Rilke, quoted in Prater, *Ringing Glass*, 59.

65. Andreas-Salomé remembered Rilke in Russia in the following words: "Dies verlieh ihm eine Ungeteiltheit von Geist und Sinnen, ein Ineinanderschwengen von beiden: der Mensch ging noch unverkürzt und unbesorgt in den Künstler und der Künstler im Menschlichen auf." [It gave him an inseparability of the spirit and the mind, a flowing together of both: the man went whole and untroubled into the artist and the artist into the man.] *Lebensrückblick,* 115.

66. Witold Hulewicz, "Gespräche mit Rainer Maria Rilke," in *Prager Presse,* 30 November 1930, as quoted in *Rilke und Rußland,* 20–21.

CHAPTER TWO

1. ". . . wir fühlten uns nicht nur in russischem 'Dienst,' sondern als Russen." Andreas-Salomé, *Lebensrückblick,* 60; Reshetylo-Rothe, *Rilke and Russia,* 37. Rudolph Binion, Andreas-Salomé's American biographer, insists that she had no contact whatsoever with the Russian population of the city and even refused to learn the Russian language, nearly failing the subject at school. See Rudolph Binion, *Frau Lou: Nietzsche's Wayward Disciple* (Princeton, N. J., 1968). Ironically, she was known among her German friends as a *Russin,* while her Russian acquaintances recognized her as a representative of German intellectuals.

2. Mikhail Bakhtin, "Response to a Question of Novy Mir," in *Speech Genres and Other Late Essays,* trans. Vern W. McGee (Austin, 1986), 7.

3. The charges of incompetent representation leveled at her by the majority of her Western biographers have to do with the unsettled issue of who is in the position to interpret other cultures competently. On this issue, see the debate currently taking place across professional and academic borders: *Redrawing the Boundaries,* ed. Stephen Greenblatt and Giles Gunn

(New York, 1992). For a comprehensive analysis of "intensive participant observation" as a new type of professional ethnographic norm in the early twentieth century, see James Clifford, "On Ethnographic Authority," in *The Predicament of Culture* (Cambridge, Mass., 1988), 21–54. Andreas-Salomé's style of participant observation proved to be very effective in making Russian material accessible to her Western audiences.

4. Critical quotations from Reshetylo-Rothe, *Rilke and Russia*, 37–38, 6. A well-known exemplar of this view about Western interpretations is Edward Said. See his *Orientalism* (New York, 1978), and the ensuing debate provoked by his study.

5. Andreas-Salomé, *Lebensrückblick*, 97.

6. Andreas-Salomé to Rilke, 26 February 1901, in *R–AS Briefwechsel*, 54.

7. Rilke to Phia Rilke, 18 May 1897, quoted in Sieber, MS. Biography, Rilke-Archiv, Gernsbach.

8. Said, *Orientalism*, 3; and his *Culture and Imperialism* (New York, 1993). For a critique of Said's one-sided presentation of Orientalism as a political phenomenon, see responses from James Clifford, "On Orientalism," in *Predicament of Culture;* and Ernst Gellner, "The Mightier Pen?" *TLS*, 19 February 1993, 3–4.

9. H. F. Peters described Frieda von Bülow in his biography of Andreas-Salomé as "Afrikaforsherin und Kolonisatorin." See his *Lou Andreas-Salomé: Das Leben einer außergewöhnlichen Frau* (Munich, 1984), 231.

10. For information on F. C. Andreas, see Götz von Selle, "F. C. Andreas," *Indogermanisches Jahrbuch* 1931:366–76.

11. Brandes visited Russia at the invitation of the Russian Writer's Society for a three-month lecture tour. In 1889 he published his impressions of Russia in which he described the post-Emancipation Russian society in frank and often unflattering terms.

12. Andreas-Salomé dedicated her book *Henrik Ibsens Frauengestalten* (Jena, 1892) to her husband with the following inscription: "To my husband. This work is something by itself, the product of coveted and honest solitude." *Lebensrückblick*, 206.

13. Andreas-Salomé, *Lebensrückblick*, 205.

14. Andreas-Salomé, *Lebensrückblick*, 97.

15. The radical change of tone in Andreas-Salomé's writing about Russia occurred in the summer of 1897, which she spent working closely with the Petersburg critic Akim Lvovich Volynsky, who was visiting her summer house in Wolfratshausen near Munich. Andreas-Salomé's relationship with Volynsky is discussed further below.

16. "Es war daß Menschliche: es war der frohe Auftrieb, die bewegte Jugend und Zuversicht, der es nichts verschlug, daß die trübseligsten und

düstersten Themen sich herausnahmen, den neuen Geist zu prädigen." *Lebensrückblick,* 97.

17. Her major Russian essays included a two-part survey of current literature and criticism, "Russian Letters and Culture" ("Russische Dichtung und Kultur I"; an analysis of the writings of Nikolai Leskov, "The Russian Holy Image and Its Poet" ("Das russiche Heiligenbild und sein Dichter"); and a critique of Russian philosophy, "Russian Philosophy and the Semitic Spirit" (*"Russische Philosophie und semitische Geist"*), which all appeared in print between 1897 and 1898. Andreas-Salomé's Russian journalistic career peaked with her essay "Leo Tolstoy, Our Contemporary" ("Leo Tolstoy, unser Zeitgenoße") (1898), which analyzed Tolstoy as a cultural phenomenon in the Russian context.

18. Stanley J. Rabinowitz, "A Room of His Own: The Life and Work of Akim Volynsii," *Russian Review* 50 (1991): 289–309.

19. Under Volynsky's intellectual guidance, she developed a philosophy in which Russians and Jews were featured as two special peoples distinguished by un-Western inwardness and depth of feeling, and she intended to write a psychological study of the two groups (Binion, *Frau Lou,* 189). And see her article "Jesus der Jude" (1894).

20. Andreas-Salomé, "Amor" (with Volynsky), *Severny vestnik,* no. 9 (1897): 1–6; Rilke, "Aller in Einer," *Severny vestnik,* no. 10 (1897). Thanks to Andreas-Salomé's intercession, Volynsky's major critical writings, including his heretical *Russian Critics,* were translated and made known in Germany.

21. Andreas-Salomé, "Rußland," part of the column "Internationalle Zeitschriften-Rundschau," *Freie Bühne* 7 (18964): 714–16.

22. "Das Bestehen und Gedeihen einer solchen Gesellschaft ist jedenfalls ein characteristisches Symptom für die gewaltige Umwälzung, die sich gegenwärtig innerhalb des russischen Volksorganismus vorbereitet." [The existence and well-being of such a society is in any case a characteristic of a powerful upheaval, which is preparing itself in the Russian folk organism.] *Neue Deutsche Rundschau,* 2 July 1896, 716.

23. Andreas-Salomé, "Russiche Philosophie und semitische Geist." In his study of the Russian Revolution, Richard Pipes insists that at the turn of the century, Russian industrial workers were, with minor exceptions, a branch of the peasantry rather than a distinct social group. See *The Russian Revolution* (New York, 1990), 107.

24. G. I. Uspensky's *Iz derevenskogo dnevnika* (*From a Village Diary*) (1889) and N. N. Zlatovratsky's *Derevenskie budni* (*Rural Daily Life*) (1882) were perhaps the finest writings in this tradition.

25. For an in-depth study of the post-Emancipation evolution of the iconography of the Russian peasant, see Cathy A. Frierson, *Peasant Icons: Representations of Rural People in Late Nineteenth-Century Russia* (New

York, 1993). A similar process had been taking place in Germany earlier in the century. John G. Gagliardo, *From Pariah to Patriot: The Changing Image of the German Peasant, 1770–1840* (Lexington, Ky., 1969).

26. "We all, lovers of the *narod,* regard them as a theory, and it seems that none of us really likes them as they actually are, but only as each of us has imagined them. Moreover, should the Russian *narod,* at some future time, turn out to be not what we imagined, we all, despite our love of them, would immediately renounce them wihout regret." Dostoyevsky, "Diary of a Writer," *Polnoe sobranie sochinenii v tridzati tomakh,* vol. 22 (Leningrad, 1981), 44.

27. G. I. Uspensky, "Pis'ma s dorogi," *Russkaia mysl'* 3 (March 1888): 161, trans. in Frierson, *Peasant Icons,* 195.

28. On the difference between Russian and middle European social relationships between town and country in connection with the failure of the Russian populist movement, see N. O. Lossky, "Kharakter russkogo naroda," *Filosofia i Zhizn',* no. 2 (Moscow, 1991): 552–56.

29. Tolstoy expressed these ideas in an argument with Gleb Uspensky, which the latter recorded in his memoir. Uspensky, *Iz proshlogo: Vospominania* (Moscow, 1889), quoted in Frierson, *Peasant Icons,* 169.

30. "Es war anregend, diese nicht alltäglichen Zusammentreffen unserer aus der Bauernschaft kommenden Arbeiter mit den Vertretern der raffiniertesten Kultur Europas mitzuerleben. Sie interessieren sich nicht für die ersten Versuche der russischen Arbeiter, aktiv in der Politik aufzutreten, sondern für ihr Sein, ihr ländliches Wesen, die gesunden Wurzel—für 'die Seele des Ackerbauern, die noch nicht endgültig verstummelt ist durch die Stadt und die Arbeiterkaserne.'" Sophie Schill, "Aus den 'Erinnerungen'," *Rilke und Rußland,* 444–45.

31. Ibid., 438.

32. Ibid., 449.

33. Andreas-Salomé, *Lebensrückblick,* 65.

34. Andreas-Salomé, "Russian Journal," early May 1900; quoted in Binion, *Frau Lou,* 264.

35. Rilke, *Tagebücher,* 133–34.

36. "Eine Ungeteiltheit von Geist und Sinnen, ein Ineinanderschwingen von beidem: der Mensch ging noch unverkürzt und unbesorgt in den Künstler und der Künstler im Menschen auf." Andreas-Salomé, *Lebensrückblick,* 115.

37. "Letzter Zuruf" (Last Call) was the title of Andreas-Salomé's letter to Rilke (26 February 1901) announcing her decision to break up their relationship. *R–AS Briefwechsel,* 53–55.

38. *Lebensrückblick,* 113. Andreas-Salomé attributed special significance to such name changes. Reverend Father Gillot, her first teacher and her first love, rechristened his eighteen-year-old charge, Louise Salomé

(called in her family "Ljola"), as Lou Salomé. She did as much for Rilke, changing the effeminate *René* to the more appropriately poetic *Rainer*. Andreas-Salomé remembered Rilke's first letter signed "Rainer," dated 5 September 1897. *R–AS Briefwechsel*, 23–26.

39. Andreas-Salomé's own stay in Italy in 1882 turned out to be decisive for her future career and intellectual development. In the house of the feminist writer Malwida von Meysenbug, she met the philosophers Paul Rée and Friedrich Nietzsche, whose intellectual influence changed the course of her life.

40. "Ein Italien Handbuch welches zum Genuß anleiten wollte durfte ein einziges Wort und ein einzigen Rat enthalten: Schau!" *Tagebücher*, 31.

41. "Statt irgendein Verhältnis zu den Dingen zu gewinnen nur Abstand merken zwischen ihrer verdringlichen Hast und dem feierlich-pedantischen Urteil des Kunstprofessors." Ibid., 31.

42. "Der Künstler soll mit einem Male so eine Art Onkel sein, der seinen Neffen und Nichten (dem geneigten Publikum) einen Sonntags spaß vormachen soll." Ibid., 32.

43. Hugo von Hofmannsthal, "Psychologie der modernen Liebe," in *Die Prosa des jungen Hugo von Hofmannsthal* (Berlin, 1930), 64.

44. Rilke, *Tagebücher*, 33–34.

45. "Ich empfind meinen Aufenthalt in Rußland als eine seltsame Ergänzung jenes florentiner Frühlings." Rilke to Frieda von Bülow, 7 June 1899, *Briefe u. Tagebücher*, 16.

46. Rilke to Helene Voronina, 9 March 1899, *Rilke und Rußland*, 87.

47. Andreas-Salomé, *Lebensrückblick*, 69.

CHAPTER THREE

1. Rilke to Andreas-Salomé, 11 August 1900, in *R–AS Briefwechsel*, 44. Moscow and Petersburg were perceived as incarnations of good and evil in the Russian Slavophile tradition. In 1863 Ivan Sergeevitch Aksakov, Moscow's leading Slavophile, sent Dostoyevsky a letter sharing with him ideas about St. Petersburg: "The foremost condition for freeing the folk suppressed spirit is this: to hate Petersburg heartily. In general, one cannot become Christian (Slavophilism is nothing but the highest Christian sermon) if one does not renounce Satan, does not blow him out or spit on him." Aksakov's letter was quoted in the first German edition of Dmitrii Merezhkovsky's study *Tolstoi und Dostojevski* (Leipzig, 1903), 254. Rilke may very well have been familiar with Merezhkovsky's book and with Aksakov's almost pagan rejection of Petersburg. Rilke's own mistrust of Petersburg's cosmopolitanism was a form of Modernist antiurbanism.

2. Rilke to Helene Voronin, *Rilke und Rußland,* 99. In her memoirs, Andreas-Salomé writes that Rilke's anxiety about finding a complete creative form for his impressions arose later in life. His Russian experience was the turning point in the evolution of his self-perception as an artist. Andreas-Salomé, *Lebensrückblick,* 141–44.

3. See Walter Benjamin, "On Some Motifs in Baudelaire," in *Illuminations,* 163.

4. Rilke, *The Notebooks of Malte Laurids Brigge,* trans. M. D. Herter (New York: Norton, 1949), 26.

5. Ibid., 26–27.

6. Reik quoted in Benjamin, "On Some Motifs in Baudelaire," 160.

7. For the description of the arrival scene, see Rilke to Wilhelm von Scholz, in *Briefe u. Tagebücher,* 8.

The actual observance of the most festive ritual in the Russian Church begins seven weeks before Easter Sunday with the Great Fast—Lent—and ends on Easter Sunday (according to the Julian calendar, the date of the Russian Orthodox Easter varies and usually falls one or two weeks after the Western Christian Easter). The ceremony is a dramatically spectacular one: Crowds of worshipers gather in the church for the midnight mass. In the last moments of Easter Saturday the icon of Christ is carried behind the altar screen. At midnight sharp the bells ring out, the altar gates are opened, and the bishops and priests come out dressed in white followed by the singing choir and the worshipers with their lighted candles. With the acolytes swinging censers, the procession files out and circles the church, stopping at each of the four corners, north, south, east, and west, then proceeds back to the entrance. "*Christos Voskresi!* Christ is risen!" The censers are swung; incense rises. Mourning is over. Christ is risen. The cry goes up all round. Everyone turns to his or her neighbor saying, "*Christos Voskresi! Vo istinu Voskres!* He is risen, indeed!"

8. "Zum ersten Mal in meinem Leben hatte ich ein unausdrückbares Gefühl, etwas wie 'Heimgefühl'—ich fühlte mit großer Kraft die Zugehörigkeit zu etwas, mein Gott, zu etwas in dieser Welt." For citation, see chap. 1, n. 65.

9. " . . . keine Osterstadt . . . das unter großen Glocken zu liegen weiß. Es ist alles Aufwand ohne Frömmigkeit, Festvorstellung statt Fest."

"Mir war ein einziges Mal Ostern; das war damals in jener langen, ungewöhnlichen, ungemeinen, erregten Nacht, da das alles Volk sich drängte, und als der Ivan Velikij mich schlug in der Dunkelheit, Schlag für Schlag. Das war mein Ostern, und ich glaube es reicht für ein ganzes Leben aus; die Botschaft ist mir in jener moskauer Nacht seltsam groß gegeben worden, ist mir ins Blut gegeben worden und ins Herz. Ich weiß es jetzt: *Khristos Voskres!*" Rilke to Andreas-Salomé, 31 March 1904, *R–AS*

Briefwechsel, 142–43. In response to Andreas-Salomé's card of 23 March 1904 depicting a Russian church at Easter, Rilke sent a long letter devoted almost entirely to the Russian Easter.

10. As Andreas-Salomé noted in her memoir: "Even what came could not change that part of our experience which had been most magnificent and most intimately part of our interior world. We had received more in Russia than Russia itself." *Lebensrückblick*, 42.

11. Sophie Schill was clearly perplexed at her German friends' lack of social inhibitions: "Die beiden bummelten durch Moskau, über den Arbat, durch Gassen und Gäßchen und hielten sich wie Kinder bei der Hand." Sophie Schill, "Erinnerungen," *Rilke und Rußland*, 444.

12. Heinrich Vogeler described the unusual sight of Rilke appearing in Worpswede in his Russian garb and cross, which even his fellow artists found quite striking. Heinrich Vogeler, *Erinnerungen*, ed. Erich Weinert (Berlin, 1952). Sophie Schill was offended by Rilke's "cheap" exhibitionism. She could not understand how he could put the sacred object on the watch chain next to other "trinkets." Schill, "Erinnerungen," 445.

13. Walter Benjamin explains the precariousness of the collector's subjective space: "Every passion borders on the chaotic, but the collector's passion borders on the chaos of memories. More than that: the chance, the fate, that suffuse the past before my eyes are conspicuously present in the accustomed confusion of these [objects]." Walter Benjamin, "Unpacking My Library," in *Illuminations*, 60.

14. "Hier zum ersten Mal kommt man vor die Dinge, gewinnt ein direktes Verhältnis zu ihnen und bleibt mit allem in einem beständigen Verkehr, der fast gegenseitig erscheint, obwhol man in jedem Sinne der Gast und der Beschenkte aller Dinge bleibt." Rilke to Voronina, 28 May (8/9 June) 1899, *Rilke und Rußland*, 98–99.

15. Andreas-Salomé, *Lebensrückblick*, 72.

16. Rilke to Voronina, 9 June 1899, *Rilke und Rußland*, 98–99.

17. Brodsky, *Russia in the Works of Rilke*, 70.

18. Andreas-Salomé, *Lebensrückblick*, 69–70. The resonance of these views with late Dostoyevsky is striking.

19. Rilke, *Tagebücher*, 233.

20. Translations from Rainer Maria Rilke, *Poems from the Book of Hours*, "*Das Stundenbuch*," trans. Babette Deutsch (New York, 1975), 5.

21. In his "Letter of the Young Worker" (1922), Rilke explained his lifelong fascination with the founder of the Franciscan order: "To take the here and now (*das Hiesige*) into your hand, fully and lovingly, . . . as ours . . . . and therefore unique. It is . . . God's most important direction, which holy Francis of Assisi meant to include in his *Song to the Sun*, . . . to point in the direction of the sun" (*SW*, 6:1115). Significantly, in *What Is Art?* Tolstoy cites St. Francis as an exception to the general corruption among Western

religious and aesthetic institutions: "Only rare individuals among the rich and the powerful, such as Francis of Assisi . . . despite the fact that their teaching undermined their privileged position, accepted Christian teaching for its vital message." *What Is Art?*, trans. Aylmer Maude (New York, 1988), 174.

22. "I am returning home at the head of the long train of shining treasures. Moscow has generously rewarded me, the Madonna of Kazan, Saint Sergius, and Saint Varvara have generously rewarded me." Rilke to Voronina, 9 June 1899, Azadovsky, *Rilke und Rußland*, 99.

23. Alienation of an individual in the city had been a familiar theme in Rilke's work long before Russia. As a military cadet, he secretly read Baudelaire's *Petits poèmes en prose*. Nonetheless, he never perceived cities as threatening human sanity—the modernist theme—until he went to Paris.

24. "Each time it occurs to me at night that you want to read him, I cannot sleep! Why? Go to the country soon, buy yourself a piece of property and wait for happiness as one waits for a harvest that has been rightly sowed." Rilke to Voronina, 27 July 1899, *Rilke und Rußland*, 105.

25. Quoted in Andreas-Salomé, *Lebensrückblick*, 116; Rilke, *Tagebücher aus der Frühzeit*, 116.

26. Rilke to Voronina, 27 July 1899, *Rilke und Rußland*, 105; *Tagebücher*, 98–99.

27. The theme of the silver clock in the living room comes up frequently in Rilke's early work. Helene and her clock reemerge in Rilke's early story "In Conversation" ("Im Gespräch") one of the three novellas in the collection *The Last Ones* (*Die Letzten*) (1898–99), and in scattered memories of his Petersburg days.

28. Rilke, in *The Enlightened Mind: An Anthology of Sacred Prose*, ed. Stephen Mitchell (New York, 1991).

29. The Russian semioticians Iu. Lotman and B. Uspensky have claimed that the myth of the diabolical origins of St. Petersburg recalls the mythologies of ancient cities like Babylon. *The Semiotics of Russian Culture* (Ann Arbor, Mich., 1984).

30. The continual hovering between genius and insanity fascinated and terrified Rilke. Lou Andreas-Salomé warned him at their separation that he was about to relive the fate of the Russian writer Garshin, who committed suicide in a fit of insanity. Andreas-Salomé to Rilke, 26 February 1901, *R–AS Briefwechsel*, 53.

31. Rilke, *Malte Laurids Brigge*, Herter trans., 147.

32. Ibid., 152.

33. Rilke, "St. Petersburg: Ein Erlebnis," in Schnack, *Chronik* 1:178.

34. Rilke, *Malte Laurids Brigge*, Herter trans., 214.

35. "Gehe denselben Weg Deinem dunklen Gott entgegen! Er kann, was ich nicht mehr thun kann an Dir,—und so lange schon nicht mehr mit

voller Drangabe thun konnte: er kann Dich zur Sonne und Reife segnen"
[Go the same way to meet your dark God. He can do for you what I can do
no longer—and for a long time now could no longer do with full commitment: he can bless you to sun and maturity]. Andreas-Salomé to Rilke, 26
February 1901, *R–AS Briefwechsel*, 54.

CHAPTER FOUR

1. Rilke later recaptured those historical events in his poems "Storm"
("Sturm") and "Karl the Twelfth of Sweden Rides through the Ukraine"
("Karl der Zwölfte von Schweden reitet in der Ukraina").

2. Rilke, letter of 31 July 1900, *Briefe u. Tagebücher*, 195–96.

3. "Dort werden Sie das wahre russische Leben kennenlernen, das einfache, unkultivierte Dorf, seinen ganzen Schmutz, seine Armut und
Unsauberkeit. Wenn Sie dort gewesen sind, werden Sie ganz bestimmt Ihre
Meinung über Rußland in vielem ändern, Sie werden sich über Ihre Begeis-
terung entsetzen und vielleicht mit einem ganz anderen Gefühl auf Ihre
Heimat schauen, wo die Leute trotz alledem wenigstens wie Menschen
leben und nicht wie Tiere." [There you will get to know true Russian life, the
simple, uncultivated village with its ubiquitous dirt, its poverty and unclean-
liness. Having been there, you will certainly change your opinion about Russia; you will be shocked at your earlier enthusiasm and possibly will look
back to your home country with quite a different feeling. There, at least,
people live like human beings, not like animals.] Sophie Schill to Rilke, 6
April 1900, *Rilke und Rußland*, 144. Phrase about "peasant expressions"
quoted in Spiridon Drozhzhin, "Der zeitgenössische Dichter Rainer Maria
Rilke," ibid., 431.

4. Rilke's Russian acquaintances frequently warned him against idealizing Russian reality. For example, A. Benois wrote to him in January 1902:
"In general, I must tell you quite honestly that I do not quite share your
enthusiasm for our motherland." *Rilke und Rußland*, 326–27.

5. Vasily Yantchevetsky, "Der Gottsucher (Aus Erinnerungen)," in *Rilke
und Rußland*, 469–70. In her study *Rilke and Russia*, Reshetylo-Rothe provides an exhaustive listing of negative Russian responses to Rilke's "uncritical" idealism, which, she claims, prove Rilke's lack of perspective on Russia.
As in Schill's case, however, this was only a "family quarrel," indicative of the
Russian desire to protect Rilke from disappointment and to encourage his
genuine appreciation of their culture. Rilke's articulation may have been
naive, but not the essence of his hopes for Russia.

6. Rilke to Alexander Benois, 28 July 1901, *Rilke und Rußland*, 298.

7. "Das Simpel und Künstlerisch Schwache." Schill, "Erinnerungen,"
Rilke und Rußland, 439. Rilke's eclectic judgments have become notorious

among critics as his "bad taste" in Russian culture. See Walter Arndt, "Rilke and Tolstoy," paper presented at the AATSEEL annual conference, San Francisco, December 1991.

8. Quoted in *Nikolai Kliuev: Stikhotvorenia i poemy,* ed. Stanislav Kunaev (Moscow, 1991), 5.

9. After the period of Stalinist antipeasant state policy in the 1930s–1950s, the peasant literary tradition resurfaced in the post-Stalinist thaw. The "village" writers who called themselves *derevenshiki* included such prominent members of the literary guild as Valentin Rasputin and Vasilii Shukshin. They promoted an environmentalist agenda by speaking out on the peasants' behalf for the conservation of nature and the preservation of the traditional village mode of life.

10. In later years, Drozhzhin's Soviet critics accused him of failing to take on a "more active, contemporary approach to life's problems. . . . And [of] limit[ing] himself to the sphere of detached moralistic interpretation." In Kalmanovsky, ed., "Introduction," in *L. N. Trefolev, I. Z. Surikov, S. D. Drozhzhin Stikhotvorena* (Moscow, Leningrad, 1963), 52. Drozhzhin was spared the fate of Kliuev and Esenin in the Soviet period by hiding away from politics in his remote village.

11. The Soviet writer A. S. Serafimovitch remembered in his diary one of Drozhzhin's visits to him in 1924: "Today, the poet Drozhzhin came to visit me and sang his songs in a strong voice as he did many years ago." Quoted in Kalmanovsky, 55.

12. Rilke to Phia Rilke, 25 July 1900, quoted in Brutzer, "Rilkes russische Reisen," 67.

13. See Kalmanovsky, in *Trefolev, Surikov, Drozhzhin,* 53.

14. Rilke went to Worpswede immediately after leaving Russia at the invitation of Heinrich Vogeler and stayed there until 5 October 1900.

15. Schnack, *Chronik* 1:115.

16. A comparison with Rilke's Bohemian style in *Larenopfer* comes to mind. The stylistic limitations imposed on Rilke by his insufficient knowledge of the Russian language have been discussed by several interpreters. Among them, Brutzer, "Rilkes russischen Reisen"; Samson Soloveittchik and Everitt B. Gladding, "Rilke's Original Russian Poems," *Modern Language Notes* 62 (1947): 514–22; and Daria Reshetylo-Rothe, "Appendix," *Rilke and Russia.*

17. "Mir ist ja Rußland doch das geworden was Ihnen Ihre Landschaft bedeutet: Heimat und Himmel." Rilke to Paula Becker, 18 October 1900, in Schnack, *Chronik* 1:112.

18. Cathy Frierson is currently at work on a study of fires and arsons in the daily life of a Russian village. Paper presented at the New England AATSEEL conference, Providence, R.I., April 1993.

19. Rilke, *Malte Laurids Brigge,* Herter trans., 16.

20. Rilke to Marie von Mutius, 15 January 1918, quoted in Betz, *Rilke in Frankreich*, 52–54.

21. "Und stell Dir vor, noch *eins*, in einem anderen Zusammenhang, eben vorher, (in den 'Sonetten an Orpheus' . . .) schrieb ich, machte, das Pferd, weißt Du, denfreien, glücklichen Schimmel mit dem Pflock am Fuß, der uns einmal, gegen Abend, auf einer Wolga-Wiese im Galopp entgegensprang—: *wie* hab ich ihn gemacht, als ein 'Ex-voto' für *Orpheus!*—Was ist Zeit?—Wann ist Gegenwart? Über so viel Jahre sprang er mir, mit seinem völligen Glück, ins weitoffne Gefühl." [And imagine, once *again*, in another connection, just as before (in the *Sonnets to Orpheus* . . .), I wrote about, I created, the horse, you know, the free and happy white stallion with the hobble on its feet, which once, toward evening, on the Volga shore, sprang in front of us in a gallop. As if I made him to be an ex-voto for Orpheus! What is time? When is the present? Over so many years he sprang into my wide open feeling with his full happiness.] Rilke to Andreas-Salomé, 11 February 1922, in *R–AS Briefwechsel*, 444–45.

22. Daniel Field, "Peasants and Propagandists in the Russian Movement of the People of 1874," *Journal of Modern History* 59 (September 1987): 415–38. Hayden White writes in more general terms on the transitional periods in history when the "lower" classes begin to share a common social sphere with their "liberators." "Noble Savage Theme," in *Topics of Discourse*.

CHAPTER FIVE

1. "Der grosser Darsteller des russischen geistlichen Lebens." Andreas-Salomé, "Russische Dichtung und Kultur, I," 883.

2. For a general biography of Nikolai Leskov and an analysis of his work, see Hugh McLean, *Leskov and His Art* (Cambridge, Mass., 1977).

The turning point in Leskov's journalistic career was a series of articles demanding an impartial investigation for the students accused of setting the St. Petersburg fires in 1861. He antagonized both the conservatives who sought punishment and the radicals who demanded total acquittal. Andreas-Salomé opened her article on Leskov with a mention of Leskov's articles on the arsons.

For a long time, Leskov's second-rate reputation stood in the way of a serious consideration of his work at home and in the West. The verdict of the literary historian D. S. Mirsky written in the 1930s continues to hold: "The Anglo-Saxon public have made up their mind as to what they want from a Russian writer and Leskov does not fit in with this idea." Mirsky's pronouncement did not apply to Germany, where, thanks to the efforts of people like Rilke and Andreas-Salomé and to Walter Benjamin's well-known essay "The Storyteller," Leskov was read between the two world wars along with Turgenev, Dostoyevsky, and Tolstoy. Among Leskov's most recent advocates in the West are Joseph Frank, "A Word on Leskov," in *Through the Russian Prism* (Princeton, N.J., 1990), 225–28; and Irving Howe, "Justice for Leskov," in *Selected Writings, 1950–1990* (San Diego, 1990), 446–58.

3. A. L. Volynsky, *N. S. Leskov* (Petersburg, 1923), 95. In her article "The Russian Holy Image," Andreas-Salomé refers to Volynsky's study as the only detailed and authoritative analysis of Leskov's work available in any language.

Volynsky began his five-part study of Leskov's career with an account of their personal friendship and of Leskov's support for the Jewish cause. At Volynsky's suggestion, Leskov wrote an essay, "Jews in Russia" ("Evrei v Rossii"), which was suppressed by the censorship and reissued only in the time of glasnost.

4. Andreas-Salomé wrote in "The Russian Holy Image": "In Leskow erhielt man den sichersten Schlüßel zu den Werken eines Pushkin, Dostojewski oder Tolstoi weil in ihm alle jene einfachen nationalen Elemente vorhanden sind." [In Leskov one most certainly receives the key to the works of Pushkin, Dostoyevsky, or Tolstoy, because he handles all those basic national elements.]

5. Until the age of sixteen, Leskov was brought up by his English aunt Polly, who introduced him to her Quaker faith. The zeal with which he later embraced Russian Orthodoxy was characteristic of a convert and his understanding of the role of religion in life was always marked by a pragmatic Quaker outlook.

6. Leskov effectively defended everyday life in his review "Graf L. N. Tolstoy and F.M. Dostoyevsky kak iereiatkhi" ("Count L. N. Tolstoy and F. M. Dostoyevsky as Hierarchs"), in *Leskov o literature i iskusstve* (Leningrad, 1984), 111–27.

7. Leskov, "Vechernii zvon i drugie sredstva k iskoreneniu razgula i besstydstva" [Evening bells and other means of eradicating debauchery and shamelessness], *Istoricheskii vestnik,* no. 6 (1882): 596.

8. Quoted in V. Khalizev and O. Maiorova, "Leskovskaja konzepzia pravednichestva," in *V mire Leskova,* ed. A. Romanenko (Moscow, 1983), 197.

9. Quoted in Walter Benjamin, "The Storyteller," in *Illuminations,* 92.

10. See, e.g., Andreas-Salomé, "The Russian Holy Image."

11. Leskov did write one novel, *Na nozhkakh* (On little legs), which failed miserably. Irving Howe offers interesting insights into possible reasons for Leskov's avoidance of anything that has to do with psychology and the novel. "Justice for Leskov," 458.

12. After his parents' deaths, he worked as a clerk and later for his uncle,

an Englishman named Scott, a Nonconformist, employed as a steward on the estates of a rich Russian landowner. This job took him all over Russia until the age of twenty-seven, when his uncle urged him to take up journalism. Leskov was thus one of the few Russian writers whose knowledge of life was based on practical experience.

13. Walter Benjamin, "The Storyteller," 83.

14. Ibid., 87.

15. For a detailed discussion of the actual debate and Leskov's participation in it, see Volynsky, *N. S. Leskov*, 131–43. Volynsky's presentation of the case has been questioned on several occasions. McLean, in his introduction to *Leskov and His Art*, calls the wayward critic "unsystematic and innacurate" and accuses him of using Leskov as a pretext for "long disquisitions on the critic's own pet ideas." My own research has convinced me that although Volynsky's opinions may not always be fair, they are stimulating and provocative. The question of accuracy is another matter.

16. N. Leskov, "Adopisnye ikony," and "O Russkoi ikonopisi," *Russkij Mir*, no. 192 (1873); "Narodnaja ikonopis'," in *Vedomosti S-P. Gradonachalstva*, no. 254 (1873), and other articles as well as miscellaneous reviews.

17. Rilke was familiar with Rovinsky's work. He wrote in a letter to Voronina: "Auch heute noch erscheinen mir diese Dinge von der höchsten Wichtigkeit, ja als das einzige, was zu erfahren . . . und die großen Bände des Werkes von Rovinski, die ich in der Kunstakademie besichtigte, genügten mir keineswegs." [Still today these things appear to me to be of the highest importance, yes as the only thing to experience . . . and the large volumes of Rovinky's works, which I examined in the art school, do not satisfy me at all.] 28 May 1899, *Rilke und Rußland*, 97.

18. N. S. Leskov, "Zhitia kak literaturnyi istochnik" (Saints lives as a literary source), in *Leskov o literature i iskusstve*, 30.

19. Walter Benjamin, "The Work of Art in the Age of Mechanical Reproduction," in *Illuminations*, 223.

20. Rilke's essays on Russian art and his *Stories of God* have been discussed in the critical literature primarily in connection with the general sources on Russia art and culture available to Rilke. Brodsky examines Rilke's Russian sources at length in *Russia in the Works of Rilke*, 96–131; see also Eva C. Wunderlich's "Slavonic Traces in Rilke's *Geschichten vom lieben Gott*," *Germanic Review* 22 (1947): 287–97. E. M. Butler found the stories "pretentious and puerile" (*Rainer Maria Rilke*, 72).

21. Rilke started working on his stories soon after he finished his "Book of Monkish Life" in 1899. The collection was published at Christmas 1900 under the title *Vom lieben Gott und Anderes: An Grosse für Kinder Erzählt*. It was revised in 1901 and in 1904, when it appeared under the present title.

22. Quotations from Benjamin, "The Storyteller," 108–9, 108.

23. Ibid., 108.

24. Presumably, Rilke borrowed the original tale from "Otchego na Russie zavelas' izmena," in Pavel Rybnikov's folklore collection *Pesni sobrannye P. N. Rybnikovym*, 4 vols. (St. Petersburg, 1861–67); and from "Comment la trahison s'est introduite en Russie," in Alfred Rambaud's *La russie épique* (Paris, 1876).

25. A. N. Engelgardt, "Iz derevni, X," *Otechestvennye zapiski*, no. 254 (January 1881): 411.

26. Benjamin suggests that all storytellers can be divided into two types: residents and wanderers. "The Storyteller," 84–85.

27. Ibid., 85.

28. Richard Pipes, "Rural Russia," in *Russian Revolution*, 91–120.

29. The story is set at the time of the Cossack rebellion against Polish rule. For the best historical analysis of the story's subject, see Brodsky, *Russia in the Works of Rilke*, 96–131.

30. Leo Tolstoy, "Christianity and Patriotism," quoted in Pipes, *Russian Revolution*, 109.

31. Andreas-Salomé, "Leo Tolstoy, unser Zeitgenosse," 1154.

32. "Russian Art" was written in early January 1900 and first published in Vienna in October 1901. Rilke claimed that at the time of its appearance it no longer represented his views.

33. Even though none of the three projects were completed, Rilke had done substantial research on them. His Rodin book and *Letters about Cézanne* took precedence over his work on Russian art.

34. Andreas-Salomé, "Russische Philosophie und semitische Geist," 40.

35. "Stiller, intimer und unliterarischer Art." Rilke to Gerhart Hauptmann, December 1901, *SW* 6:1384.

36. Rilke, *Tagebücher*, 133–34.

37. N. Gay, "Kharakternye techenia sovremennoi russkoi zhivopisi" (Characteristic trends in contemporary Russian painting), *Zhizn'* 1 (January 1899): 145–70.

38. Before Rilke's visit to Russia, Vasnetsov had been exhibited in the Paris Salon in 1877, at the international show "Art and Industry" in 1897 in Stockholm, and was elected an honorary member of L'Academie Nationale de Reims. One Western monograph on Vasnetsov had been already published: M le Baron de Baye, *L'oeuvre de Viktor Vasnettzoff devant l'école moderne de peinture en Russie* (Reims, 1895). There is no record that Rilke saw Vasnetsov's first retrospective at the Fine Arts Academy in St. Petersburg held from 4 April to 4 May 1899, open at the time of his visit to Russia. The exhibit featured thirty-eight works and was extensively reviewed in the metropolitan journals by such prominent reviewers as S. P. Diaghilev, "K vystavke V. M. Vasnetsova" (About V. M. Vasnetsova's exhibit), *Mir iskusstva*, nos. 7–8 (1898–99): 66–67. Rilke read *Mir iskusstva* and could have known or read Diaghilev's review.

39. A. Benois remarked, discussing the subject of Vasnetsov's nationalism, "the Russian spirit lies not only in this or that form but much deeper, in the artist's entire, often intangible and indefinable world outlook." *Istoria Russkoi Zhivopisi v XIX veke*, vol. 1 (St. Petersburg, 1901), 120.

40. "Seine Form is eine überlieferte. Nur ganz leise Veränderungen haben die Jahrhunderte gewagt, und man könnte behaupten, daß diese Art der Malerei überhaupt keine Entwickelung gehabt hat oder haben kann, und daß es überflüssig und aussichtslos war, darauf zurückzukommen" [His form is traditional. Hundreds of years have dared only the quietest of changes, and one can maintain that this kind of painting in general has had no development and can have none, and that it is unnecessary and pointless to come back to it]. (*SW* 5:619)

41. Already in 1901, when "Russian art" finally appeared in print after a delay of almost two years, Rilke's ideas about Russian culture have significantly changed. Vasnetsov was for him no longer a representative of the genuine Russian tradition but a contemporary imitation of it. "Der Aufsatz in der *Zeit* ist leider mit so kolossaler Verspätung erschienen, daß er nahe daran war zu verjähren" [The essay appeared in *Die Zeit* so awfully late that it is already almost outdated]. Rilke to Hugo Salus, 30 October 1901, *SW* 6:1384.

42. ". . . russischer Kunst, die mit zunehmender Nationalität sich nicht verengt, ja die vielleicht imstande sein wird, das höchste und allgemainste Menschliche auszusprechen, wenn sie alles Fremde und Zufällige, alles Unrussische ganz vergessen haben wird" (*SW* 5:504–5).

CHAPTER SIX

1. Rilke to Alfred Schaer, 26 February 1924, in *Rainer Maria Rilke, Briefe aus Muzot, 1921–1926* (Leipzig, 1937), 252–59; Rilke to Hermann Pongs, 21 October 1924, in Schnack, *Chronik* 2:948–49; Andreas-Salomé, *Lebensrückblick*, 117.

2. "Wie lange waren Tolstoi, Zola, Turgenev mir Propheten, die ein neues glückliches Zeitalter anzukündigen schienen. Aber in einer einsamen Stunde ging eine Wandlung in mir vor. . . " [How long were Tolstoy, Zola, Turgenev my prophets, who seemed to have announced a new, happy age. But once in an hour of loneliness a change happened in me . . .]. Schnack, *Chronik* 1:26. Carl Sieber, the biographer of Rilke's early years, reported that Rilke read Tolstoy's work as a student at the Linz Trade Academy in 1891–92. Sieber, *René Rilke*, 108.

3. The Russian response to Tolstoy's provocative aesthetic statement was relatively subdued. Completed in 1897, "What Is Art?" suffered such significant mutilations at the hands of its Russian editors and censors that

Tolstoy publicly disowned the book's first Russian edition. Simultaneously with writing the Russian version, Tolstoy personally supervised the book's translation into English, working closely with his English translator, Aylmer Maude. He declared the book's English edition to be the first authorized version. The book's mishandling by the Russian publishing institutions was not the only reason for its relative obscurity at home. The tradition of a utilitarian aesthetic was not new to the Russians; it had represented mainstream Russian opinion since the mid-nineteenth century.

4. Quoted in Richard F. Gustafson, *Leo Tolstoy, Resident and Stranger* (Princeton, N.J., 1989), 92–93.

5. Ernest J. Simmons, *Leo Tolstoy* (New York, 1960), 332.

6. Tolstoy, *What Is Art?* trans. Aylmer Maude (New York, 1985), 54.

7. Simmons, *Leo Tolstoy,* 541.

8. H. W. Garrod, *Tolstoi's Theory of Art* (Oxford, 1935), 10. Shaw's response to Tolstoy's definition of art was concise. He remarked, "It is the simple truth: the moment it is uttered, whoever is really conversant with art recognizes in it the voice of the master" (ibid.).

9. Part 1 of "Über Kunst" was published in the November 1898 issue, part 2 in January 1899, and part 3 in May 1899; *SW* 5:426–33.

10. *Resurrection* was serialized in early 1899 in Russia and in the West simultaneously.

11. Rilke to Benois, 28 July 1901, *Rilke und Rußland,* 295.

12. Rilke to Hermann Pongs, 21 October 1924, *Briefe aus Muzot,* 324–25. In his letter to Pongs, Rilke misstated the date of his first acquaintance with Tolstoy's book, saying that it was "before my second trip," whereas in fact the first part of the essay had been already published by the time he first went to Russia.

13. Andreas-Salomé, "Leo Tolstoi, unser Zeitgenosse," 1147; 133, appendix. Further citations in text.

14. Rilke to Lily Ziegler, 14 April 1921, in Rilke Archive, Schweizerische National Bibliothek, Bern.

15. Maxim Gorky, "Lev Tolstoy," trans. Ivy Livinsky, in *Literary Portraits* (Moscow, 1982), 95.

16. Rilke to Witold Hulewicz, 14 December 1922, *Briefe aus Muzot,* 169–70.

17. Rätus Luck, *Rilkes Schweizer Vortragsreise,* 230.

18. Richard Muther, a Breslau professor of literature, was editing a series of monographs on the arts and commissioned from Rilke a book about Rodin. Rilke, who at the time was in dire financial need, departed for Paris on 26 August 1902.

19. Rilke to Andreas-Salomé, 15 August 1903, *R–AS Briefwechsel,* 110.

20. Rilke to Clara Rilke, 2 September 1902, *GB* 1:37–38.

21. "Und nun sah ich das Haar, . . . es hatte etwas Scheues und Rühren-

des, es war Stubenhaar, im Zimmer gewaschen, verwöhnt von der Wärme der Kissen" (*SW* 6:973).

22. "Und der Mund hat eine Sprache, deren Klang gut, nahe und voll Jugend ist. So ist auch das Lachen, dieses verlegene und zugleich fröliche Lachen eines schön beschenkten Kindes." Rilke to Clara Rilke, 2 September 1902, *GB* 1:37–38.

23. "Ein künfliges Jahrhundert, ein Mann ohne Zeitgenossen." Rilke to A. Holitscher, 1902, quoted in Marga Bauer, *Rainer Maria Rilke und Frankreich* (Bern, 1931), 8.

24. The image of Rodin as an "unreflecting" natural genius who did little to theorize about his work has become accepted in art history. See, e.g., Anne Wagner's article on Rodin in *Eroticism and the Body Politic,* ed. Lynn Hunt (Baltimore, 1991).

25. "Ce n'est pas seulement pour faire une étude, que je suis venu chez vous,—c'était pour vous demander: comment faut-il vivre? Et vous m'avez répondu: en travaillant." Rilke to Rodin, Paris 1902, quoted in Bauer, *Rilke und Frankreich,* 10.

26. Rilke to Andreas-Salomé, 15 August 1903, *R–AS Briefwechsel,* 110.

27. Rilke to Hermann Pongs, 21 October 1925, *Briefe aus Muzot,* 320–37; Rilke to Clara Rilke, 5 September 1902, *Briefe aus den Jahren 1902–1906,* 35.

28. Rilke to Arpad Weixlgärtner, 12 April 1920, quoted in Luck, *Rilkes Schweizer Vortragsreise,* 176.

29. The first separate publication of the letters, *Lettres sur Cézanne,* was organized by Rilke's French translator Maurice Betz in 1944, which was followed in 1945 by a Dutch translation by C. W. Sangster, *Brieven over Cézanne.* The first German publication (*Briefe über Cezanne*) was edited by Clara Rilke in 1952, and the complete edition, published by Insel, appeared in 1962, after her death.

30. Rilke remarked after looking at Cézanne's painting *Montaigne Sainte-Victoire* that no one had seen mountains in such a way since Moses. "Only a saint can be as bound to his God as Cézanne is to his work," he wrote. Reference in Schnack, *Chronik* 1:373; complete text in Harry Graf Kessler, "Aus den Tagebüchern . . . ," in *Jahresbuch der deutschen Schillergesellschaft* 12 (1968): 48.

31. Rilke to Clara Rilke, 18 October 1907, in Rilke, *Briefe über Cézanne,* 48.

32. Rilke to Eva Cassirer, 18 October 1907, *Briefe über Cézanne,* 48.

33. Rilke to Marie von Thurn und Taxis, 14 August 1913, *Rilke, Marie von Thurn und Taxis: Briefwechsel* 1:309; Rilke to Eva Cassirer, 17 September 1913, *GB* 3:298–300; Rilke to Eva Cassirer, 2 January 1914, *Briefe 1907-14,* 324–28.

34. Maxim Gorky, *Erinnerungen an Tolstoi, Der neue Merkur,* Munich, 1920, 2d ed. 1921.

35. Rilke to Mary Dobrzensky, 11 March 1921, quoted in Luck, *Rilkes Schweizer Vortragsreise,* 129–30; see also Rilke to Lily Ziegler, 14 March 1921, and to Rudolf Zimmermann, 17 April 1921, *Briefe in 3 Bd.* (Leipzig, 1987), 2:674–75.

36. Rilke to Rudolf Zimmermann, 17 April 1921, *Briefe in 3 Bd.* 2:674.

37. Rilke to Mary Dobrzensky, 11 March 1921, quoted in Luck, "Improvisationen," 129. Characteristically, Gorky's reflections about Tolstoy's personality interested Rilke much more than the countless reviews and critical analyses of him as a writer.

38. Gorky, "Lev Tolstoy," 92.

39. Schill, "Erinnerungen," *Rilke und Rußland,* 446. Vasily Yanchevetsky entitled his reminiscences of Rilke "Der Gottsucher." It was not only Rilke's Russian friends who saw him as a "God-seeker," however. But even though Rilke was greatly irritated that such an image was promoted in Denmark by his friend Ellen Key, he never objected to this reputation among his Russian friends. For an account of Rilke's religious quest before Russia, see Wolfram Legner, "The Religion of Rainer Maria Rilke before His Visits to Russia," *Monatshefte für Deutschunterricht* 30 (1938): 440–53.

40. Gorky, "Lev Tolstoy," 93.

41. Ibid., 97.

42. Ibid., 130.

CHAPTER SEVEN

1. The idea of visiting Tolstoy was Andreas-Salomé's. She had tried to see the writer when she visited Russia in 1897, but Tolstoy was ill, and the meeting did not take place.

2. Andreas-Salomé, "Leo Tolstoi, unser Zeitgenosse," 1151, 138, appendix.

3. A. S. Suvorin, *Diary* (Moscow-Petrograd, 1923), 263.

4. Andreas-Salomé, "Leo Tolstoi, unser Zeitgenosse," 1148. Andreas-Salomé first used the explanation of inner conflicts as a primary source of creative energy in her psychobiography of Nietzsche (see *Nietzsche,* 114). She continued to use and develop this principle in her later psychoanalytical practice and in her writings on Rilke and Tolstoy.

5. E. Zabel, *Russische Literaturbilde* (Berlin, 1899), 225.

6. See S. Abarbarchuk, "Lev Tolstoi v fotografiiakh," *Novoe russkoe slovo,* 5 April 1991. These photographers were S. Levitsky, V. Prokudin-Gorsky, and Karl Bulla, as well as the professionals of the Moscow photo atelier Sherrer, Nabholtz and Co. The artists who were frequent guests at Tol-

stoy's were I. Kramskoy, N. Ge, I. Repin, L. Pasternak, and P. Trubetskoy, among others.

7. The news of Tolstoy's death spread several days before he actually died. Tolstoy's death had been falsely reported on several occasions before. On 15 September 1900 Rilke noted in his *Worpswede Diary,* in response to Andreas-Salomé's note about Tolstoy's illness: "Vielleicht haben wir doch Abschied genommen von ihm" [Perhaps we have taken leave of him]. *Rilke–Andreas-Salomé,* 46.

8. Rilke to Clara Rilke, 18 November 1910, in Schnack, *Chronik* 1:358–59.

9. Rilke to Lotte Hepner, 8 November 1915, *GB* 2:515.

10. Rilke to Frieda von Bülow, 22 April 1899, *Briefe u. Tagebücher,* 10.

11. Rilke brought with him to Moscow recommendations from Pasternak's friends in Germany, asking Pasternak to introduce him to Tolstoy. For Leonid Pasternak's work with Tolstoy on the novel *Resurrection,* see L. Pasternak, "Kak sozdavalos *Voskresenie,*" in *L. N. Tolstoy v vospominaniakh sovremennikov,* 2 vols. (Moscow, 1978), 2: 165–72.

12. *Le Temps,* 22 January 1898.

13. Gorky, 126.

14. Quoted in Simmons, *Leo Tolstoy,* 580–81.

15. Gorky, "Lev Tolstoy," 107.

16. Simmons, *Leo Tolstoy,* 580.

17. Rilke to Phia Rilke, 29 April 1898, quoted in Schnack, *Chronik* 1:84.

18. Rilke to Charles Du Bos, 30 January 1925, in Du Bos, *Journal 1924–1925* (Paris, 1931), 286 ff.

19. Rilke to Tolstoy, 31 December 1899, *Rilke und Rußland,* 112.

20. See Tolstoy to Rilke, 13 [25] September 1899, ibid., 109–10.

21. Rilke to Schill, 20 May 1900, ibid., 157; Rilke to Phia Rilke, 20 May 1900, in Brutzer, "Rilkes russische Reisen," 49; Rilke, *Worpswede Diary,* entries for 5 September and 3 October 1900, *Briefe u. Tagebücher,* 308; Rilke to Andreas-Salomé, 15 September 1900, *Tagebücher,* 234–37; Rilke to Suvorin, 5 March 1902, *Rilke und Rußland,* 336; Luck, "Improvisationen"; Maurice Betz, *Rilke Vivant,* 153; and Du Bos, *Extraits d'un journal, 1908–1928* (Paris, 1931), 286–88. Rätus Luck's commentary on Rilke's improvisations during his 1919 Swiss lecture tour provides perhaps the most telling evidence of Tolstoy's influence.

22. In recent American scholarship, the style of Rilke's letters about Tolstoy have been discussed by Reshetylo-Rothe, *Rilke and Russia,* 185; and Brodsky, *Russia in the Works of Rilke,* 171. The most exhaustive analysis has come from the Russian scholar Konstantin Azadovsky, whose essay "R. M. Ril'ke i L. N. Tolstoj" situates Rilke's relationship to Tolstoy in the context of his broader philosophical and aesthetic views. The critic A. G. Berëzina offers a reading in which Rilke figures as an unquestioning admirer of Tol-

stoy in his *Poezia i proza molodogo Ril'ke* (Leningrad, 1985). Berëzina's approach has been criticized by V. G. Admoni and K. M. Azadovsky in *Izvestia ANSSR: Literature and Language Series* 45, no. 5 (1986): 458–61.

23. E.M. Butler, "Rilke and Tolstoy," *Modern Language Review* 35 (1940): 496.

24. For Rilke's "improvisations" on Tolstoy, see Luck, *Rilkes Schweizer Vortragsreise 1919*, 126–32.

25. The Pasternaks were traveling to their native southern town, Odessa, for their annual vacation. On the platform, in front of the train, the ten-year-old Boris Pasternak saw Rilke for the first and last time. He described the meeting in his autobiographical *Safe Conduct*, portraying Rilke as an unusually gentle-looking young man, dressed in loden coat and speaking German with an unfamiliar accent. In *Ob iskusstve* (Moscow, 1990), 36.

26. Andreas-Salomé, *Lebensrückblick*, 117.

27. The revisionist feminist rereading of Phia Rilke's role in her son's life has been getting attention in recent years. Phia Rilke is now believed to have been an aspiring, able woman whose talents could not have developed in middle-class German Prague. See Tineke Ritmeester, "Heterosexism, Misogyny, and Mother-Hatred in Rilke Scholarship: The Case of Sophie Rilke-Entz (1851–1931)," in *Women in German Yearbook 6: Feminist Studies and German Culture*, ed. Jeanette Clausen and Helen Cafferty (New York, 1991), 63–81.

28. Rilke to Phia Rilke, 2 June 1900, in Brutzer, "Rilkes russiche Reisen," 49.

29. Rilke to Schill, *Rilke und Rußland*, 158.

30. In chap. 7 of her *Russia in the Works of Rilke*, Brodsky analyzes the two *Tolstoi-Schlüße* as self-contained entities. She does not discuss, however, the thematic continuity between the *Tolstoi-Schlüße* and the legend of the prodigal son, my study's main concern.

31. Although Rilke left open the question of Malte's end in the novel itself, he made it clear in his letters that Malte's outcome was tragic. Writing to Clara Rilke on 19 October 1907, he remarked: "Das die neue errungene Freiheit sich gegen ihn wandete und ihn, den Wehrlosen zerriß . . . " [His newly acquired freedom turned against him and tore him, helpless, apart] (*Briefe* 1:195). On 8 September 1908, he once again wrote: "Der Tod Brigges: das war Cézannes Leben, das Leben seiner dreißig letzten Jahre" [Brigge's death: it was Cézanne's life, the life of his last thirty years] (*Briefe* 1:235). In a letter to Andreas-Salomé of 28 December 1911, Rilke called Malte "der Untergegangene" (the annihilated one), someone who "mit den Kräften und Gegenständen meines Lebens den immensen Aufwand seines Untergangs betrieben [hat]" [managed the immense display of his demise with the help of my life forces and circumstances] (*Briefe* 1:300). Of partic-

ular interest is Rilke's draft of the novel's beginning, which was originally meant to frame the narrative. The narrator in the draft remembered Malte as someone who was no longer alive: "Wenn ich mich zwinge an diesen Menschen zu denken,—der eine Weile mit mir gelebt hat und eines Tages mein Leben verlassen hat, leise wie man ein Theater verläßt, bei offener Bühne . . . " [When I make myself think about this man—who lived with me for a while and one day left my life, quietly like a man leaves the theater during the performance . . .] (*SW* 6:949).

32. According to Ernst Zinn, Rilke gathered his information about Tolstoy's life from Pavel Biriukov's biography of the writer, *Leo Tolstoï, vie et oeuvre: Memoires, souvenirs, lettres, extraits du journal intime, notes et documents biographiques* (Paris, 1906–8).

33. " . . . daß er die ganze Welt beunruhigte um seiner Ruhe willen" (*SW* 6:970).

34. *Malte Laurids Brigge,* Herder trans., 210.

35. The disappearance of the father from Rilke's parable may justifiably be seen as Rilke's response to the "patricidal" Oedipal predilection of his age. It parallels contemporary works of which he was unquestionably aware: Dostoyevsky's *Brothers Karamazov,* Kafka's "The Judgment," Gide's *Return of the Prodigal Son,* and Franz Werfel's *Not the Murderer, the Victim Is Guilty.*

36. ". . . daß er sich bangsam zu dem fertigen Gott entsloß, der gleich zu haben war, zu dem verabredeten Gott derer, die keinen machen können und doch einen brauchen" [that he anxiously attached himself to the readymade God, the foretold God of those who are incapable of making one themselves but need one nonetheless] (*SW* 6:970).

37. "Dies alles noch einmal und nun wirklich auf sich zu nehmen, war der Grund, weshalb der Entfremdete heimkehrte" (*SW* 6:945).

CHAPTER EIGHT

1. Between May and November 1926, Rilke and Pasternak exchanged one letter each; Tsvetaeva sent nine letters and a postcard to Rilke; Rilke sent six to her (although she later claimed to have received seven and continued to call "letters" all of her subsequent writings dedicated to Rilke). The collection of these letters, edited by Konstantin M. Azadovsky, Yelena Pasternak, and Yevgenij Pasternak, has been published in German and Russian: *Rainer Maria Rilke, Marina Zwetajewa, Boris Pasternak: Briefwechsel* (Frankfurt am Main, 1983) (hereafter *R–Z–P Briefwechsel*); and *Rainer Maria Ril'ke, Boris Pasternak, Marina Tsvetaeva: Pis'ma 1926 goda* (Moscow, 1990) (hereafter *Pis'ma*). There is also an English translation: *Letters, Summer 1926: Pasternak, Tsvetaeva, Rilke,* trans. Margaret

Wettlin and Walter Arndt (New York, 1985). There are some textual discrepancies between the German and Russian editions of the letters; thus to avoid misunderstanding, all quotations will follow the letters as published in the original language. Rilke's correspondence with Tsvetaeva will be cited from the Frankfurt edition and Pasternak's and Tsvetaeva's letters will follow the Moscow edition. The English translation of letters is selective and occasionally departs from the original. Selections from these letters have also been published in French, *Correspondance à trois: Été 1926* (Paris, 1983); and in Italian, *Il settimo sogno: Lettre 1926* (Rome, 1980). For information on how these letters finally surfaced from the archives, see Patricia P. Brodsky, "On Daring to Be a Poet: Rilke and Marina Cvetaeva."

2. "Und nun will ich gleich versichern, wie die Ihre und alles, was das alte Rußland betrifft (die unvergeßliche heimliche Skaska [Märchen]), und wie alles, woran Sie mich in Ihrem Schreiben erinnern, mir nah, lieb und heilig geblieben ist, für immer eingelassen in die Grundmauern meines Lebens!" Rilke to L. Pasternak, 14 March 1926, *R–Z–P Briefwechsel*, 59.

3. For a historical survey of Russian culture in exile, see Marc Raeff, "To Keep and Cherish: What Is Russian Culture?" in *Russia Abroad: A Cultural History of Russian Emigration, 1919–1939* (New York, 1990).

4. Friedrich von Oppeln-Bronikowski, for example, used such terms as "slawischer Einschlag seines Empfindens" and "starke slawische Sympathieen" to describe Rilke's early work. "Rainer Maria Rilke: Eine kritische Würdigung (2 Teil)," *Xenien*, no. 10 (1909): 144.

5. Rilke had studied the impact of the Golden Horde on Russian cultural development, particularly on the emergence and evolution of Russian icon painting, which he later represented in his *Book of Hours*.

6. Rilke to L. Pasternak, 14 March 1926, *R–Z–P Briefwechsel*, 60.

7. Rilke to Karl von der Heydt, 3 May 1907, in *Briefe 1906–1907* (Leipzig, 1930), 253–54.

8. Rilke to Rudolf Zimmermann, 17 April 1921, *Briefe* 2:674.

9. Rilke, *Briefe u. Tagebücher*, 140. See also Rainer Maria Rilke, *Briefe zur Politik*, ed. Joachim W. Storck (Frankfurt am Main, 1992). Theodor Adorno discusses the problematics of the indirect political impact of literary art in "Rede über Lyrik und Gesellschaft," in *Noten zur Literatur* (Frankfurt am Main, 1958), 73–104.

10. "[Gorki] spricht als Demokrat auch von der Kunst, als Unzufriedener, eng und schnell Urteilender; mit Urteilen, in denen die Irrtüymer ganz aufgelöst sind, so daß man sie nicht herausfischen kann." In Rilke to Karl von der Heydt, 3 May 1907, 254 (cit. n. 7).

11. "Ist er wirklich noch . . . ein russischer Mensch? Ich fürchte, er ist sehr . . . 'Westler' und verdorben durch den westlichen Ruhm und den internationalen Sozialismus." Rilke to L. Pasternak, 10 December 1906, *Rilke und Rußland*, 353–54.

12. Maxim Gorky, "The Old Man and the New," quoted by Nina Gourfinkel in *Gorky* (London, 1960), 197–98.

13. "Ich werde nichts feiern in meinem Hotelzimmer wäre nicht der Gedanke an das herrliche Rußland, ich hätte keinen, der nur zuversichtlich und erbaulich wäre. Wie erkenn ich's nun wieder. Dieser Anruf der Regierung Vorgestern, mit der Überschrift: 'an alle, die leiden und ausgenutzt worden sind' . . . dies als Sprache einer Regierung: neue Zeit, Zukunft, endlich." Rilke to Katherina Kippenberg, 17 December 1917, in *Rainer Maria Rilke, Katherina Kippenberg: Briefwechsel* (Frankfurt, 1954), 257.

14. "Unter dem Vorwand eines großen Umsturzes arbeitet die alte Gesinnungslosigkeit weiter und tut mit sich selber unter der roten Fahne groß." Rilke to Anni Mewes, 19 December 1918, in *GB* 4:215–16.

15. Rilke received a copy of the poem from the editor of the publishing house, Reinhold von Walter, in 1921. In the 1920s and 1930s the so-called Eurasian movement emerged briefly in the Russian émigré community as a new form of Russian messianism. Eurasians claimed that under Bolshevik rule Russia was moving toward harmonious coexistence with the Asian and European peoples who lived in its territory and who had been brought together by the medieval Mongol rule. It was from this unity that salvation was to come.

16. "So wie er sich nach dem Krieg unwiederstehlich nach Paris gedrängt fühlte bis dieser Wünsch erfühlt wurde, so war er jetzt von der Sehnsucht gequält, in sich das 'russische Wunder' seiner Jugend wieder aufleben zu lassen in dem er die Erlebnisse der fernen Reisen von 1899 und 1900 wieder erneuerte." Maurice Betz, *Rilke in Paris* (Zurich, 1948), 100. Unknown by him, Rilke was suffering from leukemia, which at first he took for indisposition. He spent most of his time between his secluded residence Muzot and the health resort Val-Mont.

17. The cultural center of Russian emigration had moved from Berlin to Paris after the political and economic situation in the Weimar Republic deteriorated and became more ominous. French emigration policy was more liberal toward Russian refugees, and Russians enjoyed full residential rights there, with the exception of having to have work permits. Later, with the economic depression of the 1930s, there was a chauvinistic backlash, forcing many of the resident aliens to seek passage to America and England. For further details, see Raeff, *Russia Abroad*, 37.

18. Rilke to Nanny Wunderly-Volkart, 3 March 1925, in *Rilke, Nanny Wunderly-Volkart: Briefwechsel* (Frankfurt am Main, 1977), 2:1047–48.

19. Rilke thought highly of Bunin's story "Mitia's Love." See K. Saparov, "R. M. Ril'ke o povesti I. A. Bunina 'Mitina liubov'," in *Voprosy literatury*, no. 9 (1966): 247–49.

20. A few years later, Sazonova remembered her conversations and cor-

respondence with Rilke during his last Parisian stay. The poet seemed to her "to be drawn to Russia (as to the homeland of the Slavic world) by some mysterious blood connection full of love." Julia L. Sazonova, "Pis'ma Rainera Maria Ril'ke," *Novy zhurnal*, no. 5 (1943): 281–92. On the Sakharoffs, see Klaus W. Jonas, *Rilke und Clotilde Sakharoff: Ein unveröffentlichen Briefwechsel*, in *Monatshefte für deutschen Unterricht, deutsche Sprache und Literatur* 58 (1966).

21. "Surfacing on the stage was the arrogance of the mechanical laws of gravity, which took control over human destiny and hypocritically consented to express the futile details of the dear and sad vicissitudes of the human fate." Rilke to Nanny Wunderly-Volkart, 5 March 1925, in Schnack, *Chronik* 2:973; see also 972.

22. The estate mentioned by Rilke was Nikolai Tolstoy's. For Rilke's further reflections on puppets and puppet-play, see "Puppen," *SW* 6:1063–74.

23. *Duino Elegies*, trans. MacIntyre, 31.

24. *Malte Laurids Brigge*, Herter trans., 197. Malte imagines the actress Eleonora Duse holding up a poem as a mask.

25. As Rilke wrote of Malte's childhood. Ibid., 215.

26. "Dafür hab ich hier, zum ersten mal seit dem Krieg, die wirklichverstörenden Veränderungen im Tempo und in der Natur des täglichen Lebens zu erfahren bekommen. . . . Das Amerikanische hat die Oberhand oder das Bolschewistische. . . ." Rilke to Marianne Weininger, 26 June 1925, in Schnack, *Chronik* 2:987.

27. The two poems were Pasternak's "Nuit accablante" ("Dymnaya Noch"), from *My Sister—Life* (*Sestra moig zhizn'*), and "Départ," both translated by Hélène Iswolsky, *Commerce*, no. 6 (1925). Rilke might also have seen Pasternak's five Russian poems in Ilya Ehrenburg's anthology *Portrety russkikh poetov* (Berlin, 1922). Rilke's letter had been circulated among Pasternak's sisters before its content was relayed to Boris himself. Leonid decided to keep the original for fear that it would be either confiscated or lost in the mail.

28. Boris Pasternak to Rilke, 12 April 1926, *R–Z–P Briefwechsel*, 76–77; Christopher Barnes, "Boris Pasternak and Rainer Maria Rilke: Some Missing Links"; and Boris Pasternak, *Safe Conduct*.

Quite possibly, Pasternak wrote Rilke a letter between 1911 and 1913 which he never sent. Among his early papers are translations of Rilke's poems from *The Book of Hours* as well as individual poems "Die Stille," "Musik," "Der Schutzengel," and "Die Engel." See Christopher Barnes, *Boris Pasternak* (London, 1989), 110. "I owe you the most fundamental features of my character, the ways of my spiritual being. They are your creations," wrote Pasternak in his letter to Rilke of 12 April 1926. Although Azadovsky insists that it was Marina Tsvetaeva who "grasped Rilke's thoughts and developed the picture that was sketched by him" ("Einleitung," *R–Z–P Briefwechsel,* 45), I believe that Boris Pasternak better understood Rilke's essence when he wrote that Rilke overcame German romanticism in his work. See Barnes, "Pasternak and Rilke."

29. Rilke, *Poems from the "Book of Hours,"* Deutsch trans., 39.

30. See also Pasternak to Raisa Nikolaevna Lomonosova, 28 October 1927, Leeds Russian Archive. Quoted in Barnes, *Boris Pasternak,* 396.

31. B. Pasternak to Rilke, 12 April 1926, *R–Z–P Briefwechsel,* 76.

32. Pasternak, "Neskol'ko polozhenii," in *Boris Pasternak oblskusstve,* ed. E. B. Pasternak and E. V. Pasternak (Moscow, 1990), 146.

33. Kathrine Tiernan O'Connor, "Reflections on the Genesis of the Pasternak-Tsvetaeva-Rilke Correspondence," in *Festschrift in Honor of Vladimir Markov,* ed. John Malmstad and Ronald Vroon (Moscow, 1993). Pasternak mentions his reluctance to disturb Rilke in his letter of 12 April 1926.

34. Boris Pasternak, *Vozdushnye puti: Proza raznykh let* (Moscow, 1982), 479–80; B. Pasternak to Rilke, 12 April 1926, *R–Z–P Briefwechsel,* 75.

35. B. Pasternak to L. Pasternak, *Pis'ma,* 142; B. Pasternak, *Vozdushnye puti,* 479–83. Pasternak always imagined, he wrote, that in his original efforts and in his artistic work he was only translating or diversifying Rilke's own motifs, that he was adding nothing to Rilke's originality and was always swimming in his waters. Pasternak to Michel Aucouturier, 4 February 1959, in M. Aucouturier, *Pasternak par lui-même* (Paris, 1963), 34; see also B. Pasternak to L. Pasternak, June 1926, *R–Z–P Briefwechsel,* 177.

36. The more self-contained the life of the poet is, Pasternak claimed, the more collective, the more literary, is its story. "In a genius, the realm of the subconscious cannot be measured." *Safe Conduct,* quoted in *R–Z–P Briefwechsel,* 264.

37. Boris Pasternak, "Lyudi i polozhenia," in *Russkie pisateli—lauriaty Nobelevskoi premii* (Moscow, 1991), 242.

38. Pasternak's rendering of Rilke's *Second Duino Elegy* was apparently lost before World War I, and his remaining translations are predominantly from the earlier cycles.

In a provocative article that appeared in the journal *Sovremennye zapiski* in 1929, the leading art and literary critic V. Weidlé pointed out that the Russians had always been inspired by foreign models whose milieu they tended to disregard. Weidlé cited Pushkin's reading of Byron and the symbolists' fascination with Baudelaire as characteristic of this general trend. The question of Tsvetaeva's and Pasternak's putative "bad taste" (*durnoi vkus*) in choosing Rilke, and of Rilke's reciprocal "poor" choice of Russian models, is not new in criticism. It had already been raised by the Russian émigré critic Georgi Adamovich, among others. For a more recent discussion, see Lev Losev's "Bedstvie srednego vkusa," and Walter Arndt's "Pasternak's Versions of Early Rilke Poems," in *Boris Pasternak: Norwich Symposia on Russian Literature and Culture*, ed. Lev Losev (Norwich, Vt., 1991).

39. See K. A. J. Batterby, *Rilke and France: A Study in Poetic Development* (Oxford, 1966).

CHAPTER NINE

1. Leonid Pasternak reprimanded his son for the "indelicacy" of his request. "Is it possible that exchanges of this kind are common between you, the poets?" he asked. "We, the 'old ones,' are always 'careful' when it concerns others, possibly unnecessarily so." L. Pasternak to B. Pasternak, 23 April 1926, *R–Z–P Briefwechsel*, 80.

2. Pasternak to Selma Ruoff, 12 May 1956, *Voprosy literatury*, no. 9 (1972): 170. The German edition of letters has Pasternak writing to his sister, "Ach, was für ein Künstler sie ist! Ich liebe sie mehr als alles auf der Welt, mehr als Rilke." B. Pasternak to Josephine Pasternak, 28 March 1926, *R–Z–P Briefwechsel*, 71. The Russian version reads: "Akh, kakoi ona artist, ikak ja ne magy nel'ubit'eio sil'nee vsegona svete, kok Ril'ke." *Pis'ma*, 58. My translation is of the Russian original.

3. Rilke to Tsvetaeva, 3 May 1926, *R–Z–P Briefwechsel*, 104.

4. Tsvetaeva to Rilke, 9 May 1926, *R–Z–P Briefwechsel*, 107.

5. "I felt relieved at the thought that Tsvetaeva is in correspondence with you because, even if I cannot replace Tsvetaeva, Tsvetaeva can replace me." *Vozdushnye puti: Proza razynykh let* (Moscow, 1982), 479–80.

6. B. Pasternak to Tsvetaeva, 23 May 1926, *Pis'ma*, 110. See also Tsvetaeva to Iuri Ivask, 8 March 1935, in *Pis'ma Tsvetaevoi Ivasku, 1933–1935*, ed. Iuri Ivask (New York, 1956), 222.

7. Tsvetaeva to B. Pasternak, 23 May 1926, *R–Z–P Briefwechsel*, 148. "Du reisest immer. Du lebst nirgends, und mit Russen triffst Du zusammen, die nicht ich sind. Hör, daß Du's weißt: im Rainerland vertrete ich allein Rußland." Tsvetaeva to Rilke, *R–Z–P Briefwechsel*, 233.

8. Olga Hasty suggests that owing to "the brevity of the acquaintance and, perhaps, even more because Cvetaeva's verse—not easy even for a native speaker—proved too difficult for Rilke, he was less affected by the relationship than Cvetaeva." "Marina Cvetaeva's Encounters with Rainer Maria Rilke."

9. Rudolf Kassner, who knew Rilke well, predicted after his death that the "public would receive an overabundance of beautiful letters which he

shared with his friends." Quoted in *Rilke and Benvenuta: An Intimate Correspondence*, ed. Magda von Hattingberg, trans. Joel Agee (New York, 1987), 133.

Tsvetaeva liked to quote this coinage, "naked souls," by Marc Slonim. See *Nashe nasledie*, no. 4 (1991): 46. Azadovsky advises in his introduction to the correspondence that Tsvetaeva's letters do not belong in the category of traditional epistolary prose (*Pis'ma*, 32). G. Gorchakov presents a comprehensive analysis of Tsvetaeva's letter-writing style in his "Marina Tsvetaeva—korrespondent, addressat," *Novyi zhurnal*, no. 167 (June 1987): 151–90; and Svetlana Boym offers a provocative reading of Tsvetaeva's "erotic intersexuality" as the rebellion of a talented femme terrible in "The Death of the Poetess," in *Death in Quotation Marks: Cultural Myth of the Modern Poet* (Cambridge, Mass., 1991), 200–40.

10. Gary Saul Morson examines letters as a "boundary genre" in *The Boundaries of Genre* (Austin, 1981), 48.

11. Rilke to Nanny Wunderly-Volkart, 29 July 1920, quoted in J. R. von Salis, *Rainer Maria Rilke: The Years in Switzerland*, trans. N. K. Cruickshank (Berkeley and Los Angeles, 1966), 242. See, e.g., Rilke's letters to Franz Xaver Kappus, "To the Young Woman," to NN, to Elisabeth Schenk zu Schweinberg, and others. Also, Carl Sieber, "Rainer Maria Rilkes Briefwerk," *Inselschiff* 14 (1933): 236–41.

12. Sazonova, "Pis'ma Rainera Maria Rilke"; Klaus Jonas, "Rilke und die Sakharoffs," *Frankfurter Allgemeine Zeitung*, 28 January 1966, 28.

13. For example, the circumstances of Rilke's correspondence with Regina Ullmann, which lasted from 1908 until his death in 1926, were close to those of his correspondence with Tsvetaeva. Ullmann was a German poet and story writer who had to support her two children on the occasional income from her publications. Destitute and despairing, she turned to Rilke, who helped her to place her writings and wrote an introduction to her volume of poetry. See *Rilkes Briefwechsel mit Regina Ullmann und Ellen Delp* (Frankfurt am Main, 1987).

14. "Lettres à une amie," *Nouvelle revue française*, 1 February 1927, quoted in Betz, 197. Tsvetaeva translated and published one of these letters as *Pis'mo k drugu* (first published in *Volya Rossii*, no. 2, 1929).

15. Rilke to Tsvetaeva, 10 May 1926, *R–Z–P Briefwechsel*, 112.

16. Much has been written on the nature of masks in Rilke's work. David Kleinbard's psychoanalytical treatment is one of the more convincing. See *The Beginning of Terror: A Psychological Study of Rainer Maria Rilke, Life and Work* (New York, 1993).

17. Most of Rilke's epistolary romances started with the desire "to get out." See Storck's introduction to *Rilke and Benvenuta*, 135.

18. Rilke to Tsvetaeva, 19 August 1926, *R–Z–P Briefwechsel*, 237.

19. Rilke grew increasingly alarmed when he noticed that his style began to dominate German poetry. He warned his hagiographers that an artist always had to write in his or her own style, even if idiopathic. He refused to read any criticism about himself, good or bad.

20. In response to Tsvetaeva's words about her children, for example, Rilke told her the story of his own failed marriage and how he regretted the failure of his "long-distance" relationship with his daughter, Ruth. Rilke to Tsvetaeva, 17 May 1926, *R–Z–P Briefwechsel*, 122–26.

21. Tsvetaeva to Rilke, 9 May 1926, *R–Z–P Briefwechsel*, 106; Rilke to Tsvetaeva, 10 May 1926, ibid., 113.

22. Rilke to Tsvetaeva, 17 May 1926, ibid., 125.

23. Joseph Brodsky, "Footnote to a Poem," in *Less than One* (New York, 1986), 211–12. Anna Akhmatova likewise called Tsvetaeva "a mocking bird." Akhmatova, "Tsvetaeva," in *Sochinenia*, 2 vols., 2:208.

24. Tsvetaeva to Nanny Wunderly-Volkart, 17 October 1930, in *Rilke und Zwetaeva: Ein Gespräch in Briefen*, 169.

25. Marina Tsvetaeva, *Izbrannoiproza, 1917–1937*, 2 vols. (New York, 1979), 1:378.

26. Tsvetaeva to Rilke, 9 May 1928, *R–Z–P Briefwechsel*, 107.

27. *Malte Laurids Brigge*, Herter trans. David Kleinbard reads Rilke's novel as a chronicle of growing fear of isolation, in *The Beginning of Terror* (New York, 1993).

28. Wolfgang Leppmann, *Rilke: A Life*, trans. Alan Sheridan (London and New York, 1977), 303.

29. "To be in Rilke's company, to go for a walk with him, talk to him, correspond with him, was to be happy. But everything led back to the one central thing, to poetry." Von Salis, *Rilke: The Years in Switzerland*, 252.

30. Rilke to Tsvetaeva, 10 May 1926, *R–Z–P Briefwechsel*, 112; Rilke to Tsvetaeva, 28 July 1926, ibid., 229 (emphasis added).

31. A few years before the episode with Tsvetaeva, Rilke acknowledged this pattern in his relationships with women. In a letter to Andreas-Salomé, he wrote: "I am terrified when I think how I live from within myself, as if standing at a telescope, always looking for happiness with everyone who comes along; happiness which certainly has not been found with anyone yet. My happiness, the happiness, some day, of my loneliest hours." 21 October 1913, *R–AS Briefwechsel*, 305.

32. Claire Goll, "Rainer Maria Rilke," *Twice a Year: A Book of Literature, the Arts and Civil Liberties*, nos. 5–6 (1940–41): 370.

33. Rilke, *Of Love and Other Difficulties*, trans. John Mood (New York, 1975), 36, 37.

34. But Helene Sword argues that even the most sensitive male allies of the modernist generation failed to adequately represent the female world-

view. She persuasively reveals a hidden "male" agenda in Rilke's treatment of the Leda myth in "Leda and the Modernists," *PMLA* 107, no. 2 (1992): 305–17. But see below, n. 56.

35. Rilke, *The Notebooks of Malte Laurids Brigge*, Herter trans., 176; Rilke to a Young Woman, 20 November 1904, *GB* 1:103–4; Rilke, *Of Love and Other Difficulties*, 35; Princess Marie von Thurn und Taxis, *Erinnerungen an Rainer Maria Rilke* (Frankfurt am Main, 1966), 43.

36. Marie von Thurn und Taxis, *Erinnerungen,* 107.

37. Rilke to Mimi Romanelli, 11 May 1910, in *Gesammelte Briefe,* ed. Rilke-Archiv im Weimar, with Ruth Sieber-Rilke (Frankfurt am Main, 1987), 1:266.

38. A comparison between Rilke's and Nietzsche's views of women is one way of demonstrating how "progressive" Rilke's position on gender issues was for his time. See Klaus Goch, ed., *Nietzsche über die Frauen* (Frankfurt am Main, 1992).

39. Rilke to Tsvetaeva, *R–Z–P Briefwechsel,* 105.

40. All English-language versions of the *Duino Elegies* are from the MacIntyre translation; page numbers are given in the text.

41. Rilke, Sonnet 13, Part 2, trans. Rika Lesser in *Rilke: Between Roots* (Princeton, N.J., 1986), 56.

42. In the letter accompanying the Marina elegy, Rilke abandoned all allegory and explained to her that writing letters had become impossible for him because of his physical condition. Rilke to Tsvetaeva, 8 June 1926, *R–Z–P Briefwechsel,* 158.

43. Rilke, Marina elegy, 52–53.

44. Rilke always distinguished between the elevated singular and the belittling plural uses of the word *god*.

45. Rilke, Marina elegy, 53.

46. Before Tsvetaeva's letters became available, Dieter Bassermann, one of Rilke's most insightful readers, had concluded on the evidence of Rilke's entire oeuvre that in the Marina elegy Rilke answered Tsvetaeva's complaints about her life. Bassermann had mastered the art of guessing the originals to which Rilke was responding in his images. *Der andere Rilke* (Bad Hamburg, 1961), 228–29.

47. Rilke, "Epitaph," *in Rilke: Between Roots*, 29.

48. Tsvetaeva's words quoted in Gorchakov, "Marina Tsvetaeva—korrespondent, adressat," 179.

49. Tsvetaeva to Rilke, 14 July 1926, *R–Z–P Briefwechsel,* 173; Tsvetaeva to Wunderly-Volkart, 29 December 1931, *Ein Gespräch in Briefen,* 182. The Marina elegy was neither Rilke's last poem nor did it belong to the Duino cycle, as Tsvetaeva claimed. Rilke's last major work was a poem dedicated to Erika Mitterer, "Taube die draußen blieb, außer dem Taubenschlag" (*SW* 2:318–19). The poem was written in Ragaz at the time of Rilke's

correspondence with Tsvetaeva (20 July–30 August 1926), and its theme echoed the main message of the elegy to Tsvetaeva.

50. Tsvetaeva to Rilke, 14 June 1926, *R–Z–P Briefwechsel*, 173–74; Tsvetaeva to Pasternak, 25 May 1926, *Pis'ma*, 117; "Rilke ne pishu. Slishkom bol'shoe terzanie, besplodnoe. Menia sbivaet s tolku. Vybivaet iz stikhov. . . . "

51. Tsvetaeva to Anna Tesková, 21 February 1927, *Pis'ma k Anne Teskovoi* (Jerusalem, 1982), 49. The difference between Rilke's and Tsvetaeva's ideals for a poet's life and death remains to be examined. Even though Tsvetaeva insisted that for her no boundary existed between those two existential conditions, she clearly privileged death. Hence her ultimately narcissistic fascination with poets' suicides as their highest artistic creations. See Olga Peters Hasty, "Reading Suicide: Tsvetaeva on Esenin and Maiakovskii," *Slavic Review* 50, no. 4 (1991):838–46. Rilke, on the other hand, insisted that the poet's ideal death continues life's natural cycle. In *The Notebooks of Malte Laurids Brigge*, he created contrasting images of death: old Christoph Detlev's three-day agony spoke to everyone in the village, while the young Malte's disappearance into the city remained unnoticed. In the *Duino Elegies*, the image of "pregnant death" serves to affirm life. Even though there are descriptions of violent deaths in Rilke's work, he did not care for suicides.

52. Angela Livingstone believes that Tsvetaeva had Rilke in mind when she wrote her essays on art in the period between 1926 and 1930. *Art in the Light of Conscience*, 3.

53. Elena Korkina, "Liricheskaia trilogia Tsvetaevoi," in *A Centennial Symposium Dedicated to Marina Tsvetaeva*, ed. Efim Etkind and Svetlana El'nitskaia (Norwich, Vt., 1992), 117. Korkina divides Tsvetaeva's major lyrical poems of 1920–27 into three cycles and analyzes their gradual progression from the rejection of earthly existence to the glorification of nonbeing. See her "Kommentarii," *Marina Tsvetaeva: Stikhotvorenia i poemy* (Leningrad, 1990).

54. See Victoria Schweitzer, *Byt i Bytie Mariny Tsvetaevoi* (Fontanay-aux-Roses, 1988); and Svetlana El'nitskaia, *Poeticheskii mir Mariny Tsvetaevoi* (Vienna, 1990).

55. Tsvetaeva to Pasternak, 1 January 1927, *Pis'ma*, 203; Tsvetaeva to Nanny Wunderly-Volkart, 2 April 1930, *Pis'ma*, 226; also in *Ein Gespräch in Briefen*, 161–62.

56. "His child could not have been a son," Tsvetaeva wrote to Rilke's daughter, Ruth Sieber-Rilke, 24 January 1932, *Ein Gespräch in Briefen*, 189.

57. Tsvetaeva, "Neskol'vo Pusem Rainera Maria," in Tsvetaeva, *Ob Iskusstve* (Moscow, 1991), 288. Joseph Brodsky's reading of Tsvetaeva's "New Year's" is to me the most convincing in its fine tuning to Tsvetaeva's artistic world. And yet Rilke's role remains to be explained.

58. Marina Tsvetaeva, *Stikhotvorenia i poemy* (New York, 1983), 4:382.

59. Anthropologists differ in their definitions of the origins and nature of gift giving. Marcel Mauss describes the potlatch as a rite that implies negative reciprocity: in potlatch rich gifts are extended with the intention of obliging, challenging, or humiliating rivals by making them accept a treasure they are unable to repay. *The Gift, Forms and Functions of Exchange in Archaic Societies,* trans. Ian Cunnison (New York, 1965), 32–33. Lewis Hyde takes a more benign view of the gift-giving ceremony by showing its possible ambivalence. *The Gift: Imagination and the Erotic Life of Property* (New York, 1983), 29–39. It is appropriate to argue in this connection about the self-indulgence of poets' epistolary relationships and the sincerity of their "gifts" of poetry.

60. Tsvetaeva to Wunderly-Volkart, 12 January 1932, *Ein Gespräch in Briefen,* 185.

CONCLUSION

1. Maximillian Voloshin, "Chemu uchat ikony?" *Apollon,* no. 5 (1914): 29.

2. Rilke to Karl von der Heydt, 15 March 1913, *GB* 3:275.

3. Kahler, *Tower and Abyss: An Inquiry into the Transformationn of Man* (New York, 1957), 154, 98.

4. André Gide, *Dostoevsky,* trans. Vareese (New York, 1961), 50.

Selected Bibliography

PRIMARY SOURCES

Works by Rilke

Sämtliche Werke. Edited by Ruth Sieber-Rilke and Ernst Zinn. 6 vols. Frankfurt am Main, 1955–66.
  This is the standard edition of Rilke's works.
Das Igorlied: Eine Heldendichtung. Frankfurt am Main, 1960.
Das Testament. Edited by Ernst Zinn. Frankfurt am Main, 1974.

Collections of Rilke's Letters and Diaries

Gesammelte Briefe. Edited by Ruth Sieber-Rilke and Carl Sieber. 6 vols. Leipzig, 1939–40.
  Vol. 1: *Briefe aus den Jahren 1892 bis 1904*. 1939.
  Vol. 2: *Briefe aus den Jahren 1904 bis 1907*. 1939.
  Vol. 3: *Briefe aus den Jahren 1907 bis 1914*. 1939.
  Vol. 4: *Briefe aus den Jahren 1914 bis 1921*. 1938.
  Vol. 5: *Briefe aus Muzot 1921 bis 1926*. 1940.
  Vol. 6: *Briefe an seinen Verleger 1906 bis 1926*. 1936.
    This is the standard edition of the letters.
Briefe. Vol. 1: *1897 bis 1914*. Vol. 2: *1914 bis 1926*. Edited by Ruth Sieber-Rilke and Karl Altheim. Wiesbaden, 1950.
Briefe 1902–1906. Leipzig, 1929.
Briefe aus den Jahren 1906 bis 1907. Leipzig, 1930.
Briefe aus den Jahren 1914 bis 1921. Leipzig, 1937.
    This collection contains letters not published in *Gesammelte Briefe*.
Briefe und Tagebücher aus der Frühzeit: 1899 bis 1902. Leipzig, 1933.

Briefe über Cézanne. Edited by Clara Rilke. Frankfurt am Main, 1983.

"Ein Brief Rilkes an einen russischen Aristokraten." *Rigasche Rundschau*, 5 January 1927, 2.

Hugo von Hofmannsthal, Rainer Maria Rilke: Briefwechsel, 1899–1925. Edited by Rudolf Hirsch and Ingeborg Schnack. Frankfurt am Main, 1978.

Nebesnaya arka: Marina Tsvetaeva: Rainer Maria Ril'ke. Edited by Konstantin Azadovsky. St. Petersburg, 1992.

Rainer Maria Rilke—Lou Andreas-Salomé: Briefwechsel. Edited by Ernst Pfeiffer. Rev. ed. Frankfurt am Main, 1979.

Rainer Maria Rilke, Marie von Thurn und Taxis: Briefwechsel. 2 vols. Edited by Ernst Zinn. Zurich, 1951.

Rainer Maria Rilke, Marina Zwetajewa, Boris Pasternak: Briefwechsel. Edited by Yevgenij Pasternak, Yelena Pasternak, and Konstantin Azadovsky. Frankfurt am Main, 1983. This correspondence has also been published in Russian: *Rainer Maria Ril'ke, Boris Pasternak, Marina Tsvetaeva: Pis'ma 1926 goda*. Moscow, 1990. And in English: *Letters, Summer 1926: Pasternak, Tsvetaeva, Rilke*. Translated by Margaret Wettlin and Walter Arndt. New York, 1985.

Rainer Maria Rilke und Marina Zwetajewa: Ein Gespräch in Briefen. Edited by Konstantin Azadovsky. Frankfurt am Main, 1992.

Rilke und Rußland: Briefe, Erinnerungen, Gedichte. Edited by Konstantin Azadovsky. Leipzig, 1986.

Tagebücher aus der Frühzeit. Edited by Ernst Zinn. Frankfurt am Main, 1973.

Works by Lou Andreas-Salomé

"Aus der Geschichte Gottes." *Neue deutsche Rundschau* 8 (1897): 1211–20.

"Das russische Heiligenbild und sein Dichter." *Vossische Zeitung*, Sonntagsbeilage, sec. 2, 1 January 1898.

"Jesus der Jude." *Neue deutsche Rundschau* 7 (April 1896): 342–51.

"Leo Tolstoy, unser Zeitgenosse." *Neue deutsche Rundschau* 11 (November 1898): 1145–55.

Lebensrückblick: Grundriß einiger Lebenserinnerungen. Edited by Ernst Pfeiffer. 2d ed. Frankfurt am Main, 1974.

Rainer Maria Rilke. Leipzig, 1928.

"Russische Dichtung und Kultur, I." *Cosmopolis* 7 (August 1897): 571–80.

"Russische Dichtung und Kultur, II." *Cosmopolis* 8 (September 1897): 872–85.

"Russische Philosophie und semitische Geist." *Die Zeit* (Vienna), 15 January 1898, 40.

SECONDARY SOURCES

Works Primarily on Rilke and Russia

Anderson, Robert V. "The Concept of Creativity in the Thought of Rilke and Berdyaev." *Personalist* 43, no. 2 (1962): 226–32.

Andreas-Salomé, Lou. "Rilke in Rußland." *Russische Blätter,* no. 1 (October 1928): 14–17.

Azadovsky, Konstantin M. "Briefe nach Rußland: S. W. Maljutin im Briefwechsel zwischen Rilke und Ettinger." In *Rilke-Studien: Zu Werk und Wirkungsgeschichte,* 197–208. Berlin and Weimar, 1976.

———. "R. M. Ril'ke i A. N. Benois: Perepiska 1900–1902 gg." In *Pamjatniki kul'tury,* 75-105. Moscow, 1977.

———. "R. M. Rilke—perevodchik 'Slova o polku Igoreve.'" In *Kul'turnoje nasledie Drevnej Rusi: Istoki, Stanovlenije, Tradicii,* 217–24. Moscow, 1976.

———. "Rajner Maria Ril'ke: Pis'ma v Rossiju." *Voprosy literatury,* no. 9 (1975): 214–42.

———. "Ril'ke i Djagilev." In *Sergej Djagilev i russkoje iskusstvo,* 2:58, 376–79. Edited by I. S. Zilberstein and V. A. Samkov. Moscow, 1982.

———. "Rilke und Rußland: Zum 100. Geburtstag des Dichters." *Sowjetunion Heute,* 16 December 1975, 30–31.

———. "R. M. Ril'ke i L. N. Tolstoj." *Russkaja literatura,* no. 1 (1969): 129–51.

Azadovsky, Konstantin, and L. N. Chertkov. "R. M. Ril'ke i A. M. Gorkij." *Russkaja literatura,* no. 4 (1967): 185–91.

———. "Russkije vstrechi." In *Rajner Marija Ril'ke: Worpswede, August Rodin, Pis'ma, Stikhi,* edited by I. D. Rozhanskij. Moscow, 1971.

Azadovsky, Konstantin M., E. V. Pasternak, and E. B. Pasternak. "Iz perepiski Ril'ke, Tsvetaevoj i Pasternaka v 1926 godu." *Voprosy literatury,* no. 4 (1978): 233–81.

Barnes, Christopher S. *Boris Pasternak: A Literary Biography.* Vol. 1: *1890–1928.* Cambridge, 1989.

———. "Boris Pasternak and Rainer Maria Rilke: Some Missing Links." *Forum for Modern Language Studies* 8, no. 1 (1972): 61–78.

Blech, Hermann. "Rilke, Rußland und die slawische Melodie." *Stimmen der Freunde,* edited by Gerd Buchheit. Freiburg im Breisgau, 1931.

Böhme, Marion. "Rilke und die russische Literatur: Neue Beiträge mit besonderer Berücksichtigung der Rezeption Rilkes in Rußland." Ph.D. diss., Vienna, 1966.

Boutchik, V., E. L. Stahl, and S. Mitchell. "Texts of Rilke's Letters to Helene." *Oxford Slavonic Papers* 9 (1960): 146–64.

Brandenburg, Hans-Christian. "Rußland—das 'Gottesland' des jungen Rilkes." *Sudetenland,* no. 3 (1961): 193–98.

Brodsky, Patricia Pollock. "On Daring to Be a Poet: Rilke and Marina Cvetaeva." *Germano-Slavica* 3, no. 4 (1980): 261–69.

———. "Rilke and Russian Art." *Germano-Slavica* 2, no. 6 (Fall 1978): 411-26.

———. "Rilke's Relation to Russian Painting." *Innsbrucker Beiträge zur Kulturwissenschaft,* no 51. Innsbruck, 1981.

———. "Russia in Rilke's *Das Buch der Bilder.*" *Comparative Literature* 29, no. 4 (1977): 313–27.

———. *Russia in the Works of Rainer Maria Rilke.* Detroit, 1984.

———. "The Russian Source of Rilke's 'Wie der Verrat nach Rußland kam.'" *Germanic Review* 54, no. 2 (1979): 72–77.

Brown, Clarence. "Postmark Parnassus." Review of *Letters, Summer 1926: Pasternak, Tsvetaeva, Rilke,* translated by Margaret Wettlin and Walter Arndt. *New Republic,* 2 September 1985, 38–40.

Brutzer, Sophie. "Rilkes russische Reisen." Ph.D. diss., Königsberg, 1934. Reprint, Darmstadt, 1969.

Bushman, I. N. "Pasternak i Ril'ke." In *Sbornik statej, posveshennykh tvorchestvu Borisa Leonidovicha Pasternaka.* Issledovanija i materialy. 1st ser., no. 65. Munich, 1962.

Butler, Elizabeth M. *Rainer Maria Rilke.* Cambridge, 1941.

———. "Rilke and Tolstoy." *Modern Language Review* 35 (1940): 494–505.

Chertkov, Leonid N. *Rilke in Rußland: Auf Grund neuer Materialien.* Österreichische Akademie der Wissenschaften. Philosophisch-Historische Klasse. Sitzungsberichte, 301 Band, 2 Abhandlung. Veröffentlichungen der Kommission für Literaturwissenschaft, no. 2. Vienna, 1975.

Crowhurst, Griselids W. "Malte Laurids Brigge, Nikolaj Kuzmittsch und die Trägheit der Materie." *Acta Germanica* 8 (1973): 101–16.

Drozhzhin, Spiridon D. "Der deutsche Dichter Rainer Maria Rilke: Errinnerungen." *Das Inselschiff* 8 (1929): 225–33.

Emerson, Caryl. "Rilke, Russia and the Igor Tale." *German Life and Letters,* n.s. 33, no. 3 (1980): 220–33.

Epp, George K. *Rilke und Rußland.* Europäische Hochschulschriften. Deutsche Sprache und Literatur 1, Reihe 726. Frankfurt am Main, 1984.

Frank, Marga. "Rilke und Rußland." *Das Wort* 3, no. 7 (1938): 92–100.

Frank, Semën. "Die Mystik von R. M. Rilke." *Neophilogus* 20 (1934–35): 97–113.

———. "Rajner Maria Ril'ke i Rossija." *Rul'* (Berlin), 9 January 1929, 2–3.

Gronicka, André von. "Rainer Maria Rilke's Translation of the 'Igor' Song

(Slovo)." In *Russian Epic Studies,* edited by Roman Jakobson and Ernst J. Simmons. Philadelphia, 1949.

———. "Rilke and the Pasternaks." *Germanic Review* 27, no. 4 (1952): 260–71.

Hasty, Olga P. "Marina Cvetaeva's Encounter with Rainer Maria Rilke." Ph.D. diss., Yale University, 1980.

Heygrodt, Robert Heinz. "Rilke und Rußland." *Berliner Tageblatt,* 22 November 1921, 7.

Hkt. [pseud.]. "Boris Pasternak und R. M. Rilke." *Prager Presse,* 5 February 1932, 8.

Ilková, Zdenka. "Rilke a Rusko." *Casopis pro moderni filologii* 31 (1948): 94–108; 32 (1949): 35–37.

Ingold, Felix Philipp. "Rilke, Rußland und die 'russische Dinge.'" In *Zwischen den Kulturen: Festgabe für Georg Thürer zum 70: Geburtstag dargebracht von der Kulturwissenschaftlichen Abteilung der Hochschule St. Gallen,* edited by F. P. Ingold, 63–86. Bern and Stuttgart, 1978.

———. "Rilkes Rußland." *Neue züricher Zeitung,* 29–30 November 1975, 59–60.

———. "Sowjetische Rilke-Edition." Review of *Lirika. Neue züricher Zeitung,* 10-11 July 1976, 50.

———. "Zur Rezeption Rainer Maria Rilkes in der UdSSR: Sowjetische Veröffentlichungen zum 100. Geburtstag des Dichters." *Osteuropa: Zeitschrift für Gegenwartsfragen des Ostens* 7 (1976): 1058–63.

Isarskij, Olekha. "Rilke in der Ukraine." *Mitteilungen des Instituts für Orientforschung der Deutschen Akademie der Wissenschaften zu Berlin* 12 (1975): 28–52.

Jonas, Klaus W. "Rilke und Clotide Sakharoff." *Börsenblatt für den deutschen Buchhandel, Frankfurter Ausgabe,* Beilage "Aus dem Antiquariat," 29 (1973): 313–21.

———. "Rilke und die Sakharoffs." *Frankfurter allgemeine Zeitung,* 28 January 1966, 28.

———. "Rilke und die Welt des Tanzes." *Deutsche Weltliteratur von Goethe bis Ingeborg Bachmann: Festgabe für J. Alan Pfeffer.* Tübingen, 1972.

Kopelev, Lev. "Rilke and Russia." In *Rilke: The Alchemy of Alienation,* edited by Frank Baron, Ernst S. Dick, and Warren R. Mauer. Lawrence, Kansas, 1980.

Lavrin, Janko. "Rilke and Russia." *Russian Review* 27 (1968): 149–60.

Legner, Wolfram K. "The Religion of Rainer Maria Rilke before His Visits to Russia." *Monatshefte für Deutschunterricht* 30 (1938): 440–53.

Livingstone, Angela. "Pasternak i Rilke." *Boris Pasternak, 1890–1960,* 431–39. Colloque de Cerisy-la-Salle. Bibliotheque Russe de l'Institut d'Études Slaves, 47. Paris, 1970.

————. "Some Affinities in the Prose of the Poets Rilke and Pasternak." *Forum for Modern Language Studies* 9, no. 3 (1983): 274–83.

Luck, Rätus, ed. *Rainer Maria Rilke: Schweizer Vortragsreise, 1919*. Frankfurt am Main, 1986.

Mágr. [pseud.]. "Rilkes russische Reisen." *Prager Presse*, 19 November 1931, 8.

————. "Rilke und Rußland." *Prager Presse*, Beilage "Dichtung und Welt," 9 August 1931, 3–4.

————. "Zu Rilkes Übertragung des Igorliedes." *Prager Presse*, 1930, 1–3.

Merks, Robert. *Lou Andreas-Salomé und Rainer Maria Rilke in Rußland*. Oosterbeek, 1979.

Miller-Budnickaja, R. "O 'filosofii iskusstva' B. Pasternaka i R. M. Ril'ke." *Zvezda: Literaturno-obshestvennyj i nauchno-populjarnyj zhurnal*, no. 5 (1932): 160–68.

Minger, Karl. "Rainer Maria Rilkes Karl XII von Sweden reitet in der Ukraine." *Wege zum Gedicht* 2 (1964): 452–62.

Mitchell, Stanley. "Rilke and Russia." *Oxford Slavonic Papers* 9 (1960): 138–45.

Mühlberger, Josef. "Rilke und Rußland." *Sudetenland* 15 (1973): 161–74.

Nagy, Bela T. "Rilke und Gorki: Dokumente einer Begegnung." *Studi Germanici*, n.s., 14, installment 2–3, nos. 39–40 (1976): 297–314.

Najdenowa, Ganka. "Rainer Maria Rilke und die slawische Welt." Ph.D. diss., Berlin, 1942.

Pachmuss, Temira. "Dostoevskii and Rainer Maria Rilke: The Alienated Man." *Canadian-American Slavic Studies* 12, no. 3 (1978): 392–401.

Pasternak, Boris. Untitled pages in "Stimmen über Rilke." In *Insel Almanach auf das Jahr 1967: Rainer Maria Rilke zum vierzigsten Todestag*, 80–82. Frankfurt, 1966.

————. *Vozdushnyeputi: Proza raznykhlet*. Edited by E. B. Pasternak and E. V. Pasternak. Moscow, 1982.

Pasternak, Leonid. "Begegnungen mit Rainer Maria Rilke." *Der Literat*, 8 August 1975, 173–75.

Pelenskij, Evgenij Ju. *Rainer Maria Rilke i Ukraina*. Lvov, 1935.

Pronin, V. "Ril'ke i russkaja poezija." *V mire knig*, no. 12 (1975): 72–73.

Raab, Harald. "Rilke und die Welt der Slawen." *Neue deutsche Literatur* 5 (1957): 96–106.

Rakusa, Ilma. "Marina Zwetajewa und Rainer Maria Rilke: Auf Grund unveröffentlichter Briefmaterialien." *Neue züricher Zeitung*, 1–2 September 1979, 65.

Rannit, Alexis. "Rilke und die slawische Kunst." *Das Kunstwerk; eine Monatschrift über alle Gebiete* 5, no. 4 (1951): 13–24.

Reshetylo-Rothe, Daria. *Rilke and Russia: A Re-evaluation*. New York, 1990.

———. "Rilke's Poetic Cycle 'Die Zaren.'" In *Rilke: The Alchemy of Alienation,* edited by Frank Baron, Ernst S. Dick, and Warren R. Mauer, 137–50. Lawrence, Kansas, 1980.

"Rilke und Marina Zwetajewa: Vortragsabend in Leningrad zu einem bisher unveröffentlichten Briefwechsel." *Neue züricher Zeitung,* 28 October 1977, 37.

Rogalski, Aleksander. "Rilke i Rosija." *Zycie i mysl,* nos. 11–12 (1959): 31–44.

Röhling, Horst. "Gethsemane bei Rilke und Pasternak." *Die Welt der Slawen,* no. 8 (1963): 388–402.

———. "Pasternak und die russische Rilke-rezeption." *Die Welt der Slawen,* no. 1 (1972): 118–54.

Rozhanskij, I. D., ed. *Rainer Maria Rilke: Worpswede, August Rodin, Pis'ma, Stikhi.* Moscow, 1971.

Rudnickij, Mikhail. "Russkije motivy v 'Knige Chasov' Rilke." *Voprosy literatury,* no. 7 (1968): 135–49.

Saito, Nello. "La Russia confina con Dio: Rilke e Tolstoi." *Svizzera Italiana* 77, no. 5 (1949): 26–28.

Salgaller, Emanuel. "Strange Encounter—Rilke and Gorky on Capri." *Monatshefte für Deutschuterricht* 54 (1961): 11–21.

Saparov, K. "Rajner Maria Ril'ke o povesti I. A. Bunina 'Mitina Ljubov.'" *Voprosy literatury,* no. 9 (1966): 247–49.

Sazonova, Julia L. "Pis'ma Rainera M. Ril'ke." *Novyj zhurnal* 5 (1943): 281–92.

Schmidt-Ihms, Maria. "Die Zeitbank des Nikolaj Kusmitsch, eine Analyse." *Acta Germanica* 5 (1970): 161–75.

Schoolfield, George C. "Charles XII Rides in Worpswede." *Modern Language Quarterly* 16 (1955): 258–79.

———."Rilke, Gorki and Others: A Biographical Diversion." In *Views and Reviews of Modern German Literature: Festschrift for Adolf D. Klarmann,* edited by Karl S. Weimar, 105–20. Munich, 1974.

Sieber, Carl. "Rilke in Rußland." *Der Deutsche im Osten* 5 (1940): 307–15.

Soloveitchik, Samson, and Everett Bushnell Gladding. "Rilke's Original Russian Poems." *Modern Language Notes* 62 (1947): 514–22.

Stahl, August. "'. . . und es war die Znamenskaja': Rilke und die Kunst der Ikonenmahler." *Blätter der Rilke-Gesellschaft,* nos. 7–8 (1980–81): 84–91.

Struve, Gleb. "Iz Rainera Mariji Ril'ke." *Russkaia mysl'* 1 (1927).

———. "Koe-chto o Pasternake i Rilke." *Boris Pasternak, 1890–1960:* 441–48. Colloque de Cerissy-la-Salle. Paris, 1979.

Uyttersprot, H. "Nächtliche Fahrt." *Tijdschrift voon levende Talen* 17 (1951): 385–92.

Webb, Karl E. "The Influence of Russia upon the Young Rilke." *Modern*

Austrian Literature (special Rainer Maria Rilke issue) 15, nos. 3–4 (1982): 239–54.

Wunderlich, Eva C. "Slavonic Traces in Rilke's *Geschichten vom lieben Gott.*" *Germanic Review* 22 (1947): 287–97.

Wytrzens, Von Günther. "Zu den slawischen Rilke-Übersetzungen." *Sprachkunst: Beiträge zur Literaturwissenschaft* 10 (1979): 201–15.

Zabezhinskij, Georgij. "Rainer Maria Ril'ke i Rossija." *Sovremennik* nos. 17–18 (1967): 93–99.

Zajdenshnur, E. J. "R. M. Ril'ke u Tolstogo." *Literaturnoe nasledstvo,* nos. 37–38 (1939): 708–12.

Zarncke, Lilly. "Rilke und Dostoyevsky." *Theologische Blätter* 11 (1932): 103–12.

———. "Rilkes Frömmigkeit und ihre Beziehung zu russischem und römischkatholischem Christentum." *Zeitschrift für systematische Theologie* 11 (1933–34): 225–97.

Other Works

Admoni, Vladimir G. "Poèzija Rajnera Marii Ril'ke." *Voprosy literatury,* no. 12 (1962): 138–58.

Alpatov, Mikhail V. *Russian Impact on Art.* Translated by Ivy Litvinov. 1950. Reprint, New York, 1969.

Apollo. Special Issue on Russian Art. December, 1973.

Bakhtin, Mikhail M. *Estetika slovesnogo tvorchestva.* Moscow, 1979.

———. *Problems of Dostoyevsky's Poetics.* Translated by Caryl Emerson. Minneapolis, 1984.

———. *Speech Genres and Other Essays.* Translated by Vern W. McGee. Edited by Caryl Emerson and Michael Holquist. Austin, 1986.

Baron, Frank. *The Visual Arts and Rilke's Poetry.* Lawrence, Kansas, 1975.

Basserman, Dieter. *Der andere Rilke: Gesammelte Schriften aus dem Nachlass.* Edited by Hermann Mörchen. Bad Homburg von der Höhe, 1961.

———. *Der späte Rilke.* Munich, 1947.

Bauer, Edda, ed. *Rilke-Studien: Zu Werk und Wirkungsgeschichte.* Berlin, 1976.

Berger, Kurt. *Rainer Maria Rilkes früher Lyrik: Entwicklungsgeschichtliche Analyse der dichterischen Form.* Beiträger zur deutschen Literaturwissenschaft 40. Marburg, 1931.

Betz, Maurice. *Rilke à Paris et "Les Cahiers de Malte Laurids Brigge."* Paris, 1941.

———. *Rilke vivant: Souvenirs, Lettres, Entretiens.* Paris, 1937.

Bialostosky, Don H. "Dialogics as an Art of Discourse in Literary Criticism." *PMLA* 101 (1986): 788–97.

Binion, Rudolph. *Frau Lou: Nietzsche's Wayward Disciple.* Princeton, N. J., 1968.

Borchert, Hans-Heinrich. "Das Problem des 'verlorenen Sohnes' bei Rilke." In *Worte und Werte.* Berlin, 1961.

Buddeberg, Else. *Rainer Maria Rilke: Eine innere Biographie.* Stuttgart, 1955.

Butler, Elisabeth M. *Rainer Maria Rilke.* Cambridge, 1941.

Demetz, Peter. *René Rilkes Prager Jahre.* Düsseldorf, 1953.

Du Bos, Charles C. *Extrait d'un journal, 1908–1928.* 2d ed. Paris, 1931.

Dudkin, V. V., and K. M. Azadovskij [Azadovsky]. "Neoromanticism: Legenda o 'russkoj dushe." In "Dostoyevskij v Germanii, 1846–1921." In *Literaturnoe Nasledstvo,* No. 86. *F.M. Dostoevskij: Novye materialy i issledovanija.* Moscow, 1973.

Engelhardt, Hartmut, ed. *Materialien zu Rainer Maria Rilke: "Die Aufzeichnungen des Malte Laurids Brigge."* Frankfurt am Main, 1974.

Emerson, Caryl. "The Tolstoy Connection in Bakhtin." *PMLA* 100 (1985): 68–80.

Freedman, Ralph F. "Gods, Heros, and Rilke." In *Hereditas: Seven Essays from the Modern Experience of the Classical,* 8–14. Austin, 1964.

———. "Rainer Maria Rilke and the 'Sister Arts.'" In *Literary Theory and Criticism: Festschrift in Honor of René Wellek,* edited by Joseph P. Strelka, 2:821–47. Bern, 1984. 821-847.

———. "The Transformation of Self and the Language of Art: Rainer Maria Rilke." Lecture given at the School of Criticism and Theory, Northwestern University, July 1985.

———."Wallace Stevens and Rainer Maria Rilke: Two Versions of a Poetic." In *The Poet as Critic,* edited by F. P. W. McDowell, 60–80. Evanston, Ill., 1967.

Gulyga, Elena V. "Neskol'ko slov o proze Ril'ke." In *Stilistika khudozhestvennoj rechi, II,* 85–93. Leningrad, 1975.

Hamburger, Käte. "Die Geschichte des verlorenen Sohnes bei Rilke." In *Fides et communicatio: Festschrift für Martin Doerne zum 70. Geburtstag,* edited by Dietrich Rössler, Gottfrid Voigt, and Friedrich Wintzer, 126-43. Göttingen, 1970.

Herzog, Bert. "Der Gott des Jugendstils in Rilkes 'Stundenbuch.'" *Schweizerische Rundschau* 60 (1961): 1237–97.

Holthusen, Hans Egon. *Rainer Maria Rilke in Selbstzeugnissen und Bilddokummenten.* Hamburg, 1958.

Jaloux, Edmond. *Rainer Maria Rilke.* Paris, 1937.

Karlinsky, Simon. *Marina Tsvetaeva: The Woman, Her World and Her Poetry.* Cambridge, 1985.

Kassner, Rudolf. *Rilke, Gesammelte Erinnerungen, 1926–1956.* Pfullingen, 1976.

Das Kunstwerk. Special issue entitled "R. M. Rilke und die bildende Kunst." 1951.

Leppmann, Wolfgang. *Rilke: Leben und Werk*. Munich, 1981.

Mövius, Ruth. *Rainer Maria Rilkes "Stunden-Buch": Entstehung und Gehalt*. Leipzig, 1937.

Pagni, Andrea. *Rilke um 1900: Ästhetik und Selbstverständnis im lyrischen Werk*. Nürnberg, 1984.

Prater, Donald. *A Ringing Glass: The Life of Rainer Maria Rilke*. Oxford, 1986.

Ritmeester, Hubertin Anna. "Rilke and the 'Motherhood Debate': A Feminist Perspective on the Young Rilke." Ph.D. diss., Washington University, 1987.

Schlienger-Stähli, Hildegard. *Rainer Maria Rilke–André Gide: Der verlorene Sohn: Vergleichende Betrachtung*. Zurich, 1974.

Schnack, Ingeborg. *Rainer Maria Rilke: Chronik seines Lebens und seines Werkes*. 2 vols. Frankfurt am Main, 1975.

Solbrig, Ingeborg H., and Joachim W. Storck, eds. *Rilke Heute: Beziehungen und Wirkungen*. 2 vols. Frankfurt am Main, 1975–76.

Stahl, August. *Rilke: Kommentar zum lyrischen Werk*. Munich, 1978.

Simenauer, Erich. *Rainer Maria Rilke: Legende und Mythos*. Bern, 1953.

———. *Der Traum bei Rainer Maria Rilke*. Bern, 1976.

Storck, Joachim W. "Politische Bewußtsein beim späten Rilke." *Recherches germaniques* 8 (1978): 83–112.

———. "Rainer Maria Rilke als Briefschreiber." Ph.D. diss., Freiburg im Bresgau, 1957.

———. "Der sowjetische Rilkeforscher Konstantin Azadowskij (Eine Dokumentation)." *Blätter der Rilke-Gesellschaft* 9 (1982): 79–94.

———, ed. *Rainer Maria Rilke. Ausstellung des deutschen Literaturarchivs im Schiller-Nationalmuseum*. Marbach, 1975.

———, ed. *Rilke und Politik*. Frankfurst am Main, 1992.

Tchernosvitow, Génia. "Les derniers mois de Rainer Maria Rilke." *Les Lettres* (Paris, 1952).

Thurn und Taxis, Marie von. *Erinnerungen an Rainer Maria Rilke*. Frankfurt am Main, 1966.

Webb, Karl Eugene. *Rainer Maria Rilke and Jugendstil: Affinities, Influences, Adaptations*. University of North Carolina Studies in the Germanic Languages and Literatures, no. 90. Chapel Hill, 1978.

Index

191

Index

Index

Surikov, Ivan, 53
Suvorin, A. S., 91, 97
Svet, 53

Tchernosvitova, Evgenia, 114, 116, 125
Temps, Le, 94
Tesková, Anna, 125
Teweles, Heinrich, 6
"Three Legends of Crucifix" (Zeyer), 16
Thurn und Taxis, Marie von, 118
"To All the Toiling, Oppressed, and Deceived Peoples of Europe" (Trotsky), 105
Tolstaya, Alexandrine, 87
Tolstaya, Sofia Andreevna, 92, 95, 98, 99–100
Tolstoy, Nikolai, 52, 53, 173 n. 22
Tolstoy, Lev L'vovich, 98
Tolstoy, Leo: Andreas-Salomé on, xvii, 28, 79, 80, 81–84; Beaunier on, 94–95; Gorky on, 87–90, 95; death of, 93, 168 n. 7; on Drozhzhin, 54, 64; and Francis of Assisi, 42; on art, 80–81; Lenin on, 92; on Leskov, 65, 66, 67, 71; on peasant behavior, 64, 74, 79; meetings with Rilke and Andreas-Salomé, xv, 103, 167 n. 1; 1899: 30, 38, 94, 96; 1900: 51, 52, 97–99; influence on Rilke, 50, 79–90, 100–102; and *Notebooks of Malte Laurids Brigge*, 100–102; Rilke on, xvii, 80, 82, 84–86; Rilke's translations of, 62; Rodin, compared with, 85–86; Suvorin on, 91–92; "Tolstoy myth," in West, 92–93. Works: "What Is Art?," xvii, 80, 82–85, 156 n. 21, 164 n. 3, 165 n. 12; "The Death of Ivan Ilyich," 54; *Power of Darkness*, 30; *Resurrection*, 82, 86, 94, 165 n. 10, 168 n. 11
Trefolev, Lev, 53
Tretyakov, 76
Trotsky, Leon, 105
Trubetskoi, Pavel, 38
Tsvetaeva, Marina: treatment of Pasternak, 115, 125; correspondence with Rilke, 114–17, 122–24, 130, 170 n. 1, 173 n. 28, 177 n. 20; Rilke's elegy for, 122–24; on Rilke, 125–27; correspondence with Rilke and Pasternak, xvi, xvii, 103, 108–9, 111, 113. Works: "Attempt at a Room," 125; "New Year's," 125, 126–27;

"Poem of the End," 113; "Poem of the Air," 125; "Some Letters of Rainer Maria Rilke," 125
Turgenev, Ivan, 79, 80
Two Prague Stories, 4, 18, 97
Týl, Kajetan, 13, 14, 148 n. 46; "Where My Home Is," 13

Ullmann, Regina, 176 n. 13
Uspensky, Gleb, 29, 153 n. 29

Valéry, Paul, 109
Vasilijev, Fjodor, 75
Vasnetsov, Victor, 50, 74, 76–77, 163 n. 38
"Venerable Father and Metropolitan," 38–39
Ver sacrum, 82
Vestnik evropy, 53
"Vladimir, the Painter of Clouds," 71
Volkov-Muromzev, Alexander, 107
Voloshin, M. A., 129
Volynsky, Akim Lvovitch: and Andreas-Salomé, 26–27, 28, 66, 75, 151 n. 15, 152 n. 20, 161 n. 3; on Leskov, 26–27, 66, 67, 162 n. 15
Voronina, Helene, 33, 35, 42–47, 106–7, 149 n. 51
Vrchlicky, Jaroslav, 13, 14

Wagner, Richard, 81
"What Is Art?" (Tolstoy), xvii, 80, 82–85, 156 n. 21, 164 n. 3, 165 n. 12
"Where My Home Is" (Týl), 13
Wodak, Ernst, 6
Worpswede Diary, 97, 168 n. 7
Wunderly-Volkart, Nanny, 125

Yanchevetsky, Vasily, 52, 62
"Your Death" (Tsvetaeva), 125

Zeitlin, Mikhail, 107
Zeyer, Julius, xvi, 13, 14–17, 149 nn. 51, 55; "Aleksei, Man of God," 16; "Song of the Woe of the Good Youth, Roman Vasilic," 149 n. 55; "Three Legends of Crucifix," 16
Zola, Emile, 80
Zukunft, Die, 25